WATER BORNE

A 1,200-MILE PADDLEBOARDING PILGRIMAGE

DAN RUBINSTEIN

Copyright © Dan Rubinstein, 2025

Published by ECW Press
665 Gerrard Street East
Toronto, Ontario, Canada M4M 1Y2
416-694-3348 / info@ecwpress.com

All rights reserved. No part of this publication may be reproduced, stored in a retrieval system, or transmitted in any form by any process — electronic, mechanical, photocopying, recording, or otherwise — without the prior written permission of the copyright owners and ECW Press. The scanning, uploading, and distribution of this book via the internet or via any other means without the permission of the publisher is illegal and punishable by law. This book may not be used for text and data mining, AI training, and similar technologies. Please purchase only authorized electronic editions, and do not participate in or encourage electronic piracy of copyrighted materials. Your support of the author's rights is appreciated.

Editor for the Press: Jen Knoch
Copy editor: Crissy Boylan
Cover design: Michel Vrana
Cover photo: Kath Fudurich

To the best of his abilities, the author has related experiences, places, people, and organizations from his memories of them. In order to protect the privacy of others, he has, in some instances, changed the names of certain people and details of events and places.

LIBRARY AND ARCHIVES CANADA CATALOGUING IN PUBLICATION

Title: Water borne : a 1200-mile paddleboarding pilgrimage / Dan Rubinstein.

Names: Rubinstein, Dan, 1973- author

Description: Includes bibliographical references.

Identifiers: Canadiana (print) 20250151502 | Canadiana (ebook) 2025015157X

ISBN 978-1-77041-831-8 (softcover)
ISBN 978-1-77852-410-3 (ePub)
ISBN 978-1-77852-411-0 (PDF)

Subjects: LCSH: Rubinstein, Dan, 1973-—Travel. | LCSH: Water—Psychological aspects. | LCSH: Stand-up paddle surfing.

Classification: LCC BF789.W3 R83 2025 | DDC 155.9/1—dc23

This book is funded in part by the Government of Canada. *Ce livre est financé en partie par le gouvernement du Canada.* We acknowledge the support of the Canada Council for the Arts. *Nous remercions le Conseil des arts du Canada de son soutien.* We would like to acknowledge the funding support of the Ontario Arts Council (OAC) and the Government of Ontario for their support. We also acknowledge the support of the Government of Ontario through the Ontario Book Publishing Tax Credit, and through Ontario Creates.

PRINTED AND BOUND IN CANADA   PRINTING: MARQUIS   5 4 3 2 1

Purchase the print edition and receive the ebook free.
For details, go to ecwpress.com/ebook.

For my parents,
for all my relations.

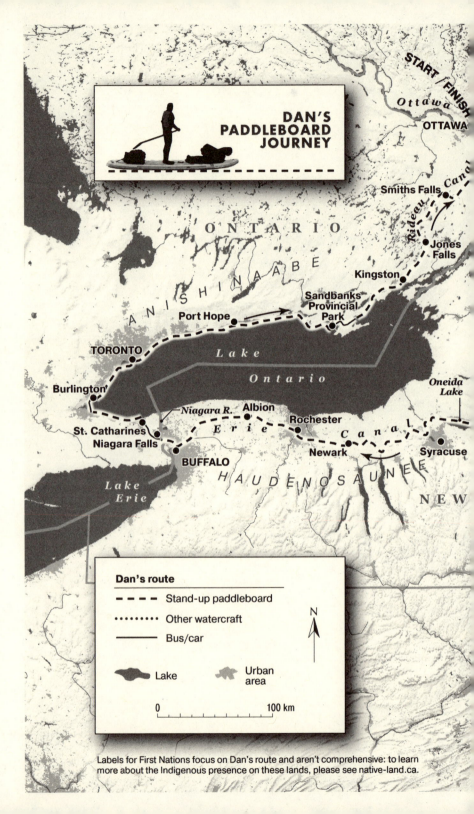

ANISHINAABE
River
MONTRÉAL
River
QUÉBEC
Hawkesbury
Oka
Lac des Deux Montagnes
Kahnawà:ke
Richelieu R.
Ile-aux-Noix
St. Lawrence
HAUDENOSAUNEE
N'DAKINNA
Lake Champlain
Plattsburgh
Basin Harbor Resort
VERMONT
Whitehall
NEW HAMPSHIRE
Champlain Canal
Schuylerville
Utica
Mohawk R.
t. Johnsville
MOHICAN
Hudson River
YORK
ALBANY
MASSACHUSETTS
Kingston
CONNECTICUT
Newburgh
Garrison
NEW JERSEY
ATLANTIC
OCEAN
Hoboken
MANHATTAN

CONTENTS

Introduction
9

Part I:
Ottawa to Montreal
27

Part II:
Quebec to New York City
87

Part III:
Albany to Toronto
175

Part IV:
Toronto to Ottawa
257

Acknowledgments
322

Works Cited
326

INTRODUCTION

"All those fishes down there in the river in the water where you couldn't see them, swimming round living out their lives feeding mating giving birth and dying — if you think about that river as a limit of existence then you start to think about the water of that river and all the waters on the earth and in earth's atmosphere, and then you have to think about all those sums of water and they are a limit of existence, too, how all of us are as limited in our native element, captives in our glasshouse atmosphere . . ."

— Marianne Wiggins, Evidence of Things Unseen

"There is a river flowing now very fast. It is so great and swift that there are those who will be afraid. They will try to hold on to the shore. They will feel they are being torn apart and will suffer greatly. Know the river has its destination. The elders say we must let go of the shore, push off into the middle of the river, keep our eyes open and our heads above the water."

— Hopi prophecy

"We really did have everything, didn't we?"

— Randall Mindy in Don't Look Up

MEASURED AGAINST THE CHRONICLES OF MARINERS WHO FOUND THEM-selves navigating inhospitable waters, my predicament isn't all that perilous. But it's getting dark, I've been on the go since dawn, a severe storm is expected overnight — and I seriously doubt that anybody has ever done, or was foolish enough to consider doing, what I am about to attempt.

Hot, hungry and exhausted, calves and fingers cramping, I study the shoreline, where a creek spills into the canal I am traveling along. A crumbling concrete wall and jagged sheet of rusty metal edge the far side of the drop. My exit.

Glancing down at the map on my phone, which glows in the smoggy twilight of Utica, New York, on a humid July night, I see that my target is close. Very close. It is time once more to summon Swamp Thing.

Let me back up for a minute. You might insist that I do.

Swamp Thing — or at least a middle-aged, five-foot-four, scruffy bearded, sweaty and sour smelling incarnation of it — had emerged for the first time the previous morning, about 50 miles to the east. A desperate measure at a desperate time. Channeling my inner bog.

It had been day three of my voyage along the length of the Erie Canal and day 34 of a larger circuit from Ottawa back home to Ottawa, via Montreal, New York City and Toronto. My vessel was a 14-foot-long, 30-inch-wide inflatable stand-up paddleboard — aka a SUP. Fastened under tie-down straps on the deck I carried three dry bags containing 60 pounds of camping gear, food, clothing, a first aid kit and other essentials, as well as an oversized backpack for lugging around the deflated SUP, its pump and a three-piece backup paddle. My route traversed a string of rivers, lakes, canals and a splash of ocean, with a few stretches over land or aboard other means of nautical conveyance. It had seemed like a fine idea when I schemed it up: intrepid paddleboarder embarks on improbable journey in his own backyard, testing the premise that "blue space" — being in or around aquatic environments — just might hold a key to human and ecological health. An absurd response, during a year of record heat, fires and floods, to absurd times. Plus, because I planned to interview people about their relationships with water and then write a few things about said relationships, I could even justify to my wife and daughters a few months of paddling as "work."

Yet on the muggy morning in question — passing through the Upstate New York village of Fultonville, named after the inventor of the steamboat but not really watercraft friendly anymore — the logistics were proving tricky. Finding places to sleep on a waterscape hemmed in by private land had been taxing throughout my trip. As was preventing my body from roasting. Equally problematic was getting my hands (and mouth) on enough food when I was propelling myself an average of 25 to 30 miles a day for weeks on end. So when I spotted one of those towering, ostrich-like highway signs advertising a fast-food restaurant, the Golden Arches called to me: calories and cold drinks were near.

I paddled to the side of the canal, removed the ankle leash that tethers me to the board and cinched its Velcro loop around a fallen log on a muddy, overgrown embankment. Then I splashed ashore, plunged into the tangle of shrubs and trees and scrambled up a steep slope on all fours. Bursting through the head-high marsh grasses at the top, a swashbuckling explorer in search of Shangri-la, or perchance an Egg McMuffin, I stumbled into the back of a Dunkin' Donuts drive-thru.

Brushing myself off as best I could, I slipped inside through the automatic doors and bought a family-sized selection of breakfast sandwiches, eschewing the orange vinyl banquettes and skulking back to my SUP to feast.

Swamp Thing had arisen.

It — he? they? do quag creatures have a gender? — became my alter ego. A manifestation of the sunbaked electrical pulses cascading inside my cranium. (Although not an entirely novel companion, my wife and daughters might say.)

Paddling all day, you have a lot of time to think. Too much time, perhaps. Sometimes I ruminate on the previous 24 hours or the 24 hours ahead or reflect on family and friends. Oftentimes I sink into the sights and sounds of my surroundings: birds and bugs, trees and train whistles, hills and valleys, skyscrapers and alleys, eddies and ripples in the water, turtles and trout drifting into view below the surface, clouds and the firmament above.

Periodically, I zoom in on the mechanics of each stroke — reach, hinge at the waist, plant the blade, pull yourself past the board, feather the paddle back, repeat — and lose myself in the metronomic, meditative cadence, zoning out and not thinking about anything at all. Paddle slips into the catch without a splash, slices through the water effortlessly. Hit it right and you feel airborne. Wavelets disperse off the nose of the board, prisms of dancing light radiating shoreward.

Sometimes, especially when tired, I distract myself with math. Three seconds a stroke. Twenty strokes a minute. One hundred strokes in five minutes, 500 in 25. Twelve hundred an hour. Three miles an hour. Four hundred strokes a mile. But you can only count paddle strokes and calculate distances for so long. Projecting my selfhood onto another entity, one better suited to this soggy terrain than an urban laptop whisperer, invoked a harmony. Not that I consciously willed Swamp Thing into existence. The epithet arose in my overheated noggin and, like it or not, we were a team. Two sides of the same coin. And really, there's a little Swamp Thing within each of us, n'est-ce pas?

Now, entering the underbelly of Utica, it's a Thursday night — maybe, I think, those details are kind of murky — and the Fultonville smorgasbord is behind me. I'd paddled more than 30 miles on another sweltering day, spotting plenty of places (a marina here, a public dock there) where I could have camped. I could also have camped at one of the three lock stations whose chambers I had transited while kneeling on my board to make like a kayak. And even at a fourth, which I arrived at after operating hours and portaged around, hauling my SUP and cumbersome gear up an eight-foot ladder and schlepping through a construction site and maintenance yard to reach an improvised upstream put-in (thankfully, a gangplank down to a floating barge, not another ladder). Yet I didn't want to tent in another thunderstorm and was determined to cover some distance, pressing onward to keep a date with a group of freshwater researchers who were expecting me at their field station two days hence.

That arduous half-hour portage, the final lock before the rust-belt city of Utica, fed me into five miles of lonesome straightaways pinched between factories and freeways, testament to the Erie Canal's commercial legacy. I knew before leaving home that my surroundings wouldn't always be pretty. Still, the cumulative toll of more than 12 hours of paddling in the sun and humidity on an increasingly industrial transect had rendered me drained and defeated. Beyond tired, I am doubting my rationale for embarking on this trip. The healing power of water? A tonic for nearly every modern ailment? A legit reason for leaving home? Whatever. My body and brain are bowed, breaking. All I want is a shower and some food, a beer and a bed. And that requires Swamp Thing.

Snugging my board up to the concrete beside Reall Creek, I detach the dry bags and swing them one by one onto the retaining wall. Then I carefully step over the jagged metal cap where wall meets canal and, more carefully, use the leash to pull the board up behind me. (Though they can puncture, inflatable SUPs can handle being dragged against or bashed into concrete and rocks. Or falling off roof racks on the highway . . . a story for later.)

A short uphill dirt path through some bushes leads from the creek to the back of a dental clinic. Carrying and dragging my SUP and dunnage, I shuttle to the parking lot behind the neighboring Rest Inn motel.

The bald, muscle-bound clerk, who speaks with a strong Russian accent, doesn't seem perturbed about the sight or smell of me, although he raises a Slavic eyebrow from behind the glass shield when I preemptively try to explain.

"I no undeerstand," he says as I mime a paddling motion. "Vat is *peedelboard*?"

An hour later, in a perfectly comfortable $72 room, the board stashed behind some garbage bins, I am clean and cool, watching bad TV, eating a turkey sub and drinking a can of cheap lager from a gas station beside the nearby interstate offramp. And I know both me and Swamp Thing will be ready to go again in the morning.

OK, before we dive any deeper, let's get to the obvious question. Why *peedelboard*?

Some might call SUP an awkward, inefficient manner of transportation. You know what? They'd be right. The physics of a paddleboarder in motion may be elegant on paper — gravity, buoyancy, Newton's third law, torque — but combine these actions IRL and it's kind of ridiculous.

You don't go fast on a SUP (not very often, anyway), and you can't carry many supplies, even if it's more laborsaving than hefting them on your back. This means you must frequently forage and are forced to rely on any amenity — or anybody — within reach. Also, as may seem obvious, unlike canoeing and kayaking, you're *standing* all day. Isn't that tiring?

Well, not really. Paddleboarding is like walking on water. Jesus allusion aside, it's a slow and eminently sustainable way to move. One step at a time, one stroke at a time. If you build up the muscle strength and a stubborn tolerance for repetition, you can do it pretty much all day. And unlike canoers and kayakers, you can shift around and stretch freely while paddling. Your hands and fingers may blister, but your knees don't lock and your back doesn't tighten.

When confronted with a headwind, however — which, per my unverified assessment, is 93 percent of the time — your body acts like a sail, slowing progress and forcing you to work harder. Because the prevailing winds on the Erie Canal blow from the west, and because the current mostly flows from the west, and because I was paddling *toward* the west on this third leg of my journey, a succession of people on the shore each day cheerfully informed me that I was going the wrong way.

These cyclists, walkers, fishers, picnickers, lock operators, canoodling couples, boaters and boat watchers meant well, frequently providing support, assistance and, just as indispensable, friendly conversation. Pretty much everybody I encountered, in fact, regardless of who or where or when, buoyed me onward, a kaleidoscopic slice of life into whose watery domain I had been granted access. Which made me wonder, after hours and hours of paddling, every single interaction mediated by water, what if the slow, hard way is not the wrong way? What if it's an essential embrace?

Since I started paddleboarding a decade ago, it has become my go-to method of moving my body and sorting out my thoughts in the natural world. I had recently finished writing a book about the transformative properties of walking, and the standard fix for a bout of writer's block or crippling doubt, going for a walk, had become a reflexive prison. Clearly, I needed another kind of kinesis. Despite living in a succession of cities on rivers, a Great Lake and an ocean, I had never owned a watercraft of any kind. I rented a SUP at a campground one summer day, then borrowed a board, then bought one, then bought another and another.

Balancing on a paddleboard, whether on glassy flats or rapids or waves, means being dialed into the moment while submitting to elemental forces. It's an intimate way to engage with water. You can carry a SUP to the shore under one arm or deflate it and tote it around on your shoulders; once aboard, you feel and need to roll with every undulation; you can jump off for a swim and climb back aboard easily, blurring the very permeable barrier between being *on* and *in* the water. You can see well, both around you and below, because your eyes are five or six feet above the surface, providing a broader perspective than one has while sitting in a boat. You see the shoreline and horizon, and when looking down, you see fish and plants and other aquatic life, the primordial soup we clambered out of on our way to becoming bipedal.

What's more, when you enter a community by water, you pull up alongside its past: harbors, piers, warehouses and gathering halls, some of which still serve their original purposes, others reimagined or abandoned. You get a sense of a place's bygone lives, its temporal trajectory, its conceivable futures. How its intertwined ecosystems — human, natural, cultural — merge and diverge. When you arrive somewhere with a paddle in your hands, you might catch the pulse of a community and see the gears of change in action. (Also: where the cheap motels are.)

In other words, SUP was a perfect tool for this particular, peculiar journalistic inquisition. And despite outward appearances and the requisite exertion, it can be hella fun.

Under the tutelage of several top-notch paddleboarders, I progressed season by season from the calm water in and around Ottawa to running spring freshet whitewater on the city's Rideau River, SUP surfing the standing waves that rise on the Ottawa River when the upstream snows melt, surfing wind-driven swells on Lake Ontario and surfing ocean waves as often as possible. I paddled every place I went and went places to paddle: Tennessee, Newfoundland, Chicago, British Columbia's Great Bear Rainforest, Belize. Whether down the hill from my house or in another country attempting saltwater circumnavigations, every outing parachuted me into a shimmering parallel world.

My SUP mentors shaped my paddling philosophy. I absorbed ideas from Karl Kruger, who lives on his sailboat in Washington State's San Juan Islands and is one of the most proficient long-distance paddlers on the planet. Karl is the only person to complete the unsupported, 750-mile Race to Alaska on a SUP (bolting up British Columbia's Inside Passage in an astonishing 14 days) and, as of this writing, is in the midst of a multiyear solo paddle through the Northwest Passage. But to him, that expedition is not a macho feat of strength and endurance: man stares down polar bears and prevails over a remote and unforgiving wilderness. Rather, it is an act of submission, of humbling oneself in the face of powerful phenomena. An escape from clocks and computers and cubicles and the confines of our landlocked, rectilinear lives. "To me, the sight and sounds of waves breaking over the bow of my board feels elemental," Karl says, "like looking at fire."

I learned as well during a few trips with Simon Whitfield, who won a gold medal in triathlon for Canada at the 2000 Summer Olympics and is now a Vancouver Island SUP guide. "Paddleboarding is defiant," he says. "It's like dancing on water." Simon fell in love with the sport after retiring from triathlon. At first, he joined the West Coast racing scene but soon found himself driving several hours to events when he would rather have been by himself on the ocean. "For me, paddleboarding is a way to figure out how I relate to the space around me," he says, explaining how SUP helped him navigate the transition away from elite competition. "When you're in wind or waves, paddleboarding is dynamic. On a calm day, it's absolute awe and magnificence."

The more I paddled, the more I experienced this splendor, and the therapeutic promise of blue space. Makes sense. In utero we gestate in a watery fluid, and after birth we're largely comprised of water. Almost all of our communities are where they are and what they are because of water. Without it, every living thing would die. Physiologically, psychologically and ecologically, there are countless ways in which blue space is healthy for humans. Researchers believe it may very well be better for us than green space and are compiling the evidence to prove it.

Mat White, an environmental psychologist at the University of Vienna, is arguably the world's leading authority on the subject. He studies what happens when we do anything (paddle, swim, surf, walk, sit) in, on or near just about any type of water, from vast oceans to urban fountains. After leading several research projects and crunching some big numbers over the past decade, Mat believes that blue space has a mostly positive and, compared to other outdoor environments, a more pronounced impact on our bodies and brains.

Water is a double-edged sword, he cautions. Drowning is the third leading cause of unintentional injury death around the world. Around two billion people don't have access to clean drinking water. Rising seas, intensifying storms, widespread flooding and waterborne diseases are among the deadliest consequences of global warming, and they tend to displace and kill those with the least capacity to escape or adapt.

These realities notwithstanding, in *Blue Mind*, marine biologist Wallace J. Nichols explains the myriad processes through which our brains get a boost from the aquatic world. Drawing on the work and experiences of neuroscientists, psychologists, artists and athletes, he details our emotional and cognitive responses to water. "Every year more experts are connecting the dots between brain science and our watery world," Nichols writes. "This isn't touchy-feely 'let's save the dolphins' conservation: we're talking prefrontal cortex, amygdala, evolutionary biology, neuroimaging, and neuron functioning that shows exactly why humans seem to value being near, in, on, or under the water." This research has implications for everything from health care and public policy to education and business, he avows, on top of our happiness and general well-being.

But I didn't need data or theories. Anxious about apocalyptical climate change, frightened by rampaging technology and the social media vortex, uninspired at work, on the cusp of 50 and wrestling with my identity as my twin teenaged daughters leave the nest, I needed to go for a good long paddle. Exotic, distant places have a strong appeal, yet I've always been drawn to journeys undertaken close to home, under my own steam. To stepping out the front door with everything I might need and completing a circle. To decelerating and reminding myself about the manna of simple things. Or swampy things.

One day in 1955 near the Dutch village of Pesse, not far from the North Sea, a farmer found something unusual in the ground during the construction of a motorway: a 10-foot-long dugout canoe made from a Scotch pine log. Dating back roughly 10,000 years, it's the oldest known boat in the world. Other ancient canoes, a couple thousand years younger, have been discovered in Nigeria, China, Egypt, Florida. Our cousins the Neanderthals likely built rafts and sailed around the Mediterranean long before we showed up on this big blue ball and started paddling logs down the river, but according to Swedish geneticist Svante Pääbo, we kicked it up a notch.

"It's only fully modern humans who start this thing of venturing out into the ocean where you don't see land," the Nobel Prize winner told the *New Yorker*. "Part of that is technology, of course; you have to have the ships to do it. But there is also, I like to think or say, some madness there." This madness is a genetic difference, Pääbo suggests, one that sent us into the unknown and ultimately "changed the whole ecosystem of the planet and made us dominate everything."

Migration can be an evolutionary force. It broadens the gene pool, gives us a better shot at survival. Our forebears kept paddling after they scattered around the globe. Indigenous Peoples from the Amazon to Australia to the Americas traveled and fished using canoes and kayaks made from wood, bark, animal skins and bones. And at least 5,000 years ago, we started standing in our boats. The great leap upward.

Peruvians paddled erect in the surf on tups made from bundled reeds circa 3000 BCE, Ben Marcus writes in *The Art of Stand Up Paddling*, noting that *tup* is one letter away from *SUP* and asking, "Who's to say that the early inhabitants of Africa — or the Netherlands, France or China — didn't stand in the canoe to better see where they were navigating, or spot rising fish and nesting birds (or infants in reed baskets), or keep their calves toned?" (The infant in question is the baby Moses, who may have been spotted bobbing about in the Nile by the pharaoh's daughter, a hyperbolic paddling magazine editor once speculated, because she was "stand-up paddling in a small boat, and so had the better perspective from which to spot the baby prophet and future Savior of the Jews.")

Conjecture aside, we do know that around 4,000 years ago, Mediterraneans started using a boat-board hybrid called the hasake to fish, transport goods and conduct rescues. "The difference is only a couple of feet," Marcus writes about the angle of incidence when you're on two legs, "but the difference in what you can see is everything." Standing on a hasake gave fisherman a good vantage for spotting prey and a steady platform for throwing spears and casting nets. Venetian gondoliers, if you're curious, have had a good vantage for spotting paying customers for about 1,000 years.

Modern stand-up paddleboarding is intrinsically linked with surfing, or wave sliding, which was central to Polynesian culture before European contact. Surfing was a spiritual art for the ancient Hawaiians, and their islands remain its mecca. But there's no evidence of anybody in Hawaii standing on a board with a paddle until 1939 when, as a black-and-white film clip reveals, Olympic swimmer and surfing legend Duke Kahanamoku stood atop an Australian surf ski — a long narrow lightweight kayak — and used a double-bladed kayak paddle to slide into the waves off Waikiki.

The link between Kahanamoku's craft and today's fiberglass-and-resin-coated foam core SUPs and carbon fiber paddles goes through Laird Hamilton. The American big-wave surfing celeb started experimenting with longboards and paddles in the mid-1990s. Soon, he was developing SUP-specific gear. There's a photo of Hamilton in September 2002 — a year after the 9/11 terrorist attacks — topping a large swell in Malibu wielding a paddle adorned with an American flag. Stand-up paddleboarding had arrived.

It takes less than 15 minutes to inflate my board to 17 pounds per square inch using a wide-gauge dual-action pump that blows air into the SUP whether you're pushing down or pulling up the handle. A metamorphosis of sorts, the rolled-up nose of the paddleboard unfurls like a prehistoric pop-art white, yellow and blue fern. Once at the recommended pressure the board feels rigid and, if you don't leave it in the sun, can remain full for a few weeks without causing damage. An eight-inch-long fin snapped into a slot on the bottom helps the SUP track straight while paddling, although one has to switch sides every dozen or so strokes to remain on bearing. If you use proper form, you'll work almost every muscle in the body, from feet to fingertips, but it's the larger ones —quads, abs, lats — that carry most of the load. Your arms are just guiding the paddle, and because of all that switching, one doesn't get beefier than the other. If you keep your limbs loose and core engaged, and you're accustomed to riding smaller, less stable boards in waves or whitewater, it's almost impossible to fall off a 14-footer unless conditions get gnarly.

Which didn't happen to me. Until it did.

My trip began in June 2023 and totaled about 1,200 miles. Four legs over four months, with a couple breaks back at home to recuperate and help handle family responsibilities. Ottawa to Montreal on the Ottawa and St. Lawrence Rivers and Lachine Canal; the Montreal area to New York City on the Richelieu River, Lake Champlain, Champlain Canal and Hudson River; Albany to Buffalo and then onward to Toronto on the Erie Canal, Niagara River, Lake Erie and Lake Ontario; and Toronto back to Ottawa on Lake Ontario and the Rideau Canal system. It included a few other lakes and rivers, a couple boat rides and a handful of overland transfers via car and bus. Inflatable SUPs are surprisingly portable, making them a versatile mode of travel. What other oceangoing vessel can you shoulder through Times Square and onto the New York City subway amid the crush of tourists?

The Big Apple — more or less the midpoint of my peregrination — was a big draw for several reasons. Foremost, it's *New York City*. Any paddler with a predilection for metropolitan backdrops would want to dip a blade. It's also the terminus of the Hudson River. Once so choked with toxic pollution that it was deemed dead (you could tell what color cars were being painted in the auto plants on its banks by looking into the river, it has been said), the Hudson helped spawn North America's environmental movement. Now it's a remarkably healthy biodiverse estuary, a cautionary tale worth investigating. (The city is also the setting for my favorite *New Yorker* cartoon, a black-and-white line drawing by Karl Stevens. Two men in suit jackets and ties are sitting at what looks like a boardroom table, with one asking the other, as if wrapping up a job interview, "And, finally, where do you see yourself in five years?" There's a thought bubble above the applicant's head: he's picturing himself standing on a floating chunk of debris, though initially I thought it was a SUP, using a chunk of wood as a paddle, amid the peaks of the Manhattan skyline, including the spire of the Empire State Building, barely rising above the floodwaters that have come. Confirmation bias, sure, but one way or another, where do I see myself in five years?)

NYC is also part of a multigenerational arc that mapped my chosen route. When my mother's family immigrated to North America from Eastern Europe in 1962, they sailed to Montreal. A relative who had already settled in the U.S. was waiting at the port and whisked them to New York City, which is where my mother met my father, a recently landed foreign student. In the late 1960s, ready to start a family, they traded tumultuous America for quiet Canada. I was born and raised in Toronto, and after chasing education and jobs around the country, I've been in Ottawa for closing in on 20 years. Connecting these dots might help me understand my place on the planet, some context for commencing the next half century of my life. Or at least the next five years.

In addition to the Hudson, just about all of the waterways on my route have an acute historical, ecological and socioeconomic resonance. The Ottawa and St. Lawrence Rivers opened the Canadian west to colonial exploitation and the genocide of Indigenous Peoples, whose ways of being and knowing settlers, myself among them, would be wise to heed. Lake Ontario and Lake Champlain — the so-called sixth Great Lake — hold wisdom about war, freedom and invasive species, as well as the sacredness and scarcity of fresh water in a warming world. The Erie Canal, an audacious early 1800s megaproject and stepping stone to Manifest Destiny, allowed New York State to blossom and burgeon; it made Manhattan the center of the world. Yet for some, commemorating its bicentennial seems to have morphed into an exercise more reflective than celebratory, as if the canal's multifaceted existence — a conduit for the passage of goods, people and ideas turned recreational ribbon — presages a new role. Moreover, the cities and towns along my route hold lessons about the interface between people and water on a continent where more than 80 percent of the population is urban.

From rural rivers to dense downtowns, these blue spaces brought me face to face with dozens of people I likely never would have otherwise encountered, both contacts I had arranged in advance to spend time with and others I serendipitously met. The former, whose lives or labor revolve around water in one way or another, inspired me with their passion and dedication to holistic health, environmental stewardship, social justice or some combination thereof. I may be starry-eyed, but they are smart, hard-working, experienced professionals; surely they can't all be wrong? The latter citizens of blue space, the folks I happened to bump into — poor and rich and every status in between, Black and Brown and white and every blended color on the spectrum, old and young, you get the idea — well, they welcomed and gave me cold drinks and snacks and confessed their fears and worries and shared their stories and glories and hugged and encouraged and cheered and teased and laughed and safeguarded and shared and restored in me the belief that when we step off the gas and drift into somebody else's sphere, there is an opening. A small opening, maybe, but an opening nonetheless.

Whether because of the slower pace it often dictates, or because it can be dangerous and deadly and the code of the mariner compels strangers to look out for each other, or because of our deep-rooted biopsychological bond to this magical molecular combination with two parts hydrogen, one part oxygen, when water is part of the picture people seem to have time and receptivity for wider horizons.

In a world gone haywire with climactic upheaval and geopolitical brinksmanship, it may seem like a finger-in-the-dike response to pluck a few plastic bottles from a river, teach a kid how to kayak or carve out a pocket-sized park beside a creek. But these are acts of enduring. At a moment when our attention is scattered digitally in innumerable directions, much to our own detriment, water is the ultimate gravitational counterbalance. It captivates and conjures kinship; it can confer pleasure and perspective by drawing our attention to the places and people where we are. And on a polarized, broiling planet, isn't this an alchemy worth investigating?

People in immediate danger from floods and wildfires don't have the luxury of inaction or despair, Rebecca Solnit argues in an essay about climate change. Yet we are surrounded by despair, "telling us the problems are insoluble, that we are not strong enough, our efforts are in vain, no one really cares, and human nature is fundamentally corrupt. Some push their view like evangelists, not merely surrendering to defeat but campaigning vigorously on its behalf."

Those pushers are often powerful white men with a vested interest in the status quo. But Solnit has seen Indigenous Peoples in the Americas — "told they were doomed and their ways were archaic" — rise up and reshape "ideas about our inseparability from and responsibility to the natural world." (Indigenous-led efforts in the previous decade have stopped or delayed at least 25 percent of American and Canadian greenhouse gas emissions.) She has seen an upswell of empowerment among women, people of color and people with disabilities, the result of movements and everyday acts of courage. "What motivates us to act," she writes,

> is a sense of possibility within uncertainty — that the outcome is not yet fully determined and our actions may matter in shaping it. This is all that hope is, and we are all teeming with it, all the time, in small ways. ... We who have materially safe and comfortable lives, and who are part of societies that contribute the lion's share of greenhouse gases, do not have the right to surrender on behalf of others. We have the obligation to act in solidarity with them. This begins by recognising that the future has not yet been decided, because we are deciding it now.

I decided to explore a frontier close to home that has become unfamiliar to many of us. A triangular swath of North America as entrancing and paradoxical as any place on Earth.

I did not set out to conquer anything, nor to put myself in jeopardy so I could inject drama into the narrative. Bolstered by white-collar affluence, I had the time and means to prepare, but really, I strung together routine, old-school activities for which many people have the capacity. Standing, sleeping outdoors, trusting strangers. A series of steps toward a distant goal. A lens into the arteries of the planet and our own bodies, the conduits through which everything grows.

If this SUP-box doesn't scare you off, in the pages ahead you'll read about my misadventures on the riparian fringe, but there are limits to how poetic one can wax about paddle stroke after paddle stroke after paddle stroke, about divine sunrises and sunsets, about the oppressive temperatures, about your scribe's oppressive smell. So I'm going to make space for the people I met and the communities I traveled to and through. To show you who and what I beheld from water level and, with gleanings from a wider scientific and literary chorus, let these stories shine.

Historian Yuval Noah Harari argues that humans don't really fight over territory or food, that divergent mythologies bring us into conflict. He's thinking about the Middle East mostly, but this notion rings true anywhere — say, along the waterways of North America, where for mile after mile I encountered cracks in a dominant narrative that seems to reward destructive behavior. "If belief in a story reduces suffering, that's a good story," writes Harari. "If belief in a story causes suffering, it is harmful. Better change that story."

But let's not put the cart before the horse here, or the peedelboard before the paddler. My night at Utica's Rest Inn is one tale among many. Yet even that stop showed me something.

In the bright blue morning, after a restful sleep, my SUP is where I had left it, watched over by two men smoking cigarettes on the second-floor fire escape. We greet each other, and after asking if it is my board, they tell me that they are living upstairs while trying to find their footing, that it is safe and quiet, and that they enjoy sitting by the canal a couple hundred feet from their temporary home because it's peaceful, calming. I tell them my name, and Sam and Jared introduce themselves.

"Where ya headed?" Sam asks, a common, albeit existential, question throughout my travels, some days asked dozens of times, regardless of whether people saw my kit on land or water. My responses varied, depending on how quickly I was moving (if I wasn't in fact slumped over resting) and how much I thought the stranger might really want to know. Sometimes my answer would be my destination that day, or the finish line of whatever waterway I happened to be on. Sometimes it was "back home to Ottawa" or "New York City," or simply "the city" (as they say on the Hudson), or some other place along the way.

"I'm going all the way," I say to Sam. "All the way to the end."

Then again, aren't we all? No matter where we're going, don't we all wind up in the same place?

"Buffalo," I clarify. "The end of the Erie Canal."

"Be careful," Jared says as I lift a dry bag onto my shoulder, showing me the wound on his arm from slipping and falling on the narrow path that leads down to the water.

"Safe travels," says Sam.

Before we pick up the story in Utica, let's paddle over into an eddy. Let's catch our breath, take a pause. Let's go back to the beginning.

PART I

OTTAWA TO MONTREAL

"Any river is really the summation of the whole valley. To think of it as nothing but water is to ignore the greater part."

— Hal Borland, This Hill, This Valley

"He who hears the rippling of rivers in these degenerate days will not utterly despair."

— Henry David Thoreau, A Week on the Concord and Merrimack Rivers

CHAPTER 1

~~~

"There is a vast, arterial power humming all around us, hiding in plain sight. It has shaped our civilizations more than any road, technology, or political leader. It has opened frontiers, founded cities, settled borders, and fed billions. It promotes life, forges peace, grants power, and capriciously destroys everything in its path. Increasingly domesticated, even manacled, it is an ancient force that rules us still."

— *Laurence C. Smith*, Rivers of Power

BY ANY MEASURE, THE OTTAWA RIVER IS ONE OF NORTH AMERICA'S GREAT rivers. Nearly 800 miles long, it drains a watershed that's 56,000 square miles (almost exactly the size of Iowa, twice as big as New Brunswick) and served as a highway into the heart of the continent after Europeans made their way up the St. Lawrence in the early 17th century. Long before that — before explorers went probing for an inland route to China and voyageurs paddled west in search of beaver pelts — the river was the home of the Algonquin people, whose predecessors had lived in the region since roughly 6500 BCE. They, too, used the Ottawa as a transportation corridor, fishing, hunting, trapping and farming along its banks and tributaries. Its name in Algonquin, Kichi Sipi, means "great river."

The city where I live, at the confluence of the Ottawa, Rideau and Gatineau Rivers, was an Indigenous meeting place well before settlers established the timber town that would eventually grow into Canada's capital. A 50-foot waterfall just west of what is now the downtown core and another not far to the east, where the Rideau tumbles into the Ottawa, across from the mouth of the Gatineau, made it a natural choice and spiritual spot to get out of your canoe and camp for a while. Indigenous Peoples traded, held ceremonies, mingled and intermarried with other kinship groups. The name *Ottawa* is derived from the Algonquin word *adàwe*, meaning "to trade," and the city is located, as the sometimes heart-swelling, sometimes perfunctory land acknowledgment at the start of most public events proclaims, on the traditional, unceded territories of the Algonquin Nation.

Colonial exploitation, political hot air and bureaucratic bloat notwithstanding, the junction of these three waterways has long been a decent hang.

Petrie Island, about a dozen miles east of downtown, is one of my regular destinations when I paddle on the Ottawa. A park that's connected to the shore by a causeway, it's the farthest I can go on a one-way inflatable SUP excursion and still catch a bus home (or, rather, two buses and an LRT train — an ordeal that can take longer than the downriver run). But I'm not riding public transportation this Monday morning in early June. Lisa, my wife, is driving me to Petrie so I can start paddling east.

"We'll be going against rush-hour traffic," I tell her, smiling sheepishly as I load my deflated board into the car. "You'll make it home in time to bike to the office like usual."

I don't point out, mind you, that she'll be bogged down in stop-and-go highway traffic on the way back. And I look the other way when we pass through a construction zone that'll delay her even more.

Considering my impending absence for most of the next four months, and the parenting and domestic load that she'll be shouldering solo all summer, this morning's drop-off is a minor inconvenience. Yet Lisa instantly and enthusiastically said "go for it" when I first mentioned my embryonic idea. Throughout two decades of parenthood together, we've taken turns springing one another for projects away from home. She's a writer, too, and, possessing an emotional intelligence far superior to mine, understands that without a creative and/or physical relief valve, my complaints, about the ennui of nine-to-five work and workaday life in general, will inevitably reach an insufferable crescendo.

We pull into a practically empty parking lot beside the beach, where the sand has been raked into a mesmerizing carpet of Zen. A good sign. Footsteps of weekend visitors expunged, a blank canvas ahead. It's mild — not too hot, not too cold — with almost no wind. Favorable conditions for the 30 miles I'm hoping to paddle today. There's a guy on the water doing some sprint training on his SUP. Another good omen. The skies are very hazy, however, choked with forest-fire smoke that has drifted into the Ottawa Valley from Quebec. I smell charred wood and get an acrid, ashy tang at the top of my throat. Local health authorities have issued air quality warnings. Schools have canceled outdoor activities. And it's just the start of a wildfire season that will ultimately become the most ruinous ever in Canada, at least for now.

Not a good sign.

But I'm not bothered by the smoky bouquet as I pump up and load my board. After months of planning, I'm stoked to finally be hitting play. And I know that regardless of the risks ahead (a rather banal list that includes sunburn, sunstroke and broken sunglasses) this is a wholly privileged endeavor. As a white man, I'll blend in more than somebody with Black or Brown skin and likely won't face the type of unwanted attention that could endanger a woman traveling alone. To ensure that my body was ready, I had the time to run, lift weights and, depending on the season, cross-country ski or paddle far too many miles for somebody with a job and a family. Even accounting for the middle-aged, not-listening-to-my-body back/leg/muscle/nerve injury that sent me to the emergency room in an ambulance less than a year ago, I'm in the best shape of my life. The credit card in the Ziploc bag that will serve as my wallet all summer helps too.

I've chosen Petrie as my launch point for a few reasons.

First, I've paddled the stretch of river from downtown to this park many times, including two training runs with all of my gear not long after the ice had melted. (I walked from my house to a nearby bus stop, rode a few blocks downhill to the Rideau, put in beside a busy bridge, ran a set of rapids and paddled about five miles to the Ottawa, portaged a mile to a rowing club and then paddled another twelve — and *then* the ungainly bus-train-bus rigamarole home, easily the hardest part, lugging my bags through the after-work transit station bustle.) So there's no need to cover this stretch again.

Second, why not prune my total distance wherever possible, within reason? Remember, this is not a man-slam-dunking-on-nature quest. My ground rules for this trip wouldn't satisfy Guinness World Records scrutineers, and I'm fine with covering most but not necessarily all of the route under my own power. Partially because I'm setting up meetings at various stops, and though I would like to surrender wholeheartedly to natural rhythms, normal people have schedules to keep and are not obstacles but central to my journey. Partially to avoid injury.

Third, Petrie makes sense because I usually stop paddling here and am always tempted to keep going. To see what's around the next bend.

I kiss Lisa and glide away from the beach under an eerie yellow dome, a blurry smudge of sun reflecting on the glassy bluish-brown water. The river is almost a mile wide here, and the lazy late-spring current doesn't provide much of a boost. Settling into a moderate cadence, my thoughts begin to wander.

After scooting past one of the ferries that make the short trip back and forth from shore to shore, I'm beside a row of luxurious houses lining the northern, Quebec side. For about two-thirds of its length, the Ottawa forms the boundary between two provinces, with residential and recreational properties on long stretches of both shorelines. Contemplating the pair of "hundred-year" floods this region has experienced in the past decade — floods that swamped several thousand homes and caused millions of dollars in damages, floods that are prompting insurance companies to stop issuing policies and lenders to stop offering mortgages — I wonder how much this jurisdictional line matters. And whether these homes (these provinces, for that matter) will even exist by the start of the next century.

In *Rising*, Elizabeth Rush travels to communities in the United States where the impacts of rising seas have been the most dramatic, from New York City and Miami to California's Bay Area, and centers the stories of the marginalized people who bear the brunt of this devastation. Although her book is largely about salt water in another country, and although people who live or have cabins on this part of the Ottawa are wealthy by international standards, the conclusions she reached apply here too: "The water will come and at some point we are going to have to admit a kind of defeat. That nothing important is ever easy or quick. That real resiliency might mean . . . learning to leave the very places we have long considered necessary to our survival."

Rush covers a broad sweep in *Rising*, from the biblical flood that begat Noah's ark to present-day economic structures. She realizes that the great flood begins not with a rainstorm but with "unprecedented population growth" and a scornful God. "I am going to put an end to all people," God says to Noah, "for the earth is filled with violence because of them." Removed from its religious context, Rush calls Noah's flood "one of the most fully developed accounts of environmental change in ancient history." Regarding our 21st-century predicament, she speculates about financial mechanisms, such as an America-wide property tax that could be collected to fund a retreat of biblical proportions away from flooding shorelines. "It would allow us to collectively practice walking away from something we desire," she writes, asking whether it makes sense to continue rebuilding in the lowest-lying areas, subjecting "the most vulnerable among us, humans and nonhumans alike, to mounting risks."

The term *managed retreat* is defined as the purposeful, coordinated relocation of people and buildings out of harm's way, rather than holding the line. It can also involve supporting ecosystem processes that mitigate risks, such as buying out homes in a floodplain and reestablishing wetlands that act as a buffer against cyclical floods. In many places — say, where a steep riverbank is eroding or where houses are submerged every couple years — this seems like a no-brainer. It's happening around the world and across North America, from Grand Forks, B.C., where the city purchased dozens of homes in a neighborhood vulnerable to recurrent flooding, to New York City, where the state acquired and demolished several hundred properties on the low-lying coastlines of Staten Island and Long Island after they were ravaged by Hurricane Sandy.

Yet managed retreat is controversial. People who build luxurious waterfront homes don't want to surrender, while others might have a cultural or personal attachment, or simply nowhere else to go. Rush paints a vivid picture of this quandary, but I identify most intensely with her passages about the weariness that stems from thinking in four-year electoral cycles instead of in multiple generations — and from the delusion that rooftop gardens can make a difference, even if they're installed atop buildings knowingly erected on flood-prone land.

"I am thinking that the belief that we can design our way out of this," she writes, "is part of the same set of addictions we must learn to give up. I am thinking about justice, and what it might look like if we thought of sea level rise as an opportunity to mend our relationship with the land and with each other."

Addressing the puzzle of global water patterns scrambled by climate chaos — flooding here, drought there, transpiration drying the land — will require countless near-impossible interventions. But despite her studied grasp of this enormity, science journalist Erica Gies believes that solutions are within reach. "Most modern humans have forgotten that water's true nature is to flex with the rhythms of the earth," she writes in *Water Always Wins*, "expanding and retreating in an eternal dance upon the land." Recalibrating our dysfunctional relationship with water, according to Gies, will help us come to the realization that "the natural systems we are destroying could be our salvation." (One of the more inventive responses to rising seas in NYC, for instance, is the Billion Oyster Project, which aims to restore the city's once teeming oyster reefs to filter pollutants out of the harbor, foster biodiversity and serve as storm barriers. We'll dive into the utility of green infrastructure later.)

My peers and I tend to respond to this era's existential crisis in pragmatic, escapist ways. For the most part desk-job city slickers, we understand that recycling, composting and driving electric cars are tiny drops in a colossal bucket; that Western nations, for all the global grief our consumeristic greed has caused, can only do so much to lower planetary fossil fuel consumption and carbon emissions with three billion people in China and India understandably striving for access to the same creature comforts that many of us take for granted. Complicit, we continue to adhere to the pleasure principle, holidaying in Europe (in the offseason, when it's not crushingly hot) or taking ski vacays at alpine resorts where there's still enough snow. On the other hand, some of the families in my circle are also growing and preserving fruits and vegetables, learning how to butcher animals and build energy-efficient structures, how to forge metals, how to fend. But even these resolute efforts won't offer much protection if our rickety food and fuel supply chains collapse. Considering the philosophical shift that Rush ponders, I wonder whether the inheritance we strive to leave behind for our children (money, real estate, a degree from a good school) will merely perpetuate our short-sighted (and possibly short-lived) habits. Whether accumulating needless things and casual air travel are compatible with empathy. And whether this voyage could lead me somewhere different.

In an essay published in *Scientific American*, environmental studies researcher Sarah Jaquette Ray suggests climate anxiety is really code for "white people wishing to hold onto their way of life," drawing resources to a dominant group and framing climate refugees as a threat in the eyes of the very people who are contributing to their displacement. "Will they be able to see their own fates tied to the fates of the dispossessed?" Ray writes. "Or will they hoard resources, limit the rights of the most affected and seek to save only their own, deluded that this xenophobic strategy will save them?" Can climate anxiety, she asks, be harnessed for climate justice?

Climate justice is a monumental challenge, a civil rights movement wrapped inside an apocalyptic threat. How does one join the cause? Different strokes for different folks, but listening to people unlike me and supporting worthy projects feels like a propitious start.

While providing no insights, my first day of paddling is a reprieve from global-crisis angst, like leaping into a lake on a suffocatingly hot day. Eight hours, 30 easygoing miles. Osprey and eagles overhead, herons and ducks and geese galore, songbirds in the shoreline trees. I swim and stop to eat a sandwich while sitting on my board, legs dangling into the water, cattails tickling my ears, holding the slightly sulfurous aroma in my lungs and feeling the loam begin to accumulate beneath my fingernails. Already, my skin seems to be developing a grungy, glistening film of perspiration, soil and eau de toilette rivière — maybe a catalyst, the moment of inception, when Swamp meets Thing. I say hello, aloud, to a fox and later bid adieu to an otter. Why not talk to animals? I'm already getting a little lonely, and hours go by when I make more eye contact with these locals than with the two-legged kind.

I reach a marina campground in a small Quebec town not long after four o'clock. Setting up my site on a grassy field beside the river is simple, and I stroll up to the main street supermarket for a cold beer to savor with the first of far too many dehydrated suppers-in-a-bag. I actually like freeze-dried camp meals. But after a few days, whether pork pad Thai or broccoli and cheddar pasta, they all start to taste the same. Worse, the plentiful gas smells the same.

By the time my bowels stop gurgling and the smoke-shrouded crimson sun dips below the hills, I'm ready for bed. Zipped into my tiny, malodourous tent, I'm drifting off to the muted sounds of FM rock radio from the car of somebody fishing on the pier. Then an HVAC unit behind the nearby fromagerie clicks into gear, and I toss and turn until the next fuzzy sunrise.

Industrial noise is still ringing in my ears as I paddle past another row of waterfront homes and cottages. People are tending to their grounds with chain saws, lawn mowers, Weedwackers. Cars and trucks rumble past on the highway. Gas-powered pumps hoover up river water for sprinklers, soaking lawns that will soon — again — need to be tamed by polluting machines. Keeping nature in check.

Yet who am I to judge? Without truckers, supermarket shelves would be bare within three days. Farmers need diesel tractors to feed us. And here I am, festooned with paddling and camping gear made by socially and environmentally responsible companies but with a nonessential carbon footprint nonetheless.

Riverkeeper organizations — nonprofit stewardship groups that watch over watersheds around the world — all espouse a similar ethos. To use it is to love it, and to love it is to want to protect it. I can justify my travels as an attempt to send others along this nautical desire line. But isn't this a self-serving instinct? Does my imported PVC trump your Weedwacker? And though I can rationalize my first-world paddle by aiming to amplify marginalized voices, the worry that my energy could be better applied elsewhere, anywhere elsewhere, continues to gnaw.

A few weeks ago, just up ahead a few miles, river right, in the town of Hawkesbury, I spent a Saturday morning participating in a pinnacle of time well spent. Ottawa Riverkeeper had organized a public shoreline cleanup, and I drove out to join about three dozen volunteers. One of the goals of every riverkeeper group — descendants of the Mother of All Riverkeepers, established on the Hudson in the mid-1960s — is to get communities engaged in their own watersheds. Research, citizen science, monitoring and advocacy are among their tactics, which help curb government policy and industrial practices. Meeting your neighbors while wrestling tires out of the muck is central to their strategy. Not only does it get you to the water, this sweat equity could also entice others down to the shore.

Armed with work gloves and plastic buckets, we descend on a scrubby patch of green, heavily treed in spots, with a rough trail snaking down to the river. Hawkesbury was chosen as today's site because there's a bridge across to the village of Grenville in Quebec. Municipalities in both provinces are working together to protect the river. "The Ottawa is seen as something that divides us," says Ottawa Riverkeeper's Renée Davies, who coordinates outreach projects. "But it also connects us. When we collaborate like this, people see how their actions can impact the entire watershed."

Cédrik Bertrand, middle-aged, lives in Hawkesbury and doesn't spend a lot of time on this chunk of municipally owned land that's maybe a dozen football fields big. But he walks here occasionally and figures if it's cleaner more people might come down to enjoy the view. "If we can restore collective pride, maybe we won't need to pick up other people's trash. Sometimes it seems like the only people who know this spot exists are the ones who come to dump garbage."

Diane Thauvette, a retired waitress who grew up in town, is at her first cleanup. She didn't come to the river as a child. It wasn't considered clean. Now she likes to picnic and walk along the shore. "It keeps me young. Body and mind."

Nearby, a woman yanks part of a car doorframe out of the ground. I'm jealous of her haul. Filling my bucket with broken glass, plastic bags, plastic bottles and beer cans, I ask Diane if she has a method for finding larger objects.

"I'm not looking for treasure," she says. "I'm not here to get rich."

Diane introduces me to a man with long hair spilling out from a ballcap, Thaila Riden, who farms and runs a community garden a few miles from the river, partnering with a food bank. He came out today despite the fact that it's a perfect planting morning. "Somebody's gotta do it," he says, "and it feels good to repair some of the damage we've caused. This is low-hanging fruit." Thaila tugs a large piece of black plastic from the ground. "Feels like I'm harvesting something."

I accompany Thaila and a teenaged boy, Jacob, scampering up an embankment where a small creek, now largely dry, trickles down slick rocks. A spring freshness scents the breeze, overriding the mulchy layer of rotting branches off-gassing at our feet. Jackpot: Styrofoam, golf balls, paper cups, rebar. There are tangles of brush and trash on the ledges, and it's invigorating to climb and reach for garbage that would wash into the river if still here when the snow melts next spring. Like a treasure hunt. And way more fulfilling than I, a river cleanup virgin, had imagined. Thaila wheels a tire to the shore just as a firefighter drives over in an ATV. We load the tire onto the cargo box, empty our buckets into a bag, then head up the slope for more gold.

Jacob is here with his mother, Alex Mallett, a bespectacled sustainable energy and climate policy researcher with whom I happen to share an employer. (The communications department at Carleton University, whose campus is cradled between the Rideau Canal and River, with a sweet set of rapids on the latter that I stare at incessantly, granted me leave for this project.) Although Alex's work involves developing and implementing policy changes to tackle system-level challenges, that doesn't alleviate her son's climate concerns. "Policy is abstract, but this is a way to switch the feeling from passive to active," she says. "Jacob tells me that he wants to see tangible action. That means focusing on things we can control. Volunteering is one of those things."

Alex believes that social norms and policy have a chicken-and-egg relationship, informing each other. "The big picture is important," she says, "but I think individual actions are also important, not only to keep us grounded but also because they can help change the norms.

"We're old," she adds. "We get complacent. We focus on our work and domestic chores. But kids, they don't think that way. They remind us that nature is everywhere, that we really need to move away from the idea that there's a barrier between urban places and wilderness. That we are not separate from nature. We're part of it."

CHAPTER 2

"I did a private SUP clinic one night for a group of six women. They were all friends, out for a good night on the lake. They were waiting for the last person to come, who was the mother of one of the students. She was probably pushing 70 and had a multitude of health issues. She wanted to be part of the social experience, but her mobility was very compromised. She basically sat on a board, and I towed her around as I taught the others. We did that for three hours. Toward the end of the night, we were getting back to the put-in and the mom looked at me said, 'I want to stand up. I'm really nervous about it.' We went around the corner, I helped her stand up and get stable, and then she paddled around the point in front of all the women, under her own power. Everybody on that dock broke into tears. I still tear up thinking about it."

— Alex Chandler, recreation therapist and proprietor of Scotian SUP

A JARRING STOP SNAPS ME OUT OF MY MEANDERING THOUGHTS. A STREAM of consciousness so absorbing, apparently, that I have run aground while crossing a shallow, sandy delta where the Rouge River empties into the Ottawa near Hawkesbury. Sometimes we are so much a part of nature we lodge ourselves into her.

A blast of thunder delivers another jolt as I step off my board onto the soft, rippled riverbed to pull it into deeper water. I knew there was a chance of storms today. Consulting the weather app on my phone regularly for wind direction and the threat of lightning is one of the keys to my admittedly limited and evidently lacking safety protocol. I haven't looked at the forecast for a while, and taking advantage of this unintentional pause to check, I discover that the smoky sky has cloaked a menacing dark red blob on the radar map that's approaching swiftly from the northwest. The river here curls to the right, to the southeast, and the wind that's funneling the storm toward me is now pushing me downriver. Figuring I've got half an hour to spare, I race past Grenville, where I had considered stopping for the night. There's a covered gazebo in a park that would have provided shelter, but there's a No Camping sign — and I don't want to bail on this tailwind just yet.

Another booming thunderclap just after I pass the village sends me scurrying to an unbroken chain of private property along the shore. Spotting a cabana with a covered porch beside a residential dock, I bellow "Hello! Hello!" There's nobody around. The wind is billowing now, swirling. I cinch my SUP to the dock and take a few halting steps toward a house up the hill, calling out greetings. Nothing. So I sit outside the cabana, getting under the roof before a barrage of hail, and wait edgily for half an hour, watching lightning put on a show and thinking I really should check the weather app more often. And that I should make more conservative decisions about when to get off my board.

In this part of Quebec, on a wobbly foundation of high school French, I'd probably be fine if spotted by a homeowner while taking shelter. "Je suis désolé. Je paddleboard a Montréal." In a place with more guns, I might have to take my chances on the water.

The other wee lesson? When the sky is full of smoke, you can't always see what's coming.

Which I promptly forget, several hours later, evening-ish, zooming toward the massive river-spanning Carillon dam, still riding that tailwind, the sky still smoky. Thunder is hard on my heels and my heart is pounding as I sprint toward a boat ramp beside the lock chamber. Not a moment too soon, I scuff onto shore, berating myself for nearly making the same mistake already. I drag my board and gear to the side of a road and barrel into a visitor center bathroom as another hailstorm begins. I'm fortunate to have this shelter but effectively trapped in its cell-like ambiance. My incarceration lasts for less than an hour, but there's nothing like a fluorescent-lit vista of urinals and cinder-block walls to make somebody revisit their life choices.

A dozen years ago, Zac Crouse wheeled his 17-foot sea kayak around this dam a few weeks into a 950-mile paddling and cycling odyssey from the upper Ottawa River to the Atlantic Ocean. He had been planning to do the trip with a close friend, Corey Morris. The men were veteran creekers — descending steep whitewater in small specialized kayaks — but Corey was swept over a waterfall and died when they were out with two others in spring 2009. Zac was traumatized by the accident, but two years later, he decided to tackle the journey solo as a tribute to his friend and as part of his healing.

Even if no man can step into the same river twice, I phoned Zac a few weeks after my trip finished. I wanted to compare notes about paddling these waters. To ask about hurdles, like the Carillon dam or the train of dark thoughts racing through his brain, he had to find a way around.

When Corey died, Zac was working as a recreation therapist in Nova Scotia. He did outdoor activities such as hiking and paddling with clients — sometimes adults and families but mostly youth — and used the sessions to help people address the problems they were facing. Unlike traditional talk therapy, moving through green or blue space together introduces shifting risks and power dynamics (especially when a parent sits in the front of a canoe and their teenager is in the rear, steering). Basic aerobic exertion plus a shared experience equals an opportunity to build rapport and have meaningful conversations. Clients can confront fears and strive toward small goals. If you're on paddleboards, you can talk about ideas such as balance and perspective.

"You're doing an activity, but there's intent," says Zac, who was introduced to me by a mutual friend, Alex Chandler, another Nova Scotian rec therapist who's also a SUP instructor. "Conventional therapy is easier logistically — for the clinician. You just sit in a room. Which doesn't really benefit the client, because it takes longer to build up trust when you're doing something unnatural."

Although he now teaches rec therapy at a university and is no longer practicing, Zac saw how kayak outings impacted his clients. "Right from the get-go, your brain is seeing patterns on the water that don't easily fall into slots and boxes. There's a calming effect. You've also got sounds and the feel of the wind; just being around that much energy has benefits that are many and varied." People with trauma often disassociate and don't want to talk or think about it. They don't want to *go there*. Meditation can be hard. But paddling might be one of the easiest ways to get into a meditative state, says Zac, who was struggling with PTSD and having daily flashbacks to Corey's death when he began his trip.

All those weeks on the water helped him manage the trauma, in concert with therapy and medication. "It gave me a purpose, something to focus on, something meaningful but also symbolic. At a basic level, it was a physical challenge, but there were higher level cognitive things happening. It was a simple, stress-free way of living, because the variables were all repetitive: move east, find a place to sleep, eat food, repeat. The problems you're solving are very basic and immediate, not future vague ones.

"You get into a trance-like state after so many hours of paddling," he adds. "The repetitive motion, the exertion, all the little things you have to pay attention to in order to make progress — those create a sense of flow. It gave me a lot of time to think and contemplate uninterrupted. I was trying to cram as many good and healthy things into my life as possible until my brain caught up to reality. Because your brain is trapped back in that moment, whatever that moment was, and the groove just keeps getting deeper and deeper. So you gotta replace that with new, different memories and try to smooth out the grooves a little bit."

Being on the journey gave Zac a novel sense of freedom (at least when he wasn't hunting down places to camp or get drinking water). It was a reset button, a break from rumination and thought loops and regret. "It wasn't magic. It wasn't like flipping a switch. But it did create a pattern of sustainable, healthy self-care.

"I don't like using Christianity as an example of anything, but the symbolism of baptism is pretty powerful. There's a reason why they use water."

Zac believes rec therapy can be more effective if it escapes the medical model, which centers on identifying and fixing a problem. "'Where are you broken?' That's the whole mindset. It's not 'How about together, collectively, we create a society where people are healthier?' What does *that* look like? How much physical activity do people need every day? How do we remove the constraints and barriers that prevent people from doing that?

"If we could zoom out a little bit, we pathologize and put the onus on the individual, which is ridiculous. We make choices as a society and then blame individuals. Essentially, the short version is don't be poor. The biggest fix for mental illness is money. Give somebody regular, consistent income and they have the time and energy to deal with the basics of life."

As a university student, Zac wondered why so many of his classmates were "so fucking calm" all the time. "Because they were rich!" he says. Because inequity contributes to chronic stress, "which can be just as debilitating as trauma."

Society can't treat access to nature as a business venture, with short-term inputs and outputs, argues Zac, because it holds so much potential. "We need to mandate public access to natural spaces. We need education, because we've become very sloth-like and sedentary and don't understand the implications. These are 50- to 100-year plans. But in a generation, we can have more active people who are less sad and more resilient and better able to handle stress. It's a start."

To a guy who loves paddleboarding, Zac Crouse's observations have a ring of the gospel. The wisdom of theory and clinical practice meshed with extreme personal experience gives him an attuned moral compass. But even as one of the converted, I didn't anticipate how his views on mental health and the pervasive impacts of inequality would cut to the heart of blue space research.

Put on your PFD. Let's jump in.

Water covers more than 70 percent of Earth's surface. It's also about 60 percent of the average human adult's body weight, although it comprises nearly three-quarters of organs such as the brain and heart. There's a nice symmetry to these numbers, all roughly in the same ballpark. Water doesn't just demarcate a decent portion of who and where we are: it's the *majority* of who and where we are.

Yet in many ways, it remains a mystery. Even though it's the most abundant liquid on the planet, we don't fully understand water's chemical structure and strange properties, at least 66 of which "differ from most liquids," writes science author and educator Rachel Brazil, among them "high surface tension, high heat capacity, high melting and boiling points and low compressibility." Frozen water is less dense than when it's in liquid form, which doesn't happen in "normal" liquids. This has something to do with how hydrogen and oxygen bond, which may also explain why water is the only known substance on the planet to exist naturally in solid, liquid and gaseous forms.

At a microscopic level, all those H_2O molecules help maintain the structure and shape of cells. They are the building blocks of our building blocks. They help metabolize and transport carbohydrates and proteins in our bloodstream — the fuel that keeps us functioning. Water helps us flush waste when we urinate, lubricates our joints and serves as a shock absorber for the brain. Every single animal and plant needs water, the latter for the life-sustaining process of photosynthesis.

The sparks that water sets off in our minds can also be explained by science. More specifically, by evolution, biology, neuroscience and concepts such as flow — a state in which people are so captivated by an activity that nothing else seems to matter.

The main job of our brains, according to molecular biologist John Medina, is to solve problems that allow us to survive while navigating an "unstable environment" (or, as I like to call it, "life"). With an endless barrage of stimuli to contend with, our neural networks have become adept at recognizing patterns and making predictions. A sudden loud noise, whether it's a lion roaring on the savannah or a bus speeding past in the city, is perceived as a threat and, boom, our fight-or-flight response kicks in.

The folks at Harvard Medical School explain this mechanism well. To paraphrase, when we see and hear that rapidly approaching lion or bus, our eyes and ears send information to the amygdala, one of the brain's main processing centers. The amygdala interprets this info and, if it perceives danger, transmits a distress signal to the hypothalamus, a command center for the sympathetic and parasympathetic nervous systems. The former makes us fight or flee from a potential threat; the latter is a network of nerves that relaxes our bodies following stressful or dangerous experiences. Once the sympathetic nervous system is engaged, it signals our adrenal glands to send the hormone epinephrine (also known as adrenaline) into the bloodstream. This sets off a cascade of physiological changes: the heart beats faster, pumping blood everywhere; we breathe more rapidly; our sight, hearing and other senses get sharper; and the release of glucose and fats prompted by epinephrine gives us a burst of energy. These instantaneous responses allow us to jump out of the way of that bus or try to evade that lion. If the threat doesn't pass quickly, the body also releases cortisol, the primary stress hormone, which keeps us on high alert until we get the all clear and the parasympathetic nervous system brings us down from the ledge. Also known as the rest-and-digest system, it basically tells the brain what our bodies are up to and then acts like a brake, dampening the stress response.

One of the challenges of modern life is that we're often on high alert: mechanical noise, highway traffic, flying through our days at a frenetic pace, whipped up by screens of all sizes. This is especially true for those experiencing trauma. In addition to technological encroachment into our time and thoughts, everything from the basic need to keep ourselves and the people we care about fed and sheltered to the pursuit of love and purpose in a byzantine and ever-changing environment can produce chronic stress. So can worries about health, money, war, climate change or racial injustice. Violence in the Middle East and Eastern Europe, an alphabet of devastating hurricanes, spiking grocery prices: there is no shortage of things to worry about. These strains, which can also result from more commonplace concerns (such as workplace conflict or a long lineup at the drive-thru), seem to be mounting in the post-pandemic, pre-next-pandemic world. Driven by factors like social media use, loneliness and a lack of access to care, the mental health crisis is real. In 2024, the U.S. surgeon general issued a warning about the harmful mental health impacts of parenting, which in turn affect the well-being of children. An activity at the core of our survival is officially a health risk. Chronic stress can lead to high blood pressure, the formation of artery-clogging deposits, poor sleep, obesity and chemical changes in the brain that contribute to anxiety, depression and addiction. All of which can literally kill us.

Hanging out in, on or around water is not an elixir, and how individuals respond to activities such as swimming, surfing or floating a boat depends on our unique psychological makeup, our distinctive physiologies and past experiences, as well as the nuances of the aquatic landscape where we are. Not to mention how much money we have, the color of our skin, our gender, mobility and so forth. But for a lot of people, a lot of different blue spaces seem to do wonders for our moods.

"Humans are hardwired to connect with water," says environmental psychologist Jenny Roe, director of the University of Virginia's Center for Design and Health. She tells me that blue space has four triggers that activate our parasympathetic nervous system. First, according to Roe, water instills a sense of being away. It can be either tranquil or dynamic, conditions that can make you introspective or dialed in to your surroundings, both of which serve as escapes from your habitual behavior. Second, blue space (especially large bodies of water) conjures a feeling of "extent," of being in a boundless environment where possibilities feel limitless. Although one can also experience these glimpses of an infinite existence while, say, hiking up a mountain, they're amplified in blue space by acts like looking to the horizon or into the depths of a lake. Third, the sounds and sights of water — as it runs over rocks, for example, or dances in the sunlight — can spark "hard fascination," a concentration of our focus through stimulation, and "soft fascination," an unconscious, partial capturing of our attention that requires little effort and frees the mind to roam. Both of these can contribute to restoration. And fourth, water confers a sense of compatibility with our location, of comfort and belonging.

Part of this affinity can be attributed to the biophilia hypothesis, the idea that our intimate relationship with the natural world is rooted in genetics. As explained by Pulitzer Prize–winning Harvard University biologist E. O. Wilson, who is often called the father of biodiversity, our universal appreciation for the shapes and colors found in nature and a spiritual reverence of animals across cultures and geographies are evidence of an innate bond forged during our evolution as a species. Ferocious predators, food shortages, frequently inadequate shelter and short life expectancies notwithstanding, living in sync with nature was foundational to human development. This sheds some light on why many people trade climate-controlled homes for sleeping on the ground inside flimsy tents as often as possible — and is surely one of the reasons why, when industrialization and urbanization started to limit interactions with our flora and fauna cousins, psychological hiccups began to proliferate.

The restorative qualities of spending time in green space are well documented. One early landmark study, published in the journal *Science* in 1984, demonstrated that patients convalescing from surgeries had fewer complications, shorter postoperative hospital stays, fewer negative evaluative comments from nurses and took fewer doses of analgesics if their rooms looked out onto a natural view as opposed to a brick wall. Five years later, in their book *The Experience of Nature*, University of Michigan psychology professors Rachel and Stephen Kaplan outlined their influential attention restoration theory, which holds that people are able to concentrate better after they spend time in a natural setting or simply look at images of natural scenes. (The Kaplans did trailblazing research on soft fascination, a key to one of Roe's four blue space triggers.)

Only recently, however, have researchers begun to zero in on what changes inside the brain when water is part of the equation. A 2022 paper published by a pair of University of California, Davis, psychology researchers, for example, concluded that even looking at a creek or pool is enough to lower blood pressure and heart rates and increase relaxation among respondents, a result they attribute, in part, to the evolutionary link between successfully detecting drinking water in arid environments and stress reduction. Taking in the sea air, strolling along a peninsula or sitting beside a pond have long been considered good for our well-being, but a series of new studies has shown how — and why — blue space appears to have a more profound impact on our bodies and brains than other outdoor environments. And how, through policy change, conservation and urban design, we can reap the holistic rewards of this eternal bond.

CHAPTER 3

"The ocean benefits human health by being a place where individuals can relax and be physically active, play, be creative, spend quality time with friends and family, and satisfy the deeply held human need to feel connected to the wider natural world around us. A healthy ocean can offer us the opportunity to not only survive but thrive. The Global Burden of Disease study points out that the disease burdens in many countries are shifting from communicable, nutritional and neonatal issues to non-communicable diseases (NCDs) (e.g. cardiovascular diseases, diabetes and depression). It is in the prevention of NCDs that living near the ocean may offer important but often unrecognised human health benefits. . . . [These benefits are] particularly strong among poorer communities with high levels of environmental and socioeconomic disadvantage, as well as during times of stress such as in financial downturns and the COVID-19 pandemic. The disproportionate benefits of coastal residence are seen globally and are by no means restricted to the Global North."

— *World Resources Institute's High Level Panel for a Sustainable Ocean Economy, "How Can a Healthy Ocean Improve Human Health and Enhance Wellbeing on a Rapidly Changing Planet?"*

WHEN I FIRST TALKED TO ENVIRONMENTAL PSYCHOLOGIST AND BLUE SPACE researcher Mat White, he had just moved from his native United Kingdom to the University of Vienna — a fitting base for a psychologist — and had recently wrapped up a leadership role in the five-year BlueHealth initiative, a European research network that examined the nexus between urban blue spaces, climate and health. BlueHealth projects relied on measures such as heart rate and blood pressure as well as surveys administered by trained interviewers and self-reported wellness. For one paper, Mat corralled big data — a U.K. census of approximately 48 million adults — and found that the closer people live to the coast, the healthier and happier they are, a conclusion he and his collaborators attributed to increased opportunities for stress reduction and physical activity. "The crucial point about that research was that it was the poorest communities and individuals who got the benefits," he told me, referring to both physiological and psychological well-being. "If you're rich, it doesn't matter how often you spend time in blue space. You're healthy and happy anyway. But if you're poor, it matters hugely."

The quality of blue spaces affects their therapeutic properties, as does how we interact with them, variables influenced by geography as well as by cognitive and cultural differences. For example, people often prefer places they visited as children, according to Mat, and there are dramatic differences between walking and sitting, and different outcomes depending on how close we live to a blue space and how frequently we visit. But on the whole, when we're near water, we tend to lose track of time and be more active, he says, and every extra minute of movement is good for our physical health. Moreover, "people benefit more mentally when they're visiting blue spaces than when they're visiting green spaces," adds Mat, although the ideal, he clarifies, is where the two spaces meet.

Natural areas often have some sort of aquatic element, from barely trickling streams in urban ravines to pounding waves below cliff-top trails. But not always. The lines between green and blue (and, in a Canadian winter, white) spaces are blurry, yet wellness surveys point to a hierarchy. In one study in the Netherlands, respondents used a smartphone app to record their level of happiness: those visiting natural coastal environments were roughly twice as happy as those in forests and three times happier than people in agricultural terrain. Manicured parks and grassy areas with low-lying vegetation typically score well, and mountains extremely well, but nothing beats water. A mountain lake, says Mat, may be the ultimate happy place.

In England, one of the projects under the BlueHealth umbrella took place in Plymouth's Teats Hill, a low-income neighborhood on a postindustrial waterfront where locals avoided the small beach because it was unkempt and strewn with trash. City council secured a grant, commissioned landscape architects and consulted the community to plan a redevelopment. It featured an open-air theater, seating, an improved slipway to make it easy to launch personal watercraft and a lawn with a view of the harbor. The cost was around $110,000 U.S., and surveys assessed the well-being of area residents before, during and after construction. Psychological health increased, as did perceptions of community cohesion. Families played in the park, seniors sat on benches and teenagers took forays onto the sea.

Similar scenes play out on freshwater rivers and at just about any blue space imaginable, no matter the salinity, from urban ponds to the greatest of lakes. More than half of the world's population lives within two miles of a body of fresh water, and many landlocked people have limited coastal access, but inland blue spaces receive far less attention from researchers than ocean environments. That's beginning to change. A 2021 Scottish study found that the presence of aquatic environments within neighborhoods, including fresh water, is associated with lower antidepressant usage among older adults.

"The goodness isn't just the water," says Mat, mentioning a study which found that people hang out by German rivers and lakes the same way they do at coastal beaches, spending quality time with one another because of the sense of belonging they feel. "It's a behavioral interaction that water encourages. This is one of the reasons we think blue spaces tackle health inequalities. They're social spaces that draw us into cross-generational play."

Blue spaces appear to promote social interactions that benefit mental and physical health "through a sense of community [and] mutual support between people," according to a 2021 paper by a team of European researchers. And by reducing air pollution and the urban heat island effect, they contribute to a healthier local environment.

The kicker to all this, the multiplier of multipliers, the shining ray of hope, is that time spent in blue space, especially by children, promotes what researchers call "pro-environmental behavior." Which is a technical way of saying "taking better care of the planet."

In a 2024 paper co-authored with Patricia Stehl and others, Mat looked at the connections between childhood exposure to freshwater blue spaces in Austria and the preponderance of a dozen different pro-environmental behaviors in adulthood, such as choosing low-carbon travel, avoiding single-use plastics, reducing energy or water consumption and participating in group activities like beach cleanups. They found a validated link. "All of the reviewers said this was a breakthrough," says Mat. "They'd never seen this before." What's more, several of these behaviors, like using less plastic, can contribute directly to preserving the ecological integrity of blue spaces, reinforcing a virtuous circle.

At a time when human contact with nature is decreasing around the world — a phenomenon among children that ecologist Robert Michael Pyle called "extinction of experience" — getting a kid to the water has the potential to help stop the bleeding. As Mat's paper declares, "Findings highlight the potential importance of childhood blue space exposure . . . and add to calls for protecting and maintaining natural water bodies and to improve their safety, as spending time around them in childhood may play a role in fostering [pro-environmental behavior] and ultimately improving planetary health."

Thud. A car door slams shut. Thud. Another. Nearby.
Lean over and look at phone.
Five-something o'clock in the morning.

Damn dam.

I was beat last night but barely slept. It hadn't dawned on me, until dawn was upon me, that this tucked-away patch of grass, under the canopy of a shaggy silver maple on an empty park-like strip of public land, was both a passable campsite *and* a national historic site. And that the Carillon lock station, part of a 200-year-old canal system built to bypass rapids on the Ottawa River, is also home to a hydroelectric generating station, whose enormous dam, nearly three-quarters of a mile long, can generate enough juice for 150,000 households. This emits a loud buzzing noise. Continuously. Which is even louder than the drone from that fromagerie's HVAC in Montebello. And not conducive to sleep if you're in a tent 300 feet from the dam.

Now a Parks Canada employee is probably striding over to inform me, somewhat redundantly at this hour, that camping is not permitted. (In my defense, I had seen the No Camping sign last night *after* I set up my tent.) I unzip the fly for a peek and see a pair of Hydro-Québec workers smoking pre-shift cigarettes outside their parked cars on the access road to the power plant.

They glance over and clearly don't care about the guy groggily crawling out of a tent in his underwear. Yet I'm awake and might as well get going. Arriving late and leaving early is a good way to avoid trouble when guerilla camping. Plus, it's not raining, at least for now, so I pack up and eat quickly (the first of innumerable peanut butter wraps I'll consume over the next few months) and launch my SUP on the downstream side of the lock.

The morning is cool. A soft drizzle begins to fall. But I have the misty river to myself, and with a light breeze at my back, distance comes effortlessly. Within two hours, there's an island portside, the three-mile-long Carillon Island Migratory Bird Sanctuary. Angling into the weedy shallows, I hear and then see a pileated woodpecker hammering away at a dead limb. To my right, a cackling rainbow of ducks: blue-winged, green-winged teal, American black. Swallows and red-winged blackbirds dart about in a tall stand of lush elm and oak, maple and aspen. I stop paddling, close my eyes and breathe in deeply. It smells musty, herbaceous and floral, with notes of clay and citrus. Forest bathing — basically, spending time amongst trees — reduces stress and helps our immune systems. We inhale phytoncides, volatile organic compounds that plants emit to protect themselves from insects and disease. These chemicals have antibacterial and antifungal qualities that can protect us from diseases too.

"Think of [forest bathing] as a prescription with no negative side effects that's also free," suggests the New York State Department of Environmental Conservation.

I breathe in deeply again.

Off the eastern tip of Carillon Island there's a four-mile crossing to Pointe-aux-Anglais, an apt waypoint for an anglais, with a wide detour to the north if I want to stick closer to the shoreline. The wind has picked up — it's blowing pretty hard now that I've poked beyond the lee of the island — but it's coming from the west-northwest and pushing me more or less *where I want to go.*

Did I tell you how rare it is for this to happen when you're on a SUP? How some cosmic law dictates thou shalt always have to contend with a headwind or a crosswind. (Unless you purposely seek out a downwind trip in, say, Maui.) So I head into the open water, paddling hard and surfing swells for one of the first (and, sadly, one of the last) times on this journey. A 14-foot board loaded with gear keeps its speed in a tailwind and planes atop small waves when you catch them. It's tricky to stay balanced as I corkscrew down some of the faces and fight to keep my bow aiming in the right direction. It's also adrenaline-rush thrilling. Whooping loudly, I zip across the yawning bay in less than an hour and discover, just beyond the tip of the point on the far side, the sheltered basin of a sailing club. Had I approached by road, this private dock would have been off-limits, but nobody sees me pop in for a pit stop.

After another, shorter wind-aided crossing, I'm paddling tight to the shore at a brisk pace. A steep, heavily treed hillside rises from the water's edge, and I notice cabins perched on stilts, camouflaged by the dense foliage. Then what looks to be an ad hoc marina at the base of a precipitous dirt road. This stretch of riverside feels different than what I've seen so far along the Ottawa River: dug-in, defensible.

I pass within a few feet of a dock beneath one cabin and see a man watching me from a porch high above. I wave, but he doesn't respond. And then it hits me, as I reach a string of houses with manicured lawns, pools, fountains and fake palm trees on the outskirts of the village of Oka: those were the Kanesatake Lands. Which puts me a stone's throw from the forest where, in 1990, Kanyen'keha:ka (Mohawk) protestors were embroiled in 78-day-long standoff with police officers and soldiers — "one of the most significant acts of armed self-defence in Canada by Indigenous peoples," writes artist and activist Gord Hill, a member of the West Coast Kwakwaka'wakw Nation, and an encounter that "set the tone for Indigenous resistance . . . to this day."

CHAPTER 4

"My memories of that summer at Kanesatake are so different from the stories told by the media. Their attention was focused on the barricades. To most of them, this was a just a cop story: the police and soldiers were there 'to restore law and order,' to put things back the way they were. But most of the people behind the barricades were my family, friends and relatives. And they didn't want things to go back to the way they were. They knew that would mean a certain and steady ride down a one-way street to an oblivion called assimilation."

— Dan David, from the foreword to People of the Pines

HOW DOES ONE BEGIN TO UNRAVEL WHAT HAS COME TO BE CALLED THE Oka Crisis? By starting with the arrival of colonial forces in North America and their ruthless dispossession of Indigenous Peoples. The same old story, whose local details belie a broad resonance, like ripples emanating from a stone dropped into a river.

On this particular river, in 1717, land was granted by the king of France to a Roman Catholic order, the Sulpicians, who established a mission at Oka, northwest of Montreal. The Mohawks who settled there a few years later believed the land had been set aside for them, Geoffrey York and Loreen Pindera write in *People of the Pines*. They had been hunting, fishing and trading in the St. Lawrence Valley since the 1500s and were related to earlier Indigenous Peoples who had lived there for thousands of years.

Mohawks in Oka contested control of this land, first to the Sulpicians and the French; then to British, after they had defeated the French; and eventually to Canadian authorities and courts, after this young dominion was established in 1867. All of their claims, at least nine formal appeals over 150 years, were rejected. Meanwhile, the Sulpicians were selling lots to white settlers, with Mohawks relegated to a patchwork of properties west of the fledgling village. By the mid-1940s, the Sulpicians had sold all of their land and moved on, and the nearly 265 square miles the Mohawks once lived on had been whittled down to just two.

In 1959, in a wooded area known as the Pines, whose ownership had long been in dispute, a nine-hole golf course was built adjacent to a Mohawk burial ground. Thirty years later, the mayor of Oka announced plans to add nine more holes and a luxury home development. Despite a campaign calling for a delay and the provincial government expressing concern, construction was set to start in spring 1990. That led to a Mohawk barricade on a dirt road leading to the Pines. Warriors from nearby communities, including Kahnawake and Akwesasne, joined the blockade. Men with AK-47s conducted patrols and took up defensive positions in bunkers and in the trees.

Tensions throughout the region had been rising for decades. Inspired by the American Indian Movement in the United States, which called for armed resistance from Indigenous communities to fend off government interference, there was a steady stream of conflicts between Mohawks and police in Quebec over issues such as law enforcement and revenue from gambling and cigarette sales — proxy battles not only for self-determination but also self-preservation. (*People of the Pines* reports that one Kanesatake man whose slot-machine operation had been raided was using the proceeds to pay the salary of a Mohawk-language kindergarten teacher at the local elementary school.) There were flashpoints on both sides of the border: Mohawks occupied an abandoned summer camp in the Adirondack Mountains and held it for three years; an international bridge was blocked; a National Guard helicopter flying over a Mohawk community in New York was shot at, triggering a standoff for several days.

Which made Oka a tinderbox.

On July 11, 1990, Quebec provincial police descended on the barricade in the Pines with a front-end loader and about 100 members of a tactical squad to enforce a court injunction. With tear gas in the air and a chopper overhead, a brief firefight ensued. One officer was shot and killed in the chaos.

The police retreated hastily and set up a checkpoint to control people traveling around Kanesatake and Oka. The force's abandoned vehicles were used to bolster the barricade. Across the river and 25 miles to the east, Mohawks from Kahnawake seized and shut down the Mercier Bridge, a major commuter artery across the St. Lawrence into Montreal. In the Pines and on the bridge, both sides settled in. Dozens of Mohawks were camping in the woods in Kanesatake: men, women and children. Up to 600 people took turns on duty on the bridge. As the days dragged on, residents of the nearby south-shore city of Châteauguay became increasingly irate about their route to jobs in Montreal being blocked. There were violent, racist confrontations daily. The RCMP, Canada's national police force, was called in to support the Quebec police; a total of about 2,000 officers were deployed. Then, in mid-August, the army took over. About 4,000 soldiers arrived with more than 1,000 vehicles, including tanks, armored personnel carriers and artillery pieces, as well as ships patrolling the Ottawa and St. Lawrence Rivers.

I didn't know much of this history when I paddled into Oka. I turned 17 in 1990 and remember fragments from the TV news. That a police officer had been killed. Intense stare-downs between soldiers and bandana-veiled warriors with nicknames like Lasagna. That it was over a graveyard and a golf course. But none of the details, nor the context, were familiar to me. As is, I suspect, the case for many non-Indigenous Canadians, especially if we're not from around there. But when you immerse yourself in a place, these distant and not-so-distant layers of the past rise to the surface and propel you toward an inevitable inflection point: willful ignorance or reckoning?

~

Today, the village of Oka, on a midweek afternoon in June, is quiet and pleasant. There's a small beach and boat launch beside the ferry pier, a library with pristine bathrooms across the street and a café up the road. Very welcoming for waterborne visitors. Much more so than, say, Oka Provincial Park, a couple miles farther east and my destination for the night.

I try to book a campsite online, pecking away on my phone while drinking an Americano at a picnic table outside the library. But I'm not a phone guy, and it doesn't work. So I paddle to the park, pull my board onto a sandy beach and walk more than a mile to the front gate, where I'm told that I'll need to go to an office in the middle of the campground to pay for a site. Another mile on foot later, I'm told to go to the general store, where, finally, in my broken French, heels blistering in my damp water shoes, I'm able to secure a spot fairly close to the shore.

The campground is almost empty, I notice as I lug my dry bags to the site. It's raining now, dusk is approaching and the mosquitoes are attacking ferociously. I set up my tent in an itchy-and-scratchy frenzy; shove dry clothes, food and a book into a bag; and make a beeline for the place communautaire, an insect-free indoor space.

There's only one other person in the enormous room. An enormous man, forearms covered in tattoos, wearing a grubby hoody and sweatpants. I say hello, he nods, and I take a table near the far wall. Tired but dry, I'm content to read and enjoy this modicum of comfort. He seems engrossed by his phone, and I wonder why he's here. Most campers this time of year have trailers or RVs; why would anybody choose to tent and, like me, be forced to hide from the bugs? After nearly an hour of silence, he says, "The Wi-Fi here sucks. You getting a signal?" I tell him that I'm not online and ask what brings him to the park.

He clears his throat. "I, um, got on my bike a month ago in Moncton to ride to the West Coast. And now I'm here."

"What inspired that, if I may ask?"

"Well, where do I begin . . ."

I walk across the room, introduce myself and ask if it's cool to sit down. Chris Aubichon shakes my hand.

For the next three hours, Chris tells me his story. He had been living in New Brunswick, working as a property manager, and decided to make a dramatic change. A former ward of the state, he was abused horribly as a child and, after selling drugs and collecting debts for bikers, did time in youth custody. He has anxiety, depression and diabetes, plus a bad back and bad knees. But in the face of all this, now in his mid-40s, Chris wanted to go back to school and become a social worker — and thanks to a recent legal change in British Columbia, where he grew up, postsecondary tuition is now covered by the government for former wards of the state, no matter how old they are. So he bought a cheap mountain bike and, without training, cobbled together some camping gear and started pedaling toward the Pacific.

"Why bike?" I ask.

"Because it's an insurmountable challenge for *me* to do 3,500 miles on a bike," he says in a deep gravelly voice. "I'm six-foot-five, 320 pounds — I'm the last person on earth you would think could be capable of doing this. The man who can accomplish this is ready to make an impactful change in his life, and other people's lives too.

"I know I'm bright, but I'm developmentally delayed by about 15 years," Chris continues, telling me that he wants to show his daughters what's possible. "As a teenager, dealing with sexual, physical and emotional abuse, I wasn't capable of going to school. Now I'm ready. Potential is one of those arbitrary bullshit things. What is potential? You can't see it, touch it, weigh it. I believe there's more to me, more I can do to be helpful."

I ask Chris about his family, and he says that his maternal grandmother was a member of the West Coast Tla'amin Nation. She tried to outrun intergenerational trauma in Vancouver, which is where his mother was born and swiftly adopted into a white family. He tells me about his sister, who has been nagging him to share his story on social media, to talk about his struggles with mental illness, about his daily battle to keep his shit together. But he doesn't think anybody will care. And despite his transparency with me tonight, he usually doesn't open up to strangers.

In more than three decades as a journalist, I've interviewed lots of people who've been dealt raw hands, but I've never heard anybody express themselves with such incise honesty.

"Listen to your sister," I suggest to Chris.

Somewhere in the pine forest of Oka, thousands of mosquitoes flap their wings.

(Spoiler alert — Chris makes it to the coast and is going to school! His ride takes three months and there are crushing setbacks, such as his bike and gear being stolen. But he starts posting regularly on Instagram [@nothingfancy_justpedal], attracting a large following and a slew of media coverage. Hundreds of strangers help Chris with hotel rooms, restaurants, home-cooked meals, a new bike and camping equipment. "We're fed horror stories about the world, but there are so many good people out there," he says. "It's a cliché, but just talk to people and you'll see that they're good." Some of these folks, in turn, have been inspired by Chris: they've bought bikes, they're rebuilding relationships, they're getting off the couch. "All because of what I did; I'm probably the fattest man to ever bike across Canada!")

There's no industrial noise tonight near my tent. Just chittering racoons, which smell food in one of my dry bags and are trying to claw through the coated nylon fabric atop the picnic table. I yell at the four sets of eyes illuminated by my headlamp. They go right back to clawing. Worried about a puncture, I step outside, gather a few chunks of wood and hurl them at the racoons. They scamper off into the bushes, then return in a few seconds. More throwing, more scampering, more returning, more clawing and a torrent of cursing ensues. I jam the food bag into the foot of my tent, stack the other two in the tiny vestibule and fruitlessly attempt to sleep with a stockpile of wooden projectiles at the ready.

Drowsiness is the least of my problems in the morning. There's a hard wind from the northeast and I've got a six-mile southeast traverse across Lake of the Two Mountains right after leaving this park. Riding a tailwind on a SUP is a blast. Energizing endorphins can kick in when you're fighting a headwind. But crosswinds are bloody awful. Especially when I can see the opposite shore and know it'll take more than two hours of ceaseless paddling on one side of the board to get there, with regular muscle-draining sweep strokes to recalibrate. And that I'll have to battle to stay balanced in messy two-foot waves. And that any short break or attempt to work different body parts by switching sides briefly will shunt me back upriver.

Half an hour into my crossing, talking to myself out loud because there are no animals in the middle of this enormous lake on this bracing day, I switch to distraction by singing. Springsteen's "Born to Run" is the only song with lyrics I might be able to fumble through. But I stop at the fourth line; "suicide machines" hits a little close to home, though I'm not in any real danger. Worst-case scenario: I end up on the other side of the river, upstream from Oka, and either hunker down or, somehow, make my way east by road. Either option would be a gut punch to my confidence, but just as I start to ponder what those next steps might be, Chris Aubichon pops into my brain.

If he has the grit to bike across the country, surely I can cross this lake.

Bellowing at the wind, my gaze lasers onto a house on the far side and I maintain my line across. It's the hardest paddling I've ever done. For now.

At the eastern shore of the lake, I approach a highway bridge that's under repair. A construction worker in a boat motors over and tells me, in French, not to go under the bridge. Maybe. I think. Doesn't matter. Still shaking with adrenaline, I point to where I'm headed and proceed beneath a shower of sparks.

My next stop is Sainte-Anne-de-Bellevue, another Parks Canada lock station, at the western tip of the Island of Montreal. Even though it's early afternoon, I'm thinking about camping here. Until a young lock operator politely informs me that camping is not permitted. So I sit on a bench, eat some lunch and turn to outernet.

Outernet is a term that Lisa coined. It's the opposite of the internet. You get information by — shudder — talking to people.

Tamas Buday Jr., a Canadian Olympic canoer turned SUP coach and racer, paddles over from his nearby home for a prearranged chat. I had wanted to ask him about his love for the water; now I want to pick his brain about where I can sleep tonight.

Compact and muscular, with a wide smile, Tamas tells me about his competitive career and a switch to SUP that, now in his late 40s, keeps him young. "It presented a new challenge. The technique is different than canoeing. This sport makes me feel like a kid." He's seen SUP help people he paddles with navigate rough waters, such as deaths in the family and divorce. "You can paddleboard in almost any conditions. It can be a sanctuary."

Speaking of which, Tamas opens the map app on his phone and shows me a tiny uninhabited island a few miles to the east. "You should be good to camp there. Probably."

CHAPTER 5

"I got a funny story for you. I was down in South Carolina for a paddleboard race. We were out for dinner beside the ocean. One of my friends saw one of the other people at the restaurant flick his cigarette off the patio and onto the street. At the end of dinner, my buddy picked that cigarette butt up, put it on the guy's table and said, 'Please, next time, just throw it out in the garbage.' Both of them had had a few drinks. The guy got a little upset. He started making fun of us: 'You paddleboarders, why don't you go hug a tree.' We were very calm at first, but garbage like that ends up in the ocean. The guy was drunk and started pushing people around. There were a lot more of us, but we didn't want any trouble. Then some of the girlfriends got into it, and my friend pushed the other guy to the ground. We didn't want to get into it; we were racing the next day, and this was the U.S. The police were called. 'Assault this, assault that.' We didn't want trouble. But when you love the water, when you love nature, it can carry you so far you get into a fight. We got away without charges, and I got a story to tell."

— *Tamas Buday Jr., SUP athlete and coach*

TUCKED BELOW THE NORTH SHORE OF LAKE SAINT-LOUIS, WHERE THE Ottawa joins the St. Lawrence, Dowker Island is encircled by marshy areas and short cliffs. Except, I discover as I poke my way around the perimeter, for a small bay, facing northeast, where a staircase of large limestone slabs leads out of the water. An obviously used campsite — flat grassy spot for tent, fire ring made from rocks — is tucked into the trees. I stash my board and bags out of sight, just in case, and wait until dusk to set up. A police boat passes a little too closely; I crouch behind a shrub until the engine trails off and the loudest sounds are from wavelets lapping on the shore. The wind has diminished to a breeze that's keeping the bugs away, and the smoke of the past few days is gone. The evening air feels languid, tranquil. I've never had an island to myself before.

The lights of Montreal twinkle to the east as a dark curtain descends.

I wonder what my mother saw as she approached the city, from the other direction, on October 10, 1962. Canadian Thanksgiving. She was 20 years old and had just spent eight days with her parents and younger brother sailing across the Atlantic, from Gdansk, Poland, aboard the MS *Batory*. My grandparents, Tyla and David, are from a small town in eastern Poland. They were just friends, not yet 20, and fled east together into what was then the Soviet Union when the Nazis invaded in 1939. Their saga is a book unto itself. My mother was born on the run, in Georgia, and returned to Poland with her family in 1959. But it no longer felt like home. America beckoned.

I'm asking my mother questions about her voyage on the *Batory* as we sit on a bench beside the Rideau River in Ottawa a couple months before my departure for Montreal. She's got a wicked sense of humor, and perhaps because of the hardship she endured while growing up, nothing seems to faze her. But even though childhood memories don't appear to rekindle trauma, she doesn't freely talk about the past.

"Oh no," Ma says when I pull out a notepad and digital recorder and she realizes there's an ulterior motive to this relaxing walk. "You tricked me! Where's my paddleboard so I can get away?"

Slowly, with a few detours, I pry out some details. An ocean liner that had been pressed into naval service in the Allied fleet, the *Batory* resumed its passenger run across the Atlantic after the war. "We were not the first class," Ma says, "but we weren't the lowest class. We were the middle. Our portholes were just above the surface, so after the people underneath us drowned, we would be the next."

Ma doesn't remember much about the voyage, mostly that she had somewhere to sleep and food to eat. "I don't know why all this got wiped out of my mind. I was just going with the flow. Shortly after I got off the boat, it was gone. I guess that's my tendency. When there's stuff that I don't think is important, I don't store it."

Jenny, the wife of my grandmother's recently deceased first cousin, met them at the port in Montreal and took them by taxi to the airport, and soon they were in her house in Brooklyn. Two weeks later, my mom moved in with Jenny's son and his wife, Ralph and Bunny, on the other side of the Hudson River in Hoboken, New Jersey. She started working as a laboratory technician at the Stevens Institute of Technology, where Ralph was a physics professor, and learned how to speak English from his young children. Because she had gone to college in Poland, Ma was able to start graduate studies at Stevens a year later and eventually earned a PhD in geophysics.

Don't worry. There won't be a quiz about my family tree. But you'll meet some of these people later, including those kids who taught my mom English. And you'll meet the handsome physics grad student Bunny introduced to my mom. Just be patient. New York City won't paddle to itself.

I phone my mother before going to sleep on Dowker Island, hoping to draw out a few more anecdotes about her arrival in Montreal. But she turns the tables on me, looking up my location online and deluging me, her nearly 50-year-old son, with questions about whether I'm allowed to be here and is it safe and where am I going next and what did I eat.

For much of her career, Ma worked in remote sensing. I ask whether the satellites she used to study ice cover in the Arctic have been redeployed to keep tabs on me.

"I think drones would be better," she replies. "Lower, closer."

"If you're going to go to the trouble of spying on me, you could at least use your drones for food drops."

Throughout the rest of my trip, poring over Google Maps, the Weather Network and restaurant menus on her laptop, Ma responds to my social media updates with a barrage of texts. Where exactly is my tent? Is it raining? Hot? Cold? Windy? How is my back? What's for dinner? The barbecue place: Did I get the brisket or the pulled pork? What about sides? The fried okra?

Her cyberstalking is reassuring. As if she's traveling with me and watching over me at the same time.

Large bodies of water are rarely dead calm. The six-mile crossing from Dowker Island to the south side of the St. Lawrence is trippy, more airplanes overhead than boats down here with me. Two hours by myself in the middle of an immense river on a gunmetal-gray morning, the only dry land a tiny rock-rubble islet covered with guttural-grunting cormorants, their fishy, ammonia-rich guano salting the air.

On the opposite shore, about a mile shy of Kahnawake, I skirt an entrance to the St. Lawrence Seaway shipping channel. This section of the seaway, a nearly 200-mile-long series of locks between Montreal and Lake Ontario, opened in 1959, giving ships access to the Great Lakes. If rivers are arteries to the heart of the continent, this was a big-ass bypass.

To pull off a feat of this scale, ordinary citizens, naturally, had to make sacrifices. Building the seaway was divisive, I had learned during its 50th anniversary, in 2009, when my first major assignment as an eager youngish editor at a magazine was to shepherd a cover story about the project onto the page. (That story, by D'arcy Jenish, was part of a partnership between our organization and the St. Lawrence Seaway Management Corporation, winner's history writ large.) "Decades of wrangling between political factions and competing economic interests preceded construction," a sidebar to the main article read, "but the impasse was trumped by the North American steel industry's need for an efficient marine transportation system to supply plants with iron ore from newly opened mines in Labrador and eastern Quebec." Once all that iron ore (and stone and sand and salt and other bulk cargo) was unloaded in industrial ports such as Cleveland, Detroit and Chicago, holds were filled with grain from the U.S. Midwest and Canadian prairies for the return trip east and export overseas. The same sidebar (cringingly headlined, by me, "The river giveth and taketh away") reports that hydro dams created a 30-mile-long lake upstream from Cornwall, Ontario, flooding six villages and three hamlets and displacing more than 6,500 people. But it doesn't say a peep about Kahnawake, even though the federal government expropriated around 1,300 acres and a trench was blasted through the Mohawk community's waterfront.

Although ships have a smaller carbon footprint than trucks or trains, and although the seaway has bolstered GDP on both sides of the international border, the waterway opened with tremendous hoopla but "never lived up to its hype," Dan Egan writes in *The Death and Life of the Great Lakes*. The main problem was that its lock chambers were designed to match the locks on the Welland Canal, which links Lake Ontario with Lake Erie, circumventing Niagara Falls and opening the door to the rest of the Great Lakes. But they were smaller than the locks on the Panama Canal, which meant they could not accommodate the majority of the world's oceangoing fleet and "were obsolete," Egan writes, "almost before the freshly poured concrete could dry."

An average of only two overseas freighters reach the Great Lakes every day during the nine-month, ice-free shipping season, and these are not the Panamax-scale container vessels that carry most of the world's cargo, but smaller 1930s-sized lakers. Beyond this inherent inefficiency, ships that ply the seaway have long "been hauling something not listed on their manifests — noxious species from ports all over the world that are inexorably unstitching a delicate ecological web more than 10,000 years in the making." Ah, yes, invasive species, the most famous of which may be the minuscule zebra mussel, one of many animals and plants that was able to migrate upstream thanks to this manufactured waterway. "It turns out the seaway's most important import could not be bought or sold," Egan writes. "And it can't be killed."

Eurasian milfoil is another invasive that has choked North American lakes and rivers after hitching a ride in the ballast water of ships. A rapidly growing weed that's native to Europe, Asia and northern Africa, the so-called zombie plant aggressively outcompetes native species and forms a mat of vegetation on the water surface, preventing sunlight from penetrating. This shades out other plants, blocks fish, tangles propellers and swimmers, and when the milfoil rots, it can reduce aquatic oxygen levels.

It also stops my SUP as I paddle toward Kahnawake. I'm in Recreation Bay, a marshy finger of water between the town and Tekakwitha Island, a mile-and-a-half-long landform that was created in the 1950s when rock and clay from seaway construction were dumped onto a group of five small islands, creating one larger arid island. The shipping channel runs along Tekakwitha's northern shore, and the bay that I'm painstakingly bashing my board through is on the south side of the island. Stopping frequently to clear clumps of weeds from my fin, I finally reach the dock at the Onake Paddling Club.

CHAPTER 6

"What do I want to see in 50 years? Well, I hope that my great-grandchildren's children's children will be able to see something. They are the faces yet to come. If you knew who your great-grandparents were and also your great-grandchild, you're smack-dab in the middle of seven generations. Which is where I am. I have two great-grandchildren. I think about them. I know the difference in this environment from the time that I was a child. I know how differently it feels on my skin when the sun is hot. I do worry. Some people say if we don't get it right in 50 years, we're done. Some people say we're already done. We're at a point in history where humankind is capable of destroying this planet, but Creation will not allow that to happen. We wouldn't be the first extinction to come along. This place will continue. It may need to heal, it may need to recover, it may need to get rid of some things, including us."

— Ross Montour, Kahnawake Council Chief

THE TWO GARAGE DOORS ON THE FRONT OF THE WIDE YELLOW BUILDING are open, and the Onake Paddling Club's manager lets me leave my SUP and paddling gear inside amongst dozens of canoes and kayaks. Then I phone Robert Rice, who picks me up and drives us back to his comfortable B&B on the edge of town. "Make yourself at home," he says after helping carry my bags to an upstairs bedroom. "There's juice in the fridge and a hot tub in the backyard."

Robert's sister Linda is visiting, and after I'm settled, I take a stool at the kitchen island and ask them what Kahnawake was like when the seaway came through. Displaced residents were pressured to accept meager compensation, he says, and there was no real benefit to locals. Just freighters gliding by on their way somewhere else. They can't say much from personal experience, however, because they were born and raised in Brooklyn.

I had heard about the legendary Mohawk ironworkers, men like Linda and Robert's father, whose fearlessness, strength and skill — and the need to support their families — made them ideal candidates for the dangerous job of building the steel skeletons of many of New York City's landmark skyscrapers and bridges. The Empire State Building, the original World Trade Center, the George Washington and Verrazzano-Narrows Bridges: Mohawk "skywalkers" stood on narrow scaffolding hundreds of feet above the ground, hammering and welding steel beams into place. Their aptitude for this type of work was first noticed in the 1880s, when a train bridge was being constructed across the St. Lawrence at Kahnawake. At night, curious, they would climb the structure. "Let's put rivet guns in their hands," remarked a foreman who noticed their sure-footedness and daring.

Within a few decades, around 700 ironworkers from Kahnawake alone were commuting to New York or living with their wives and children in a Brooklyn neighborhood that came to be known as Little Caughnawaga, the anglicized name of Kahnawake, a community that thrived into the 1970s.

Indigenous people in Canada or the United States are allowed to work in either country under the Jay Treaty of 1794, which, among other things, codified their right to employment on the other side of the border. Mohawks helped build vertical cityscapes not only in New York but also in places like Chicago and San Francisco, an Indigenous presence in urban America that wasn't reflected in the popular culture of the time. This "notion of Indigenous absence," writes Canadian history and Indigenous studies professor Allan Downey, a member of the Dakelh Nation, "led generations of scholars and policymakers to relegate Indigenous existence and history to the periphery of these 'civilized sites of modernity.'" This exclusion masked a significant development: urban spaces and jobs were cultivating a reimagined spirit of Indigenous nationhood.

I absorb this rich history from Chief Ross Montour, the son of an ironworker, while sitting on a bench outside the paddling club on a Friday evening. Long silver hair tucked behind his ears, Ross is one of 12 Chiefs in the Kahnawake band council. His portfolio includes both environment and Indigenous rights and research, a distinction that blurs as he patiently answers my questions.

When Ross was a young child, the weedy bay we're looking at now was open water. There was a wharf, a beach and a ferry to Montreal. People swam, paddled, fished. Around the corner, there was a store where kids bought sodas; the woman who owned it would drag a log across the road in summer to prevent cars from speeding past. Then: cranes, constant blasting, piles of rubble and broken rock everywhere. The artificial island, a convenient place to dump excavated material, significantly restricted water flow along the town's shoreline. There is a small gap between the island and the mainland with a narrow road bridge. When the downstream locks are opened, there is a draw from the shallow bay, but for the most part, the water is stagnant. That's one reason why there are so many weeds.

Some of Ross's relatives lost their homes to the seaway, including his great-grandfather. There was anger, he says, and the Chiefs did everything they could, but the government was intent to get its way, despite all the people living along the St. Lawrence. Like the rail lines, highways and hydro corridors that cut through communities, Ross sees the seaway as part of a colonial continuum. The settlement called Kahnawake itself has been moved several times. (Kahnawake means "by the rapids," which are about half a dozen miles downstream.) "In this country, sadly, it's not unusual," he says. "It's just the way things have been done."

In his role as environment Chief, Ross attends consultations on projects that could impact the community, such as a proposed port expansion in Montreal, or industrial developments that could affect fish. These hearings are typically limited in geographic scope, he says. "They're not looking at the big picture; they're checking-the-box type things. It doesn't matter whether we fish for this species or that species or in this location or that location. It's about the life of the river and everything that lives in it. When we talk about all of the elements of Creation, we're talking about responsibility. As human beings, we have to think about how we interact with them. Because if we don't, in the end, will we survive?

"We say that everything has life. Everything is made up of atoms, everything is made up of energy, everything is connected to the other. Our responsibility for the environment doesn't end at the boundary of the reserve. It goes beyond that."

Ross shows me a video on his phone shot two days ago: the Manhattan skyline is burnt orange in the middle of the day, the worst air quality ever recorded in the city because of smoke drifting down from wildfires in Canada. Earlier today, he was at a meeting about logging as 300 fires burned in Quebec alone. "There's a disconnect," he says. "This is the most remarkable year in a remarkable decade of fires, but there's still debate about whether this is due to human-caused climate change or part of a natural cycle so let's carry on. How do we not connect these things?

"Part of the challenge now for Indigenous communities is what we say we believe compared to how we actually treat the environment. Have we become just as consumeristic as everybody else? That's a question we have to ask ourselves."

Just before he goes, Ross points to the bridge that connects Tekakwitha Island to the mainland and tells me about a skirmish that took place in the waning days of the Oka Crisis.

Most of the media attention was focused on the blockades in the Pines at Kanesatake, but as July bled into August, the mood was getting more ugly and violent by the day in Kahnawake. Police set up barricades between Mohawks and mobs from Châteauguay, and there were riots just about every night, with the anger of the city residents increasingly directed at the police. Food was scarce on the reserve, and supplies had to be snuck in through the forest or by boat. Anybody who left Kahnawake — for medical appointments in Montreal, to visit family in Kanesatake — risked not being able to return. Replacing police with soldiers in mid-August eased tensions somewhat, and two weeks later, after strained negotiations, Mohawks agreed to dismantle their barricades on the Mercier Bridge. Once they were down, a brief flare-up led to a military raid in search of weapons in Kahnawake, and troops kept their armored vehicles in the reserve, occupying about half of the town. Meanwhile, in the Pines outside Oka, by mid-September, hundreds of soldiers had completely surrounded the last few dozen Mohawk warriors, women and children holed up inside a treatment center. With the siege in its final stages, the army conducted a series of searches for weapons in Kahnawake. On September 18, 1990, dozens of soldiers and police officers landed at the western end of Tekakwitha Island in helicopters and boats.

As they advanced toward the bridge, about 300 men, women and children came from the other side to stop them from entering the community. The soldiers tried to put up razor wire, swung rifle butts and fired several volleys of tear gas as they were hit with rocks and fists. More helicopters landed on the island until there were nearly 150 soldiers in the melee. Seven hours later, the troops retreated and were airlifted away.

"We're not known, historically, to be passive," Ross says. "Mohawks are a fairly assertive group of people."

The Oka Crisis had a "profound effect" on Indigenous Peoples across Canada, Gord Hill writes in an essay he contributed to the book *Setting Sights*. Although most acts of Indigenous resistance today do not involve weapons, Oka revitalized a "fighting spirit and warrior traditions" that have come to define pipeline and rail blockades and other recent protests in defense of land and water. It also prompted a change in response tactics: the quick deployment of heavily armed police, instead of soldiers, to portray conflicts as criminal rather than political, coupled with the restriction of media access, attempts to control the narrative and influence public perception. Yet this doesn't detract from Hill's pithy conclusion: "What was especially inspiring about the Oka Crisis was not only that armed warriors confronted police and military forces, but that they also won. To this day, neither the golf club expansion or condominium project has been built."

Resistance takes many forms. Sometimes it involves a paddle.

Maris Jacobs was eight years old when her mother first brought her to the Onake Paddling Club on an early summer morning. A shy, anxious girl, she had tried a few different activities — figure skating, T-ball, theater — but none of them took. That first day of paddling camp was stressful, scary. But soon, the fear faded. Unlike more structured sports, kayaking was something that she could work on individually while still part of a wider group. "You're out there by yourself in a boat," she says, "and you have to learn how to balance while you're moving."

Maris and I are talking outside Onake the morning after my conversation with Ross Montour. Now in her late 20s, petite with a quiet intensity, she's a coach after about a dozen years as an elite competitor. Kayak racing was her thing. She'd arrive by 8 a.m. and stay on the water until dark. "Kids often don't feel they fit in anywhere, but I developed a community here. It started to feel like who I was when I was really young. It was something I came to rely on. It built my confidence."

That buoyancy carried over into other aspects of Maris's life, such as public speaking and school. She went away to university in Syracuse, New York, and now works for a Kahnawake consulting and communications firm. But from spring through fall, she spends a lot of time on the water with teens who are training at the club. She sees herself in these young athletes and has developed more patience, empathy, humor and leadership skills through coaching.

Onake was started in 1972 as a way to help local youth reconnect to their culture and to the water, a relationship that the seaway impeded. Kahnawake's Alwyn Morris, who won gold and bronze medals in kayaking at the 1984 Olympics, began his career here. But the emphasis isn't on winning races.

"We don't just want to produce good paddlers — we want to produce good community members," says Maris. "We want the kids to learn how to be respectful, how to be team players, how to be supportive toward one another. Kids who are healthy, who care about the water and care about the environment.

"Growing up, I wasn't sitting in my kayak thinking, 'Wow, I'm really connecting with my ancestors right now.' That's not what you're thinking, but it's what you're doing. That knowledge was passed down for centuries. I think about this bay and what it was. It's still here and we're still using it and we're still welcoming people here. I don't think about this all the time. But it's there. When I'm paddling, there's just something that feels like home."

I get into a small outboard with Maris and fellow coach Lanhotonkwas Goodleaf for this morning's session. There are eight teenagers in four canoes, getting ready for the upcoming North American Indigenous Games. They paddle away from the dock, under the bridge to Tekakwitha Island and into the shipping channel, where the water is much less turbid than the bay. Lanhotonkwas hollers instructions, and the canoes take off. "Alright, stay focused on technique," he yells to be heard above the engine. "I want to see crisp switches, paddles going straight in and stirring the pot on the way out. Hit it, hit it." This outing — a couple miles west in the channel and then returning via the bay, early on a Saturday when some of the paddlers might prefer to be sleeping in — is more to train their minds than their bodies, he tells me, "so they can push when they're tired."

I ask about the odds of happening upon a freighter in the channel, and Lanhotonkwas says there's no regular schedule: "It's not like a train. Just expect one to come about every half hour." As if on cue, the Polsteam *Iryda* approaches from the west, a 650-foot-long bulk carrier. The canoes angle toward the side of the channel but don't slow down, and Maris waves at the ship as we pass. "We have to deal with the wash from these big boats," she says. "That teaches kids how to paddle in rough conditions." (Lanhotonkwas says he used to kayak alongside the freighters when he was a teenager, getting close enough to whack them with his hand. With a smirk, he also tells me "some kids" shot at them with BB guns.)

We follow the canoes out of the channel entrance into the open St. Lawrence, then U-turn back toward town through the bay. The pace drops as canoes encounter milfoil and other plants. Even though the community recently acquired a weed-cutting boat, it can't keep up with all the growth, exacerbated by agricultural runoff that enters the bay from the Châteauguay River, which flows past farm fields before emptying into the St. Lawrence not far upstream.

"The weeds make it more difficult to train, that's the hardest part," Maris tells me once we get back to the club. "I didn't think about colonization and environmental racism when I was a 10-year-old, but it's still impacting us. We're sending kids out into the seaway. They have to learn how to paddle around ships and yachts and Jet Skis. You take a group of 15 kids out there with one motorboat, and it becomes a safety issue.

"But we have to live up to our name here in Kahnawake," she adds. "We're by the water. That's who we are. Just the act of opening the doors of the club in the morning, having people come here to paddle, introducing kids to the water, that's an act of protection unto itself."

Paddling is more reflective than many aspects of modern life, Maris says. Sometimes she gets lost in the way her boat is cutting through the water. When she hits a perfect stroke, there's "no sploshing or splashing, no kerplunk," she says. "You can't hear anything. It's like a knife going through a soft stick of butter." A few times in her training days, when she was in the bay or in the seaway, when the water was flat and there was no wind, no noise, "it felt like I was flying," she says. "I was buzzing, like I was not even in the boat. My muscles just took over and did the work for me. It was the best."

Maris introduces me to one of the paddlers, Rotshennón:ni Two-Axe, a 19-year-old sprint canoe racer (who went on to win six medals at the Indigenous Games a few weeks later). A premed student at McGill University in Montreal, he also trained at a camp where Olympian Tamas Buday Jr. coached. ("He was our tutor," Tamas told me. "Our kids were doing homework, and Rotshennón:ni was helping everybody.

I asked if I could call him by a nickname. He said, 'Nope, this is our culture and you have to respect that; you have to learn how to pronounce my name.' So we did.")

Paddling gives Rotshennón:ni a reset from the busyness of everyday life. Although it's difficult to juggle studying and training, canoeing has helped him manage stress and excel academically. "It's a grounding activity to come back to, spending some time outdoors and on the water after being stuck in books," he says. "We can't change the seaway now, but we can continue to claim this space. The big ships are just more obstacles we have to manage. Finding our way and adapting is something we've had to do for a long time."

CHAPTER 7

"We were a people who used the rivers as highways. They were our trade routes, how we made our livelihoods. That connection was severed by the seaway. Having opportunities to spend time near water is important for establishing a new relationship. It's not going to be the way it was in the past, so we need a new way to understand the water. We need to rediscover it."

— Cole Delisle, *Kahnawake Environmental Protection Office*

AFTER THE PADDLERS STOW THEIR BOATS AND HEAD HOME, I'M ALONE outside the club. This is my first day *not* paddling since leaving Ottawa, and the fatigue is catching up to me. Weariness notwithstanding, I feel a perplexing desire to take my board out for a spin. But it's not as strong as the desire I have to lie down on the grass, close my eyes and drift off.

Suddenly there's a shadow over me. "Dan?"

Cole Delisle, an environmental project coordinator with the Kahnawake Environmental Protection Office (KEPO), has agreed to show me how the community has reclaimed Tekakwitha Island and nursed life from a rocky, barren place.

We walk over the bridge and sit down on a bench by a new beach, one of the first things locals wanted to see on the island. Building it involved cutting into the shoreline, which consists of boulders from seaway construction, and trucking in sand, plus adding breakwaters to prevent the sand from being sucked into the shipping channel when the locks open. Prior to its construction, there was no decent place to swim outside in Kahnawake since the public pool fell into disrepair and was demolished more than 20 years ago.

The whole project, restoring both the island and bay, began when representatives from Onake asked KEPO if anything could be done to improve paddling conditions, explains Cole, a tall, soft-spoken and bearded millennial with a tattoo of a raven on his right forearm and another on his left. When the band council's environmental office began investigating how agriculturally rich sediment had altered the bay's aquatic chemistry and hydrodynamics, people started looking more closely at the island. Tekakwitha had always been unforgiving habitat for plants and animals because of its rocky shoreline and hard flat ground with poor soil. Like the bay, it had been overrun by invasive species, including eastern cottonwood and sumac trees. After about a decade of study and planning, work began during the COVID-19 pandemic.

Cole and I start walking along the multiuse path that runs the length of the 115-acre island. We're immediately swathed in a canyon of green under a gentle shower of cottonwood fluff, the snow-like seeds piling along the edge of the trail in drifts. He points out some of the trees that have been planted, among them balsam fir and several different types of maple, and a long list of poetically named native plants that have been added to the mix: swamp rose, fragrant water-lily, red-osier dogwood, mountain holly. We're also enveloped in birdsong, and when I ask Cole what I'm hearing, he names species such as killdeer, yellow warbler and cedar waxwing — calls he can identify not through some mystical knowledge but thanks to the birding app on his phone.

In addition to removing invasive species and planting native ones, both terrestrial and aquatic, workers hired by KEPO created wetlands with changes in elevation to mimic natural topography, with low-lying parts open to inundation from the bay. In some places, they dug; elsewhere, they added hills, molding the terrain to be irregular and blend into the landscape. They built bank swallow habitat: eight-foot-tall sections of concrete wall with sandbanks on both sides and holes drilled into the concrete for nesting, something that will hopefully encourage birds to build more nests in the adjacent sand. They assembled rocky hibernacula for snakes to shelter in and created nesting sites for painted and snapping turtles by shaping the shoreline so it slopes gradually to the water, then adding topsoil as well as native shrubs and plants.

To make the island more attractive to human visitors, stone staircases were built to allow people to step down to the water's edge, and benches surrounded by plantings were sprinkled around. There used to be a dirt rut boat launch near the entrance to the island; it was reinforced so people can get onto the water without damaging the shoreline.

When the project first started, Cole remembers walking through Tekakwitha's wetlands. They were flat, strewn with garbage and populated mostly with invasive species. "It really wasn't a great place to be," he says. "The island has always been the party spot. People come here to have fires and drink. We wanted it to be more than that." The community holds a gathering on the island every July, the Echoes of a Proud Nation Pow-Wow, which draws thousands of visitors and was started as part of the healing after the Oka Crisis. A few weeks after my visit, Kahnawake's first ever Pride parade ends with a sober dance party at the beach.

The restoration project comes with funding for 10 years of monitoring to keep an eye on how the naturalized wetlands evolve over the years; to count the number of turtles, snakes and other animals on the island; and to assess the impact of seasonal flooding as well as the growth and health of various plant species. Already, even though work is still underway, there are more people walking and biking on the island. And on a recent spring morning, when Cole was laying down roof shingles in the snake hibernacula to give them places to warm up in the sun, he heard hundreds of frogs singing from the wetland.

"I can't wait to see how much this place changes over the next few years," he says. "There will be forests and biodiverse marshes. It'll be completely different than how it was before. It'll be a place with purpose. We shouldn't forget the history of the seaway and why this project was done, but hopefully it doesn't sour this place. Hopefully animals will treat it like a natural island."

Cole heads home after we walk back to the paddling club. He has family visiting from the U.S. and they're heading to a picnic spot on the St. Lawrence, an area with flat rocks on the wall that separates the open river from the shipping channel. It used to be a short walk from town; now one must drive six miles west to the lock, cross a bridge and drive six miles back to get there. I'm tempted to ask Cole if I can join but don't want to impose.

Sitting on a bench overlooking the bay, concepts of restoration and reconciliation percolate. Reconciliation can be defined as the restoration of friendly relations, so it shouldn't be a surprise that many Indigenous people feel there must first be a settling of disputes, because the relationship has never really been good. But how can we take this step if we don't spend time with one another? I'm thinking as well about environmental reconciliation. About reacquainting ourselves with the land and waters so our actions and decisions are informed by firsthand knowledge, by a blend of Indigenous and Western worldviews. By what the Mi'kmaw call Etuaptmumk: two-eyed seeing.

Chief Ross Montour walks by with his dog and stops for a chat. An older man with white hair rolls up on the bike path on his ATV and pulls over. We talk about the river and ironworkers for a while. He's mildly curious about who I am and why I'm here but seems more interested in telling stories. Which is perfect, because I'm here to listen.

Afterward, I stroll to a nearby park, where a girls' baseball game is underway on a diamond whose third base line runs along river. I buy a hot dog at the concession stand and watch the game for a few minutes from the bleachers, then start walking toward a store where I can buy a pair of sunglasses to replace the ones I broke yesterday. (Take note: sunglasses replacement number one.)

A pickup truck slows near the sidewalk, and the driver leans out the window. "Hey! I saw you at the baseball game," he says. "Do you need a ride somewhere?"

I might have encountered these friendly folks in any small town, but the fact that we were near the water in Kahnawake could have something to do with it.

It's almost the end of the first leg of my journey, the proof-of-concept stage, and I'm surprised more than anybody that it actually worked. I made it to where I wanted to go, met the people I wanted to meet and haven't succumbed to any debilitating ailments. My experiences so far are giving me glimpses of resilience in the face of both short- and long-term challenges. Of people who are keeping the fire burning or coaxing flame from the embers.

Many of us in the Western world are suckers for truisms about nation-making and mankind's dominion over the land. I certainly was while editing that article about the St. Lawrence Seaway. Some stories slice through those myths. Paying attention to the past gives us a shot at avoiding the same blunders. But which past? Whose past? Because where and how we look just might shape where we're going.

I'm blessed with another placid day when I set out back across the St. Lawrence to Montreal the morning after my visit to Tekakwitha Island. I had been warned about this stretch of river: it gets windy and the waves can be big. Boat traffic! Currents! None of these hazards materialize, and a long, uneventful paddle brings me to the mouth of the Lachine Canal, which leads downtown.

Eight miles long, the Lachine is so named because when Europeans were stopped by the nearby rapids on the St. Lawrence, they were poking around for a route to China ("la Chine" in French). The canal opened in 1825, built to sidestep that whitewater and provide access to markets for manufacturers. The increasing size of ships and opening of the seaway in the 1950s made it obsolete. The area around the Lachine fell into disrepair, and part of the waterway was filled in. It closed to navigation in 1970. But a pedestrian and cycling path was built a few years later, and the canal reopened to pleasure craft in 2002.

On this sunny Sunday afternoon, the path, which alternates between park-like stretches and warehouses and factories behind chain-link fences, is busy with walkers, runners and riders. It's hot, humid and the water looks too dirty to cool off in. My tempo wanes. Even though I've got a hotel room booked tonight a short walk from the end of the Lachine and a bus trip back home tomorrow for a 10-day breather, I'm starting to worry about all the miles ahead of me this summer and the concrete corridors I'll have to traverse on other canals. If this short stretch is tough, how will I handle the longer, rougher and more searing days on deck? Will this grand tour, like some of my previous ill-conceived hiking exploits, also end in mission failure? Will I need, at some point, to call for a ride home?

As I approach downtown and the shipping terminals of Montreal's old port, I see more of the transformation that has taken place since the canal was rewatered. Misgivings evaporate; observance takes hold. There are trees and resting areas and throngs of people. There are patios and condos at the foot of lively, vibrant streets; some of the buildings are new while others are repurposed industrial behemoths. It's a vibrant place and an example of what can happen when a 200-year-old canal is reimagined.

Everywhere around me on this muggy, smoky evening there are people. Families with toddlers kicking soccer balls and millennials on blankets with bottles of wine. Some people fish, others kickbox, others beatbox. Sitting beside the water, on funky wooden furniture, on grass that has already started to brown. Seeking a bit of cool as the sun drops. Pulled here by the most powerful magnet imaginable.

PART II

QUEBEC TO NEW YORK CITY

～～～

"My life amounts to no more than one drop in a limitless ocean. Yet what is any ocean, but a multitude of drops?"

— David Mitchell, Cloud Atlas

"He recognized something essential about moving water, which is not merely a conveyance but an equalizer — an urbanizing force on the prairie and a rural belt in the city, machine in the garden and garden in the machine."

— Ben McGrath, Riverman

CHAPTER 8

"Our curiosity about water's true nature is not idle, nor an indulgent wish to return to the past. Water seems malleable, cooperative, willing to flow where we direct it. But as our development expands and as the climate changes, water is increasingly swamping cities or dropping to unreachable depths below farms, generally making life — ours and other species' — precarious."

— *Erica Gies*, Water Always Wins

HERE'S SOME ADVICE THAT COULD COME IN HANDY IF YOU FIND YOURSELF paddling over the American border in the rain anytime soon. Before our phones got smarter than we are, one would have had to radio U.S. Customs and Border Protection (CBP) to report a nautical arrival on a waterway without a staffed crossing and, if asked, present for an in-person inspection at a nearby port. Now there's an app called CBP Roam for "pleasure boaters," which is a lovely term but one that doesn't exactly convey what I'm doing at this particular moment. Which is kneeling on my board under a bridge, trying to peck my passport information and mode of travel details with wet fingers onto a wet phone.

Length of boat: 14 feet. Flag country: Canada. Name of boat: *Swamp & Circumstance?*

The phone and I are wet because this bridge just shy of the border is a *train* bridge and slats don't make for an effective roof. So, if you're ever in this boat, so to speak, might I suggest selecting a better spot than I chose (say, a *road* bridge) to signal my imminent international incursion and cue up a video call with a CBP officer.

The virtual and literal gatekeeper on the other end of my sodden screen — I can't see him, but he can see me — doesn't sound concerned about the drowned muskrat ducking under a bridge nor its mode of travel. I swivel the camera around my setup and give props to Badfish, the Colorado company that gave me my SUP, figuring that a dash of "Buy America" patriotism might trump the fact that I'm piloting a vessel that, to some, is akin to a blow-up toy.

"OK, go ahead," he says. "They might want to talk to you at the customs dock at Rouses Point, but you're fine on my end."

A few hours earlier, under the late-June daybreak drizzle, I had paddled away from my wife and daughters at a floating hotel on Quebec's Richelieu River, southeast of Montreal, a dreamy spot to spend the last night we'll have together for the next couple months. From the rooftop deck of our shipping-container-like unit, lying back in beanbag chairs under a shaggy carpet of pink clouds, we had a close-up view of Île aux Noix, a small chunk of land that played an oversized role in the American Revolutionary War and War of 1812, as well as earlier colonial conflicts between the British and French. There's a historic fort on the island, but when I paddled over for a peek, the dock was restricted to official boats, and I didn't want to get busted by redcoats in period uniforms while sneaking in through the bushes.

Although Île aux Noix was a "soggy, mosquito-infested trap," historian Jack Kelly writes, American generals used it as a base for attacks on Montreal and Quebec City in 1775 and, a year later, to recuperate while retreating south. Nearly 1,000 of their men died of smallpox and other diseases and were buried on the island. After the U.S. gained independence, the British took over, built fortifications and, starting in 1812, used it to supply their ships for a series of battles on Lake Champlain.

There were a *lot* of significant skirmishes and military developments in the late 18th and early 19th centuries along my route to New

York City. Without key victories on Lake Champlain, America may not have become America quite as quickly. The village of Whitehall, at the top of the Champlain Canal, which links the lake to the Hudson River, considers itself the birthplace of the U.S. Navy. And the Hudson has been called "America's River," a prime-time theater for everything from revolutionary triumphs to industrialization and Gilded Age opulence. We'd be wise to keep an eye on the rearview while racing ahead, but peer deeply into these turbid waters, because some patterns reveal themselves in subtle ways.

The first thing I see after the border is Fort Montgomery, a stone garrison jutting out into Lake Champlain that was built during the Civil War amid rumors of a possible British invasion. A faded For Sale sign advertises an asking price of $2.95 million. Crumbling and overgrown with greenery, historic preservation will likely be too costly, but the site reportedly has potential as a winery or wedding venue. Whatever its next chapter holds, the fort does not deter me from paddling down the middle of the channel where the Richelieu River emerges from the lake. Half a mile later, the man on the dock far off to my right, who appears to be wearing a blue uniform, and now appears to be waving his arms — and hollering something that sounds a lot like "Hey, you! HEY, YOU!" — confirms that a stop at the customs post is in order.

I paddle toward the CBP station, tickled that in an era of drone surveillance, motion-activated cameras and AI up the wazoo, a yelling dude remains the last line of protection. Like the video call officer, this sentry doesn't seem overly curious about somebody attempting to enter his country on a SUP. He and his colleagues would have to mount the slowest pursuit of their careers if I tried to outrun their awaiting speedboat.

"Um, do you have a passport?" he asks when I finally reach the dock.

"Yes, sir," I reply, rooting around inside a dry bag and handing it to him.

"Did you use the app?" he asks while casually flipping through the small blue booklet.

"Yes."

"Great! Just show me the code from the app, and we'll send you on your way."

I had assumed that staff here would have received an electronic notification that some idiot paddler was cleared for ingress. Even my mother, who texts me as I'm restowing my passport, seems to know my precise location. Then again, borderlands, like the fringes of any river, lake or ocean, are transition zones. The rough margins where change comes slowly, from the friction of daily and seasonal cycles. Or in a tremendous burst, like water breaching a dam.

Ten miles to the west of Rouses Point, Roxham Road was one of the most notorious border crossings on the continent about a decade ago. More than 100,000 asylum seekers, primarily from Latin America, the Middle East and Africa, walked into Canada from the U.S. over a roughly six-year span. Thousands had been bused to New York City from states such as Texas, taken Greyhounds to Plattsburgh, New York, and then taxis or Ubers to the country road that offered a loophole in the Safe Third Country Agreement, which requires people to seek refugee status in the first "safe country" where they arrive. Because Roxham Road wasn't an official port of entry, they could step into another political jurisdiction and file claims for asylum.

These arduous journeys took place largely over land, but before rail, roads and ride-sharing, water was the only highway. Half a dozen blocks past the customs dock, there's a two-story red brick house overlooking Lake Champlain. Built more than 200 years ago, it was owned by a local customhouse collector and was an important stop on the Underground Railroad.

A diverse network of routes, safe houses and supporters, the Underground Railroad helped enslaved people in the South escape to free states or Canada. Compared to other parts of the U.S., not much is known about its presence in Upstate New York; the Fugitive Slave Act of 1850 made it illegal to help freedom seekers, so people didn't necessarily trumpet their participation. Between 1830 and 1860, up to 5,000 mostly Black enslaved women and men escaped the country every year, estimates the Underground Railroad's most prolific regional chronicler, Tom Calarco, the author of six books on the subject. Completed in 1823 to bring goods to market, the 60-mile-long Champlain Canal served as a lifeline for thousands. Freedom seekers hid on boats, throwing dogs off the scent. Some worked as laborers in canal towns until it was safe to keep moving. The "conductors" who ferried them from station to station, between hidden rooms and root cellars and barns, were Black barbers and ministers and families, as well as Quakers from the surrounding farms and ship-owning abolitionists.

A reverend in the Hudson River community of Troy, New York, reported helping 22 people in two weeks. In an abolitionist newspaper published in 1848, Calarco found reports of a "neat, swift, little dayboat" that could make the trip from New York City to Troy in nine hours. This steamer was "the fastest boat on the river," with a hold designed to conceal passengers.

Just west of Lake Champlain, at the North Star Underground Railroad Museum, Jackie Madison, the president of its parent historical association, strives to unearth and preserve these stories. The canal and lake were a "mainline on the railroad," she tells me, and freedom seekers used whatever means of transportation they could. Jackie, who retired to Upstate New York, applies her volunteer energy to her fellow Black Americans. But she can't stop thinking about the migrants who are using the Champlain corridor to travel both north and south today.

"There are families, young children, babies — it's sad that people are uprooting their lives and have to find new homes. They don't know how things will turn out, and sometimes it doesn't turn out well, when all they're hoping for is safety.

"This has been the way into and out of the U.S. for a long time. A lot of people coming through this route now are on the fringes of society. Which is where slaves were. It's the same old tale repeating itself. Somehow, we need to change this story. The silver lining during the Underground Railroad was that people stepped up and helped when they could have looked the other way. They put themselves at risk. A lot of people doing a little adds up to a big change."

Noting that the ideas that emerged from the Underground Railroad inspired Thoreau's essay "On the Duty of Civil Disobedience," which in turn influenced Martin Luther King Jr. and Gandhi, Calarco calls it "the best example in our history of individuals acting out of a passionate belief" that we all are created equal, "that the dictates of their conscience, of their moral prerogatives, of higher laws, take precedence over others."

The rest of my first day in America is pleasantly uneventful. The rain stops as I pick my way from point to point down the forest- and farm-lined western shore of Lake Champlain, covering 25 miles in eight hours, and I pull onto a sandy beach at the Monty's Bay campground well before dark. I pitch my tent, chat with Sheila and Cindy in the office/shop about the fishing tournament on the lake this weekend — a pair of locals are in the running for a grand prize of $90,000 — and treat myself to a burger on the patio of a snack bar just down the highway.

Dawn breaks smoky. Carrot-shaped Lake Champlain is huge, more than 100 miles long and nearly 450 square miles in size, with New York's Adirondack Mountains rising to the west and the Green Mountains of Vermont to the east. Paddling south, the mountains are concealed by haze, thicker now than it's been at any point on my trip.

Rounding Cumberland Head, a bulky peninsula projecting out into the lake, I carefully time my dash past a ferry terminal and aim for Plattsburgh. It's about three miles across a yawning bay from the headland to the city, and I can't see a thing.

By some small miracle, the smoke isn't making my asthmatic lungs wheeze, but it does ramp up my epochal worries. How much forest has burned since I pushed off onto the Ottawa River? How much is burning now? Looking out into the gray void, listening to the sporadic, piercing cries of gulls, our fitness as a species feels fragile.

I pull out my compass and paddle due west. Suddenly, somewhere in the abyss, I hear an outboard motor. A small boat zips past me, also bearing west. Then another, another, another: a procession emerging from the brume, each vessel with two people aboard wearing matching logo-adorned jerseys. Each vessel speeding by a little too close for comfort. Half an hour later, I start to see the outline of Plattsburgh and realize these boats are heading to the marina, and when I arrive, the water between the docks roils with fishing boats racing to the weigh-in at the end of their tournament.

For me, the tally is 19 miles down, seven to go. Back on my board by midafternoon, I skim the shoreline south toward Valcour Island, where the state's conservation department maintains a couple dozen primitive tent sites. Ringed by rocky outcrops and sandy beaches, the island is just a mile off the mainland, a quick hop to the boathouse where an ecologist from SUNY Plattsburgh has agreed to meet with me at 9 a.m. tomorrow.

I pass a group of sailboats and pontoon cruisers moored in a bay on the western side of the island, several of which are blasting loud music. By the time I've selected a site on a limestone point about a mile away from my neighbors and pulled my SUP onto the rocks, the music has stopped and the boats have departed. The island appears to be empty a few days before the start of prime tourism season. Let's see Ma try to find me here!

My home for the night features a hearth-like firepit overlooking the lake and four hand-hewn tables, which is like winning the lottery for an organization-aholic like me. I leave my food and cooking gear on the table closest to the firepit, spread my paddling clothes to dry atop another in the dining room, drop my tent and sleeping kit on a table tucked into the trees at the back of the site and set up my office (notepad, pen, phone) on a standing-desk-like board atop a magnificent stump pedestal. There's even a yoga-ready grassy area off to the side for stretching and a rock-slab deck by the water's edge.

I swim and then eat my beef-chili-in-a-bag beside the lake. The breeze is building, the smoke clearing. I manage to stay up late enough to watch the hills morph from amber to red.

CHAPTER 9

"When you take a risk, you have to trust that someone will come to your aid; and when it's your turn, you will help someone else. It's better to face your fear than to run from it because running won't make the problem go away."

— Maria Ressa, How to Stand Up to a Dictator

AT 8:30 A.M., THE SOUTHERLY WIND IS WHIPPING. IT'S A BATTLE TO GET TO the boathouse — still preferable to my regular Monday morning commute — but I arrive a few minutes before Tim Mihuc motors in at the helm of an aluminum skiff. With a bushy white beard and a jaunty Indiana Jones hat, Tim looks like the kind of professor who would rather be outdoors than in a classroom. This is helpful, because I'm the kind of learner who would also rather avoid classrooms. Director of the university's Lake Champlain Research Institute, Tim is here with a pair of students and a research assistant, and despite the choppy conditions, they're scheduled to do some sampling at one of their data buoys a little south of Valcour Island.

"Jump in," he says without killing the engine. "Bring your PFD."

As we bounce toward the buoy, Tim explains that today's task is to collect zooplankton and phytoplankton samples at five-meter increments down to the 50-meter lakebed. Maddy, Marshall and Zach each have a different gauge of net, so they can haul up different sized organisms. Once we're tied to a mooring, it gets busy in the boat. Tossed around by swells, Tim labels sample bottles as the students prepare their rigs. The metal ring that holds Marshall's 500-micron mesh to a winch pops off and disappears into the water.

"Where's the connector?" Tim asks.

"It shot off and fell into the lake," Marshall says.

"Fuck. Why?"

"It exploded."

"Exploded?"

"Well, violently shot off."

"OK, we've got a toolbox. Let's come up with a solution."

The species they collect will be counted and identified back in the lab, allowing the team to estimate the density of various populations at different depths. Because each species occupies a unique ecological niche — some zooplankton eat phytoplankton, some zooplankton are eaten by fish — keeping track of their numbers can indicate shifts in the lake's overall ecology and predict future changes. For example, certain fish not having enough food.

Level by level, the students dip and raise their nets. It's painstaking work, but the hands-on experience they're getting will give the students the skills — and hopefully the desire — to pick up where their professors leave off. That's one of the main missions of the institute. Another is to assemble a multiyear dataset. Combined with continuous weather reports and water temperature readings recorded by a descending chain of probes, it will help researchers assess the impact of climate change on the lake's thermal structure and on the biota that have adapted to live at specific depths.

Climate change is bringing more frequent and intense storms to Lake Champlain, says Tim, and higher temperatures are "thickening" the layer of warm water near the surface. Less winter ice cover means more evaporation, which impacts the thermal regime as well. And the stratified layers of water at different temperatures appear to be mixing more often than conventional wisdom held, releasing nutrients from the lake bottom. Understanding how a complex web of species responds to these shifts illuminates global change at a local scale. These findings, in turn, can inform research on other lakes, Tim says, "to get at the broader picture of how freshwater systems are faring."

As a whole, Lake Champlain is faring well. Monitoring programs show that despite generations of agricultural runoff, phosphorus levels are stable, keeping algal blooms under control. There are invasive species — including the fishhook water flea, discovered by Zach during his master's research — but not as many as in the Great Lakes, because this lake is not as interconnected. Municipalities still draw their drinking water from the lake. And it appears to have the carrying capacity to handle the current load of boaters and fishing tournaments.

"They're here because it's a healthy fishery," says Tim. "Recreation is a good use, as long as it doesn't become overuse and degrade the system."

Maddy shows Tim the sample she has drawn from 30 meters down.

"Holy crap!" he says, pointing to floating flecks of black rubber. "We call them nurdles. There are a ton of them in the lake. We've been seeing them for a year, and we see them all the time. This is from the middle of the water column, where fish are swimming around."

Tim doesn't know what the nurdles are or where they're from. They look like the little rubber nubs on new tires, like bits of preproduction plastic that could be melted down to make something. "It's clear they're getting through treatment plants. This is concerning. They're in the planktonic food web, and somebody is consuming them."

Microplastics are a major environmental issue. They're in the water, the air, our bodies. They're tiny, everywhere and bad for our health. Microrubber poses a similar threat. It seems like an insurmountable problem, but Tim tells me about a new project on the lake: sampling for nurdles at 15 different sites to assess their spatial coverage. "If we can find where they're concentrated, we can try to track the source."

As we return to the boathouse, Tim pivots from ecologist to amateur historian. This combo makes sense. Both are methodical pursuits, one shedding light on relationships between living things and their environment, the other sharing stories about connections between past and present. In this narrow strait between Valcour Island and the mainland, Tim says, one of the first naval battles of the Revolutionary War took place in October 1776. Benedict Arnold, before his name became synonymous with treason, commanded the American fleet. With the British in pursuit, Arnold's ships holed up near the boathouse. When the British passed the tip of the island, running into the type of southerly wind that's battering us today, the Americans engaged. Outnumbered and outgunned, the Americans took heavy casualties, then retreated south on a moonless, foggy night. Arnold's men intentionally ran their ships aground and scuttled the wrecks, escaping back to Fort Crown Point by land. But they had held off the British long enough to prevent them from reaching the Hudson Valley before winter and threatening New York City. Lose the battle, win the war.

Tim and his crew roar away, and I have a decision to make. Fast. It's 12:15 p.m. and the windspeed is 15 miles per hour, gusting to 25, from the south-southeast — precisely the direction I'm going. There's not much shelter on this side of the lake, barely any bulges of land to tuck behind, and there are thunderstorms in the forecast. I *could* fight my way south. But the wind that's feisty enough to stop a navy isn't expected to let up until tomorrow night, and I'm 40 miles from where I'd very much like to be tomorrow night: a historic resort on the Vermont side whose owner has agreed to put me up.

Forty miles is probably beyond my range in a headwind, and Lake Champlain is notoriously dangerous for paddle craft when the wind blows, especially this wide-open central part, the Broad Lake, where five-foot whitecaps and tumultuous nearshore conditions are frequent. Ottawa paddling legend Max Finkelstein was windbound on Champlain for two days while leading a voyageur canoe expedition from Canada's capital to Washington, D.C. Still, when I ran my proposed route by him, his immediate response was "sounds like fun."

SUPing south today would not be fun. But there's a southbound train leaving Plattsburgh at 2:45 p.m.

It's seven miles from the Valcour boathouse back to the Plattsburgh marina, which is just a couple blocks from the Amtrak depot. My hastily-coming-together plan is to catch a train to Port Henry, New York, near the bottom of the lake, then paddle north toward the Basin Harbor Resort with the wind at my back. I inhale an energy bar, chug some water and start stroking pell-mell north. The wind is hitting me just enough from the side — the pesky E part of SSE — that I have to fight the swells as well as the clock, digging hard on my left side, head down. I'm beat when I land on the beach beside the marina nearly two hours later. Which is where the real rush begins.

Deflating a 14-foot-long SUP, rolling it up as tightly as possible and loading it into its backpack is a demanding task. There's a lot of air to squeeze out. Do it poorly and there won't be room in the bag for two three-piece paddles, a PFD and pump. All of which has to fit to make walking with the board on my back and three dry bags over my shoulders remotely feasible. By 2:30, covered in sand and sweat, I start scurrying crab-like toward the station.

In the marina parking lot, I see a sunburned, 60-something man smoking a cigarette and tending to his ramshackle sailboat.

"Would you be able to give me a ride to the train?" I ask. "Please?"

He looks at me, grunts and nods toward an even more ramshackle car with Quebec plates.

"Merci!" I say as he opens the overflowing trunk and begins removing bags and boxes to make room for my gear.

We reach the station five minutes before departure time, and I start unloading my bags. Another car pulls up and a white-haired man leans out the driver's window.

"Here for the train?" he asks.

"Yes," I reply, stomach sinking.

"It's been suspended. Since Friday."

Friday. The last day I checked the schedule. Fuck. And now what? I'm even farther away from that high-thread-count sheet than I was this morning. Why did I waylay myself, blindly expecting to waltz onto a train? Why did I backpedal instead of moving *forward*?

The bearer of bad news, who turns out to be the station's kindly caretaker, Roger, explains that because of the extreme heat of the past week, northbound trains on this line, which links New York City and Montreal, had to travel exceedingly slowly once they crossed into Canada due to track conditions. The 50 miles from the border to Montreal was taking four hours, rendering the trip unviable and making trains turn around at Albany. It's disturbing to find out that global warming may be incapacitating our low-carbon transit networks. But I don't dwell on this dire vision, distracted by my more immediate pickle.

Roger lets me into the 140-year-old red-brick station to fill my water bottles. Rough stone blocks form one of the interior walls. This used to be a seawall on waterfront, I'm told, but the area was filled in for rail and road. "I don't know why they did that," Roger says. "They wouldn't be able to get away with that today."

Dejected, I sit outside and cogitate. There are no other trains, buses or ferries from Plattsburgh that could help. But one county to the south, I see on my online map, there's a small ferry from Essex, New York, to Charlotte, Vermont. If I can get across Lake Champlain and lop off some distance, I can work my way down the more sheltered eastern side of the lake to the resort.

There's just the wee matter of getting to Essex.

How hard could it be to hitchhike, I'm mulling when Roger pops outside with a business card. "Local guy has a ride service. Maybe he could take you somewhere?"

Nobody answers the phone, but a ray of golden light strikes me, a heretofore heel-dragging Luddite in the gig economy. Uber. I had downloaded the app before leaving home and use it for the first time ever. Terry will be here in 13 minutes.

Covering in 30 minutes a span that would've taken me many hours is discombobulating, but the sting is softened by easy conversation while sinking back into the upholstery on a twisting highway through the trees.

Terry was born in a mining village up in the Adirondacks that's now a ghost town near a hiking trailhead. My daughters and I snooped through that tract of tumbledown buildings during a camping trip when they were young. Small world: we might have been in Terry's bedroom. He tells me about some of the passengers he's had in recent years: Columbia University journalism students filming a documentary about Champy, Lake Champlain's mythical sea monster; carloads of refugees bound for Roxham Road, whom he was driving to the border twice a day.

At Essex, the lake thins to three miles. After devouring a plate of fish and chips and waiting out a string of storms at a restaurant inside a two-century-old sloop trade warehouse, I pay $5.25 for the half-hour ferry to Vermont, inflate my board on a construction company's dock beside the landing and, hugging the shoreline, paddle to a boat launch — the only public land in the area. As expected, there's that all-too-familiar sign: a picture of black tent inside a red circle with a thick red diagonal line over the tent.

Seeking local knowledge, and banking on Vermont's reputed hippy, chill vibe, I approach a guy who has just finished backing his boat into the water.

"Think it'd be cool to camp here?"

"You should be fine," he says, looking me over. "Nobody will bother you."

I set up my tent beneath the skirt of a cedar and am eating dinner when he returns. We sit on curbstones and talk. Friendly chatter about sailing and paddling. But I get the sense that maybe he's a tad too friendly. I mean, I'm flattered — Swamp Thing's aura, apparently, has yet to ooze forth — but I mention my wife in an anecdote to clarify my status.

Increasingly loud thunder signals another round of rain. Time for sleep.

The wind is still steady from the south-southeast in the morning. But it's only 15 miles to Basin Harbor, and neither the S nor the SE will be much of a factor on this stretch of the Vermont shore, where the lake kicks westward, like the toe of Italy's boot. With no interviews booked until tomorrow and accommodation prearranged, I'm off the clock.

I paddle slowly south, sheer cliffs giving way to cottages, farms and sprawling estates, and slip into the wide grassy mouth of a creek. Sitting on my board for a snack, listening to birds chirp and warble, a wave of serenity washes over me. I stop in a state park picnic area and rehydrate a package of pasta with spicy sausage, rather than my usual scarfed midday repast of peanut butter wraps and energy bars. Driving here from home would've taken just a few hours; arriving mostly through my own exertion makes the meal taste that much better. As an innkeeper once said to me in Wales after a long day of hiking along the coast to reach my lodging, "You've earned your pudding." After eating, I paddle across the bay to a secluded rocky cove, take off my shorts and T-shirt and swim. Lying down on the warm rocks to dry, I feel like I was born to do this. Like I've never not been doing this.

Six miles down the shore, I paddle into a tiny round bay for something I've definitely never done: watch a dude valet park my SUP. Pulling up to the edge of a busy complex of docks, a young man in a golf shirt steadies my board as I step off, then carries it to a rack on the side of the harbormaster's shed. The service is excellent at the Basin Harbor Resort, even if no guest has ever checked in via paddleboard. More folks use the airstrip out back.

Wrapped around its eponymous bay, the 700-acre property consists of a white clapboard main lodge, dozens of cottages, an armada of Adirondack chairs, lakeside cocktail hour and elegant dining. Soon I'm sinking into a plush bed upstairs in the Homestead building, circa 1792, where well-dressed housemates heading out for a wedding rehearsal dinner make me feel out of place, but sloping floors and a rocking chair on the covered veranda conjure a familiar at-sea sensation.

Basin Harbor has been welcoming guests since Ardelia Beach opened up her farm to visitors in 1886. Today, the fourth generation is at the helm. Bob Beach — soft-spoken and refined — considers his family stewards of the land. "I don't feel that we own it," he tells me. "In the grand scheme, we're just here for a short amount of time and hope to take good care of it as best we can."

That sense of responsibility sparked the Lake Champlain Maritime Museum, which Bob cofounded in a transplanted stone schoolhouse in the neighboring harbor in 1985. Its original mission to preserve and share the cultural and natural heritage of the lake has expanded to include a focus on social and environmental justice, on repairing the harm caused by history being told from a singular dominant perspective. "It's a work in progress to remain relevant in today's society," says Bob. "We want to be forward-thinking, but also to preserve the past. Everything is an evolution."

In the morning, I watch Bob deliver a history lecture on the front porch of the main lodge — the nearby town of Ferrisburgh was an important stop on the Underground Railroad, he tells 15 or so guests, and free Blacks settled and intermarried in the area — then I walk to the museum.

There are a lot of old boats on the campus, which has spread out into 18 buildings scattered around a grassy, treed lot. There are several displays about the Revolutionary War, but also an exhibit marking the 50th anniversary of the Clean Water Act of 1972, the most significant law governing water pollution in the U.S. And the stone schoolhouse, my first stop, is devoted to the Indigenous Peoples of Lake Champlain, with an exhibit exploring the experiences of the local Abenaki Nation during the COVID-19 pandemic: paintings, stories, a beaded stethoscope and mask. "Abenaki families turned to traditional medicines and other cultural practices for comfort and survival," reads the introduction, "connecting with nature and small family groups."

Outside, there's a full-sized replica of the *Philadelphia*, one of the American ships sunk in the Battle of Valcour Island, and an open-sided workshop where at-risk youth build 32-foot boats. They select the trees, cut boards at the on-site sawmill, forge nails at the blacksmithing shop and row the finished boats together. "This isn't history to put on the shelf," museum executive director Chris Sabick says as we walk around the grounds. "We're trying to include diverse programming and more voices, not just old white men."

Down at the lake, floating beside the dock, a ghost under the gray sky, there's another replica: the *Lois McClure*.

CHAPTER 10

"Between the birth of the environmental movement and today, the conversation has evolved from a paternalistic, stewardship-based model of ecological activism to include questioning the very ethics of bringing more people into the world — asking not 'How do we save the planet?' but 'Should we even be here?' Of course, back in the dawn of Earth Day celebrations, few were talking about parts per million and carbon footprints; the ice caps might have been melting, but that had yet to make the nightly news. Both our impact on the planet and our awareness of it have grown exponentially since. But the distance between these two rhetorical positions, each outlining how to care for the more-than-human world, is so great that it makes me wonder what else, in addition to the climate, has changed."

— Elizabeth Rush, The Quickening

WHITE WITH GREEN TRIM, 88 FEET LONG AND 14.5 AT THE BEAM, THE *Lois McClure* is a clone of an 1862 canal schooner — the workhorses of the region's shipping heyday. Pulled along canal towpaths by horses and mules using 300-foot-long ropes and raising sail in open water, hundreds of these boats carried iron ore, lumber, marble and agricultural products south from mines, forests and farms, loading up with manufactured goods, spirits, coffee, coal and sugar for the return north. Built by museum staff and an army of volunteers, the *Lois*

McClure was launched in 2004 and for 15 summers set forth on annual multimonth public tours, propelled by a tugboat, along the interconnected waterways upon which I'm paddling. Down to New York City, west to Buffalo, up to Montreal and Ottawa.

"I was worried that people wouldn't give a shit," Art Cohn says to me over lunch at the resort's pub after I leave the museum. "Where are the guns? The swashbuckling stories? Why did you bring me a truck? Who was going to care, other than maritime nerds?"

A muscular 74-year-old with a deep voice and unmistakable New York City accent, Art cofounded the museum with Bob Beach. They make an unlikely duo: Vermont gentry and a working-class Jew who grew up in veterans' housing projects in Queens and Harlem. But when Bob wanted to learn more about a shipwreck in Basin Harbor, he turned to the nautical archaeologist running a nearby diving business, and they bonded over a shared love for history. Art had worked as a commercial diver, salvaging shipwrecks, but became increasingly distressed by the plundering. Lake Champlain's cold dark fresh water holds an estimated 300 shipwrecks, and that heightened his interest in preservation.

Ten years of in-water archaeology helped Art draw up the plans for the *Lois McClure*. He didn't intend to join the yearly voyages but ended up on the permanent crew. "I had to go with the boat. I was too emotionally attached not to." They stopped at a couple dozen ports each season, welcoming more than 300,000 visitors aboard before the final pre-pandemic run in 2019. The goal was to show what life had been like on the water, to reintroduce the region's history and aquatic ecology. "There wasn't a lot to read. The boat was the exhibit. We wanted people to ask questions. It really was — is — a quest to give perspective."

A conversation about loads of lumber might lead to talk about clear-cutting; a question about families who worked on the boats could segue to women's rights. "Unintended consequences," says Art, "is a big concept we can all learn from."

Crews cooked and slept on the boat, and Art always ate dinner on deck. Locals would come to the harbor or lock station to hang out in the evening, to make sure their visitors were comfortable, to trade tales. Rekindling one of the original roles of these waterways, an aquatic 19th-century internet was carving out a new niche. People handed over nautical knickknacks and century-old ship's diaries they'd dug up from basements. They came bearing casseroles and homemade apple pies.

Art became a volunteer firefighter after watching emergency responders stream into the World Trade Center on 9/11. He has pulled bodies from the water and serves on a critical incident debrief team. But he fights back a tear when recounting the sheer joy of traveling by water. "It was poetry. It was as good as it gets. Everybody adopts you. It's the way we want the world to be.

"The canal has always adapted to its era," Art continues. "Now it's become one of the most important recreational and historic waterways in this part of the world, and you can move stuff on it that you couldn't move any other way. I don't know what extraordinary projects will be facilitated in the next few decades because we had the foresight to maintain and operate this waterway for 200 years and counting."

After buying my meal, Art clears the diving gear off his passenger seat and shuttles me to a supermarket so I can pick up a few staples. Now that the *Lois McClure* has been retired, he has more time for archaeological dives. "I find it therapeutic," he says. "Being surrounded by a fluid, being able to control your buoyancy. If I'm stressed or have a headache, it doesn't matter — I always felt better coming out of the water than when I went in."

He also has more time these days for terrestrial research, such as a journal article he's writing about links between the Beach family and the Storms, who lived beside Basin Harbor and, in 1802, may have become the first Black family to own land in Vermont. When Bob's grandfather Allen Penfield Beach was born in the lodge in 1886, a doctor declared him stillborn. Thirza Storms, a nurse in attendance, contravened medical protocol, as well as race and gender norms, and continued to work on the baby. She saved his life.

Art is not holding back his emotions as he shares this story. "I'm advocating for the simple connections between human beings and with our history," he says elegiacally, voice cracking, "and with the things we've done right and done wrong."

Breaking camp in a hotel room with a coffee maker and bathroom is simple, and nobody is outside yet as I leave Basin Harbor. The lake is just as quiet. Not a single boat moving. The sky is devoid of smoke or storms, and I've got a clear sightline on the high peaks of the Adirondacks, waves of jagged dark green cutouts fading to the west.

There are no running gun battles as I head south above legions of sunken cannonballs, just me swatting at a bee with my paddle, killing it, then apologizing to its tiny carcass before a burial at sea. It takes four hours to reach Crown Point, a pinch a quarter mile across where Benedict Arnold decamped after the Battle of Valcour Island. This is a change of scale from the wide-open upper part of the lake. Imposing bluffs and mansions give way to modest homes and the tang of manure from shoreline farms. The water is now greenish, sediment-choked and chalky, not the clear blue of the past few days. Well-fed and rested, I'm cruising.

Just north of Fort Ticonderoga, where Arnold retreated after abandoning and torching Fort Crown Point, I see the smokestacks of a paper mill — the first mill of my trip. I also see a wooden tour boat taking visitors onto the water.

"You going to the city?" the captain asks.

"Yep," I reply, awaiting his exalting admiration.

"I passed a guy last week doing the exact same thing."

That would be Massachusetts paddleboarder Phil Katz, who departed Burlington, Vermont, a few days before I reached Lake Champlain, en route to NYC. Phil and I had talked on the phone, and he gave me some intel on the conditions ahead. For instance, where not to set up a makeshift camp because it's too close to a biker clubhouse.

The tendril at the bottom of Lake Champlain turns and constricts until finally, after 37 miles, just before sunset, I see a jumble of masts on the Vermont side and a pair of four-story buildings set back in the steeply sloping hillside.

The lake is barely 800 feet wide here — half the width of Crown Point — which has made it a natural crossing for more than two centuries. The first building, a boarded-up brick and stone structure, was constructed as a warehouse in 1810 by merchant Walter Chipman. Schooners and sloops stopped to unload goods; flour, glass, nails, molasses, paper, rum, salt and snuff were transported inland by horse-drawn wagon. A ferry, one of the earliest on the lake, began plying back and forth to New York in 1820. Passengers could hop onto a stagecoach on either side: west to Rochester, east to Boston. They could catch boats sailing north to Quebec or, once the Champlain Canal opened in 1823, south to New York City. Another warehouse, built from stone quarried on the property, went up in 1824 to handle the additional trade resulting from the canal. The bustling tavern where two bartenders were in constant service is gone, as are the hotel, church and school, but the 1824 building is now home to the Chipman Point Marina.

Chip Taube runs the marina — his name a happy coincidence — but is busy fixing a rental houseboat, so his wife, Michelle, points me to a picnic area where I can tent. We walk into the water-level floor of the building, which is crammed with antique furniture and curios and serves as the office and shop. The low ceilings are held up by rough wooden beams, the doorways framed by marble lintels, the floorboards wide and well-worn. A cup of coffee costs 25 cents, ice cream bars $1 and muffins $1.25. "Help yourself if there's nobody around," Michelle says, "just leave the money in this jar."

I had been in a bit of a bleary stupor when I arrived, wiped out by a long day in the heat, but this warm welcome and the homey atmosphere perk me up. The showers are one floor up a tight staircase in a whitewashed, warmly lit space full of century-old chairs and lamps. It feels like stepping into a time capsule, a historical village for tourists. Except it's not a cordoned-off facsimile. And the water pressure is excellent.

When I'm clean and have answered the latest round of my mother's questions about my whereabouts, I bump into Chip's mother. Pat and her husband bought the business 30 year ago. She describes the good old days: boaters hanging out on shore barbecuing, kids swimming and fishing, a spirited book club, a loaner car. "Do you need to go into town?" she asks. "You can use my car."

Heartened by her offer but already loaded down with supplies, I ask Pat how the marina has changed over the decades.

"Well, people don't spend the night as often as they used to. They boat for the day and go home, and their kids just sit on the porch so they can get Wi-Fi on their phones. And people *argue*. I know we always had Democrats and Republicans, but there was never any mention of politics. People came here to be on the water, and that's what we offered: a place to relax. Now people fight about politics, and friendships have ended. It's sad. That's not what we're here for."

Pat lives on the third floor of the building, which, because it's snug to the slope, has a ground-level entrance facing away from the lake. She sits at the wheel of a golf cart and gracefully executes a three-point turn to drive uphill. It's quiet after she pulls away, just fish leaping for insects and splashing back down into the water.

Morning. Mist burning off lake. Twenty-five-cent coffee. Mist burning off brain. A tapered gorge with marshy elbows and forested hills. A hint of peat and resin hanging in the air. Eagles, crows, turkey vultures, me.

I stop to banter with three men on the porch of a fishing cabin and, removing my ballcap to wipe the sweat from my brow, watch my sunglasses fly off the bill. Diving into the murk, I'm too slow to save the quickly sinking shades. Without pause, one of the men gives me his. After paddling away, I realize they are prescription bifocals that I can't use. But it's the generosity that counts.

It's the hottest day so far. Do I sound like a broken record? Are we too complacent about records being broken? In the narrows below Chipman Point, I cool off with frequent plunges in the increasingly opaque water. Lifting myself onto the SUP after a swim, I see a large snake swim past. A few minutes later, I startle (and am startled by) a school of long thin fish with pointy snouts and spikey dorsal fins.

They're basking just below the surface and thrash the water as they dive. These encounters don't dissuade me from submerging my body; despite a row of sharp cone-shaped teeth, the longnose gar is harmless. But it's only the last day of June: I'm nervous about the heat and watercourses ahead.

At the bottom of the lake I paddle up the Poultney River to Whitehall, the northern end of the Champlain Canal.

The canal — a shorter second banana to its east-west counterpart, the Erie — blazed an all-water route from New York City to Lake Champlain, Canada and beyond. Until exactly 200 years before my visit, the voyage south entailed a short portage from Lake Champlain to Lake George at Ticonderoga (an Iroquoian word for "between two waters"), then a longer carry to the Hudson River. Have you ever hefted a canoe on your shoulders along root-covered and mosquito-swarmed trails? Portaging isn't always enjoyable. For example, if you're packing cannons. Sixty miles long, the Champlain Canal provided a critical link.

A link that's technically not open to paddleboards. Regarded by some as toys for a weekend at the lake, SUPs are treated differently than canoes and kayaks; regulations prevent us from entering many locks. A pair of New York canal system's communications people had assured me, however, that if I kneeled on my board and wore my PFD, lock tenders would grant me passage. So I call the number in my guidebook for C12, the northernmost lock, and tell the woman who answers that I'm paddling southbound and will be at her lock in five minutes.

"Good timing," she says. "We've been shut for repairs all day but have just reopened. I've got a lock full of boats going north and you can enter the chamber after they leave."

It's a little intimidating to wait at water level for a pair of 20-foot-tall metal gates to swing open but reassuring to know that this is a time-tested design. The provenance of today's locks goes back to Leonardo da Vinci. In the 1400s, he improved upon the vertical "guillotine gates" of 10th-century Chinese canals by sketching the first miter gates, which swing open. Meeting at a 90-degree angle and forming a V shape, miter gates take advantage of upstream pressure to make a waterproof seal and require less energy to move than gates that close to form a perpendicular barrier. They revolutionized canals, which swept across Europe and around the world, transforming global trade and geopolitics.

Lesser known among da Vinci's countless inventions are both a wheeled paddle boat and a stand-up pedal boat. The Leonardo Museum in Venice has wooden models of both designs — evidence of how prolific he was and, I avow, of the crucial role of standing in the evolution of paddle craft. So I suspect the ultimate Renaissance man wouldn't blink an eye if he saw a guy on a SUP slide into C12 after half a dozen motorboats churn out.

The backwash inside the lock is black, speckled with sticks and goose droppings; the smell is earthy, pungent. It feels like a giant's bathtub, if the giant lived in a dank basement apartment. I grab one of the slimy ropes hanging down the left side of the lock, and the gates start to close. A minute later, water begins to bubble into the chamber through several tunnels. Inch by inch, my board rises 15½ feet.

On the upstream side, I tie onto a ladder up a concrete wall where a couple of boats are moored. First order of business: public washroom! I ask a police officer getting into his vehicle, and he directs me to the pavilion in a nearby park. "There are showers there too," he says.

"Are you saying I need a shower?"

"Nope, that's not what I'm saying. Only you can make that decision."

The pavilion is empty, and I decide why not? The shower is refreshing. Then I'm right back in the same grimy clothes and steamy afternoon.

Next on my agenda: history!

Whitehall was a strategic spot for colonizers. British captain Philip Skene established a town here in 1759 and called it — wait for it — Skenesborough. He built sawmills, a forge and shipyards, carving out a little corner of empire for the king. But when the Revolutionary War broke out, American forces led by our friend Benedict Arnold and Ethan Allen raided the town. They commandeered ships and, in the summer of 1776, built a few more, using the burgeoning fleet to capture British-held forts at Ticonderoga and Crown Point and launch attacks in Quebec. The renamed town considers itself ground zero for the U.S. Navy, although the military doesn't recognize it as such, citing a continental congress vote to procure two armed vessels in Philadelphia in 1775 as the moment of inception, while honoring "the significant naval roles that many other towns played in the American Revolution" and not declaring any as the sole place of origin.

I check out the remains of a schooner that did battle on Lake Champlain, then walk the short main strip beside the water. Restored red-brick buildings line one side of the street and house the essentials: bank, bar, café.

A couple blocks away, the rest of the town appears to be struggling. Houses in varied states of disrepair: some falling apart, others burned down. People sit on stoops smoking, waiting out the late-afternoon sauna. Cars on blocks, babies crying. Once an industrial and shipping hub where silk mills employed more than 1,000 people, nearly 30 percent of Whitehall's 2,500 residents now live below the poverty line. A few years ago, its overdose rate was five times higher than the county average. A local white judge was removed from the bench for pointing a loaded handgun at a Black defendant in court. Life here looks hard.

I procure a new pair of sunglasses and a sandwich at a busy convenience store on the highway that's now Whitehall's commercial center — "Land and ocean temps soar," a headline on the TV news screams, "is planet past the point of no return?" — and head back to the spruced-up waterfront to sit in the shade.

Is this a mirage? A tenuous blue veneer screening the harsh reality? For the past few weeks, looking at maps, Whitehall seemed alluring, even romantic. Although I see just a small snapshot, my layover in town is demoralizing. Retreating to this bench, my thesis may have been sunk already. Is it utter naivete to think blue space can make a difference?

When the sun droops and temperature cools ever so slightly, I embark on a six-mile paddle to lock C11. I had initially planned to camp at C12 but now want to shoot through the clammy Champlain Canal onto the breezier Hudson. On my way out of town, I see a guy throwing sticks into the water for his pit bull to retrieve.

"Is it safe to swim here?" I ask.

"I've swam in this," he says. "I wouldn't eat the fish though."

"So, I can swim?"

"Well, there's a sewage treatment plant just up the way . . ."

"So, I should wait until I pass it?"

"Smart boy."

My evening paddle — post sewage treatment plant, post quick dip — is ethereal. Surrounded by thick, tangled vegetation, nobody on the water or shore. A straight shot south, a slight bend, another straightaway: a lonely cleft in the middle of nowhere.

Two guys in jeans and pressed button-up shirts sit on the grass beside the only bridge over this stretch of canal. Dark complexions, dark hair. They don't look like they're from around here, though I don't know if anybody from this century would.

"Where are you going?" I ask.

"Canada," one of the men says.

"Where are you from?"

"Mexico," says the other, smiling wearily.

I drag my board onto a small island at lock C11, right across from the floodlights of a correctional facility. Setting up my lightweight tent, blowing up my lightweight air mattress, I picture men going to sleep in their cells just a couple hundred feet away. And men walking to an unknown future.

CHAPTER 11

> *"In America, which was not settled until the waterways of Europe had been in use for years, the opening of waterways closely followed the cutting of roads through the wilderness and in turn the railroads antedated the canals by only a short time. These are circumstances which have given to America a peculiar history of rapid development."*
>
> — Roy G. Finch, *"The Story of the New York State Canals"*

BEEP, BEEP, BEEP. MY ALARM GOES OFF AT 4:30 A.M., AN EARLY START TO BEAT the crushing heat. Also, it's tricky getting onto the water on the upstream side of this lock, where there's a vertical ladderless drop. I slowly lower my board using the leash and then cautiously squeeze myself onto a notch in the wall so I can retrieve my bags — a maneuver best attempted before the lock tender arrives for duty.

The air is still cool and fresh as I set off. A fawn sips in the shallows. A train whistles and clatters by. Two cyclists flicker through the trees and vanish. I spark a small stampede of cattle in a wooded field. Few are the waypoints for keeping tabs on distance along this unvarying, forest-fringe byway, just the occasional road bridge and a countdown of numbered locks.

At C9, Damien, three weeks into his first season with the Canal Corp., hands me two bottles of cold water and tells me he's found his dream job: "This is it, man. You're outside all day, watching eagles, talking to folks out here fishing. It doesn't get any better than this. Except what you're doing. And you don't get paid for that."

The section from C9 to C8 is the summit of the Champlain Canal. From C8 onward, the water drops until it reaches sea level at Troy, a tidal estuary that stretches more than 150 miles up from the Atlantic. But I'm getting ahead of myself, and a mean headwind has slowed me down.

Sharing the chamber with a sailboat at C8, I ask the woman at the wheel, half joking, half pleading, whether I can hitch a ride.

"We can throw you a towrope," she says with a laugh. Then the gates open, and they motor off.

Below C7, the Hudson River merges with the canal, which follows the river course for its remaining length, diverting around waterfalls and rapids via locks. Despite the signs warning of legacy PCBs in the Hudson, I swim. Short-term exposure is not a concern. Just don't eat too much local fish. Or dig in the dirt.

At C6, two million gallons of water surge out the chamber in six minutes, dropping me 19 feet. Veteran lock tender Randy gives me more cold water and a warm bottle of Dos Equis that my friends in the sailboat had left on the wall. (Locking through is free on the Champlain and Erie; some boaters leave tips.) After listing all the roles he's had on the canal over 30 years, from carpenter to "rover," driving up and down the line to lock through barges at all hours, Randy tells me he came aboard when he was going through a custody battle and needed a gig with benefits. He got the job and custody of both children.

"You never know what's going to happen at a lock," Randy says. "Last night, I was putting a barge through and seven Canada geese swam into the lock when I opened the gate. The barge came in and the geese stayed right there, and when I opened the other end, they swam out. I've never seen that before. I've seen ducks land in the lock but not swim in and out. I've seen dead deer— they must have fallen in trying to get away from coyotes and drowned overnight. But these geese *knew*. When the lock was full, they turned around and faced the other door just when I was about to open it."

Randy was born and still lives near the canal. "When I was a kid, I used to ride my bike to watch all the jet-fuel barges. They were all lit up at night. They lit up the whole trailer park when they passed by."

It's dusk when I bump into the floating dock just above C5. I drag my board and gear up a knoll and dump them beside a bench. There's a small dark-wood pavilion tucked into a pocket of trees a few feet away: curved slotted roofs splayed wing-like above a seating area, like a phoenix rising. Down a slope through a tunnel of willows I come across a labyrinth, a spiraling circular path formed by recycled slate roofing tiles, recessed in an amphitheater surrounded by a grassy berm. There's a playground beside the labyrinth: boulders, a sandbox in an old satellite dish, repurposed construction tubes, a slide built into the hill, flowers and shrubs flitting with butterflies. A large pavilion with a three-tiered metal roof abuts the playground. The bathroom is locked, but I find the key taped to the back of a bench.

Kate Morse left it here for me. She's the executive director of the nonprofit that runs Hudson Crossing Park, a once befouled island between the Hudson and the canal channel that now feels like a fairy tale.

In addition to letting me camp and agreeing to tour me through the park in the morning, Kate has also given me a dinner recommendation. I walk a mile into the village of Schuylerville to a brewpub that overlooks a pond-like turning basin on the old Champlain Canal, whose original course was rerouted in the early 1900s. Of more immediate interest, the pub serves Laotian food. I order a heaping dish of noodles and, the second it arrives, a side of spring rolls.

"Put on a lot of miles today?" the bartender, Max, asks.

"Yep," I reply through a mouthful of noodles. "Paddling."

"You gotta see what I got for my birthday!" he says, showing me a picture on his phone of a gleaming wooden canoe, a surprise gift from his girlfriend, who drove up with it earlier today on the roof of her car.

"You gotta pop the question," I say.

"I know. I know."

Max has something else to show me and beckons me to follow him outside. He points down the road. "That's the Surrender Tree."

After eating, I walk past the spot where a British general signed the Convention of Saratoga under an elm in 1777, capitulating to the Americans in what an interpretive panel declares to be "the turning point of the American Revolution."

It's pitch-black and I amble back to the park through the sultry night along the towpath. A constellation of fireflies sparkles in the woods to a soundtrack of peepers, bullfrogs and cicadas. There are a handful of houses on a thin strip of land between the old and new canals, their warm yellowish lights flickering dimly through the trees like candles, homesteads from another era. I close my eyes and can practically hear the clip-clop of horses and mules pulling canal boats two centuries ago.

Less than 20 miles north of Schuylerville, between 1947 and 1977, a pair of General Electric manufacturing plants dumped roughly 1.3 million pounds of PCBs into the Hudson River. Polychlorinated biphenyls are highly carcinogenic chemical compounds that accumulate in water, sediment and wildlife. At the top of the food web, eagles were particularly susceptible. Their America-wide population crashed from an estimated 100,000 nesting birds in the late 1700s to just over 400 known pairs in 1963. It began to rebound when the pesticide DDT was banned in 1972, then soared after PCBs were banned in the late 1970s, although it was too late to stop contaminated deposits from washing downstream on the Hudson.

Toxic pollution shut down commercial fisheries, and nearly 50 years after the GE plants in Hudson Falls and Fort Edward were closed, people are still advised to limit their consumption of fish from the river, the greatest health risk to humans, with other forms of exposure to present-day concentrations not considered overly harmful. In 1984, a 200-mile stretch of the waterway, from Hudson Falls to the Atlantic Ocean, was designated a federal Superfund site, the largest in the country. This allowed the U.S. Environmental Protection Agency to compel those responsible to clean up their mess. To date, GE has spent an estimated $1.6 billion dredging and removing PCBs from the Hudson. But hotspots remain. In late 2023, a group of environmental organizations that keep an eye on the river released an independent scientific assessment which found that the dredging "has failed to ensure the protection of human and environmental health because the concentration of toxic PCBs in the river's fish and sediment remain higher than anticipated."

This was the burbling backdrop 25 years ago, when the 42-acre island I'm camping on — a parcel of forest and former farmland hived off the mainland by the canal — had become a dumping ground. People tossed fridges, couches and televisions out of their trucks; teens partied, lighting fires and leaving behind smashed bottles and beer cans. A community group suggested cleaning up the New York State Canal Corp. property and creating a park, but the response from many locals was doubt and derision. "It's impossible," said one. "It'll never happen."

That didn't deter the school groups and scout troops who convened to remove garbage. Barrels containing mysterious substances were hauled out of the wetlands. Kids teased Kate Morse, who was hugely pregnant at the time and couldn't bend down to pick up trash. She remembers a group of students coming across a fish one day that had somehow become trapped in a small pool. "Once the kids noticed it, everything else stopped and they dug a little canal to save it. They fought a little tiny battle for that fish and figured it out. The fish survived. It seemed like an insignificant act, but it reflects something bigger."

In 2003, a nonprofit was incorporated, and Hudson Crossing Park was born. Volunteers asked community members what they wanted to see. An old bridge across the Hudson, closed and slated for demolition, was repurposed for active transportation. A playground was built using natural and upcycled materials, and the adjacent pavilion was erected. Somewhere for kids to play, somewhere for parents to sit. Two miles of trails were mapped out. "It's amazing what can happen," says Kate, "when people with imagination aren't afraid to roll up their sleeves."

~

Kate and Mike Bielkiewicz, chair of the park's board, are giving me a tour in the pouring rain. We walk along a sensory trail, a wide crushed-gravel surface suitable for visitors with mobility devices, lined by a string of large wrought-iron bird sculptures — here a heron, there an osprey — so people with visual impairments can tactilely experience the birds they hear. Dropping down a set of stairs to a secret garden, bright orange lilies and painted rocks ring a stone bench under a wooden arbor. A 12-year-old girl built the steps so visitors could access this tucked-away spot. We reach the Dix Bridge and walk halfway across the Hudson, just downstream from a set of rapids. This was the first free bridge in the area when it was built in 1895. Tired of paying tolls, businesspeople pooled their funds and made their own crossing.

"It's a huge piece of the puzzle," says Kate, explaining that the span is part of the Empire State Trail, which runs from New York City to the Canadian border and west from the Hudson to Buffalo. "And it's a beautiful view, even in the rain."

Despite the downpour, we keep running into people, out with their dogs, who want to chat. After stopping at a pollinator garden and a self-serve kayak rental kiosk, where anybody with a smartphone and credit card can unlock a boat, we retreat to the pavilion. Like proud parents, Kate and Mike share more of the park's birth story.

Schuylerville was similar to Whitehall before this project started, says Kate, who is wearing a pair of green overalls, her shoulder-length hair tucked behind her ears. It was rough: a couple of antique shops, a tattoo parlor and "a big bar that nobody wanted to walk past."

Once a thriving mill town, Schuylerville had three grocery stores when Mike was a kid. There were hotels, a hardware store, clothing stores, newsstands. "Things went south in the '70s, '80s and '90s," he says. "There weren't a lot of lights on."

Writer James Howard Kunstler had bought a house in Schuylerville, and in a 1990 *New York Times* article he used the community as a dartboard for everything wrong in America. Cyclical poverty, drug addiction, teenage pregnancy, a "general air of rot and disrepair." For most inhabitants of Schuylerville and other old industrial towns on the

Hudson, he wrote, "the decade-long fiesta of capital gains known as the Reagan Years might have taken place on another planet." Kunstler attributed this decline to the shuttering of factories; to chain stores undercutting local merchants; to landlords who purchased decaying buildings, fixed them shoddily with government grants, then rented apartments to families on welfare. Still, strolling along the towpath, overgrown with honeysuckle thickets, geese honking overhead and the river flowing nearby, he sensed a latent energy.

"What remains," he wrote, "is the Hudson River, source of all the town's past wealth. . . . Today, the life of the town could hardly be more disconnected from the river. Schuylerville, and towns like it in the Hudson and Mohawk valleys, changed because their local economies ceased to matter, and it is only now beginning to dawn on us that you cannot have a community without a local economy." Subsisting on products made by corporations based elsewhere, Kunstler argued, makes a place a colony. Small towns need to reinvent their economies and rely on local assets. "To me, a plausible future for the town is one in which people rediscover the river's value and harness its power to make something useful in a way that is not harmful and wasteful. And in the process, perhaps, rediscover their own value."

Hudson Crossing Park is just one factor in the community's resurgence. Real-estate pressure in New York City has sent tens of thousands of homebuyers up the Hudson Valley, where old houses with good bones abound. This has led to displacement, gentrification and soaring prices in some towns, in particular those closer to NYC. But elsewhere it has fueled a more gradual transformation: young people with energy and ideas putting down roots. Schuylerville has an art gallery now, a bike shop, a café, the brewpub. And the park is pivotal.

Much more than a physical space, it hosts recreational and educational programming that's inclusive, mostly free and often has a subtle sustainability message. There are interpretive nature walks, school and summer camp visits, foodie fundraisers, concerts, cleanups, winter carnivals, native plant sales. It belongs to the community, Kate says, and has awakened a spirit of camaraderie and possibility.

Kate is the only paid staff at the park, which is funded by grants and donations, an annual budget of roughly $120,000. But about 300 individuals volunteer in one capacity or another. On our walk, she pointed out a giant cottonwood that had fallen in a storm. A local came by with his tractor to remove the debris; another came with his chainsaw to carve a face into the stump. Schuylerville's mayor mows the lawn and trims trees. "Everything you see," Kate says, "assume it was done by volunteers."

Part of the vision for Hudson Crossing Park was for it to be an economic driver. Visitors who come to spend time in its green and blue spaces might pop into town for lunch, stay for dinner or spend the night. "We need to look at our waterfront for its natural and heritage value," says Mike. "We need to recognize our waterfront as the resource that it is, one that transcends politics."

In the waning months of the Biden presidency, with another potential Trump term on the horizon, our talk turns to politics. Republicans in this part of the state tend to be old-school, says Kate. Live and let live. "They're the farmers who work hard every day and may not agree with what their neighbors are doing, but they're not going to get into it. They're socially conservative, but they complain about the same things I complain about.

"I would say the vast majority of people who use this park are conservative. They love it, but when they see things on paper, it becomes a source of political drama. It's turned into this ridiculous dialogue: we don't need green spaces, we're surrounded by green spaces. And sure, when I grew up, I could walk across my neighbor's farm. I didn't worry about property lines. We live in a very different world these days, to the extent that, in a nearby town, a girl was murdered because she and her friends pulled into the wrong driveway."

That tragic killing, a little north of here in Hebron, happened in early 2023. A group of teens were shot as they turned around. Kate knew some of the kids in the car. "This is the world we're living in now. The argument that we're surrounded by green space is no longer valid."

One of the biggest social benefits of Hudson Crossing Park, as blue space researcher Mat White might say, is the mixing that it encourages. It's a neutral space where all are welcome. "You meet people on the trail who you're not necessarily going to meet in your circles," says Kate. "You get that gentle reminder that there are people in this town who haven't been here for generations, there are people in these communities who might have accents or look different than you do, and they're your neighbors. White people aren't the first people who loved this space — we're *really* not the natives — and we're not the only people who love this space. It helps filter through all of the noise and humanizes the shared experience."

Kate is quiet for a few seconds, then continues. "Everything about this place is replicable. I will happily give away every secret we have. But really, every community has people with vision and people with know-how. It's just a matter of pulling together and chipping away at what you want to see. All our ideas might not come to fruition. Things might not happen today or tomorrow. But we're still going to dream about them, and we're still going to work hard.

"Each piece of this park was created by somebody who asked, 'What does this situation need? Let's take care of it.' When I think about things on this scale, I'm optimistic. I may not be able to fix all of the problems in the world, but I can fix some of the problems in this part of it. And there are a lot of people trying to do the same thing."

CHAPTER 12

"Perhaps the time is ripe for reconsideration of an ideal that has fallen out of favor: manual competence, and the stance it entails toward the built, material world. Neither as workers nor as consumers are we much called upon to exercise such competence, most of us anyway, and merely to recommend its cultivation is to risk the scorn of those who take themselves to be the most hard-headed: the hard-headed economist will point out the opportunity costs of making what can be bought, and the hard-headed educator will say that it is irresponsible to educate the young for the trades, which are somehow identified as the jobs of the past. But we might pause to consider just how hard-headed these presumptions are, and whether they don't, on the contrary, issue from a peculiar sort of idealism, one that insistently steers young people toward the most ghostly kinds of work."

— Matthew B. Crawford, Shop Class as Soulcraft

KATE AND MIKE LEAVE THE PAVILION JUST AFTER NOON. I'M BUZZING FROM our conversation, but the rain is still pelting and the glow fades fast. My decision to hastily decamp under this roof with my breakfast and leave the tent standing means four hours of squandered drying time. I'm picturing myself shoving wet gear into dry bags and paddling until dark to make up for this late start . . . and then my phone rings.

It's Rob Goldman, the owner of the New York State Marina Highway Transportation Company, which runs tugboats throughout the region. He and I had been corresponding about me doing a ride-along, ostensibly to learn more about inland shipping but really as an excuse to take a shortcut. Rob was unreservedly game, but it didn't seem like my timing would dovetail with any of their scheduled transits.

"Where are you?" he asks.

"Hudson Crossing Park. Right across from lock C5."

"A southbound tug will be there in half an hour. Want a lift?"

"Absolutely! But I've got a 14-foot paddleboard."

"Um," Rob replies, sounding mildly annoyed, "we've got a barge."

Packing up a campsite in a downpour is a small price to pay if you're about to hop onto a working tugboat — an immersion journalist's and tired paddler's double jackpot. I corral my gear, zip across the canal and pile my bags and board beside the water. A few minutes later I hear a low rumble and see an enormous blue barge with a red open-top container on its deck. The tug at its rear has a matte black base and boxy cabin beneath a hydraulic wheelhouse that, when raised, makes the *Edna A* look like a postmodern metallic peacock.

Nautical nomenclature notwithstanding, it's typically more efficient to push than pull, though back in the day tugs weren't tall enough to see over their cargo, so they only pulled from the front, like horses. The barge glides toward the lock mere inches from the wall. "Throw that on there for me," says a burly man with a radio clipped to his shoulder, tossing me a thick ringed rope that I drape over a metal cleat (my sole tangible contribution as a passenger). Engineer Chris Caprio helps me lift my SUP onto the barge, then we step over a small gap onto the tug and into a cozy galley.

"Want a coffee?" he asks, grabbing a mug from the wood-paneled cupboard.

"Yes, please."

"Take a seat," Chris says after pouring.

"I'm good."

"Sometimes," he says, nodding at a bench beside the table, "it's the best place to stay out of the way."

We lock through and motor south at five knots, the equivalent of 5.75 miles per hour, not quite twice my average paddling speed. (Traveling at one knot means you'll cover one nautical mile per hour, Chris explains. A nautical mile equals one minute of latitude or 1.15 land-based miles, making it the preferred measure for travel by air or water.) I sip my coffee and look out the window, watching the trees and clouds knot by.

Marine shipping is significantly more fuel efficient than moving the same amount of weight by road, and it's better than rail as well. It's slow, however, and as with trucks and trains, burning diesel to power a big boat releases greenhouse gases and other pollutants. Only certain products make sense to ship on canals these days: the load of high-friction crushed granite that the *Edna A* is shepherding today, from an upstate New York quarry down to Long Island for use in highway and bridge construction; other bulk aggregates, such as sand or salt; and unusually large items, like the dozen 2,000-barrel fermentation tanks, manufactured in China, that were barged to a brewery in Rochester, or a new pedestrian bridge that was barged to Buffalo. But Goldman's company seems to have found a niche, and there's work afoot to electrify the industry. There are even start-ups experimenting with sail freight, including the *Apollonia*, a 64-foot schooner that, since 2020, has hauled more than 200,000 pounds along the Hudson — coffee beans, lumber, flour, beer, cheese, pumpkins, cider, furniture — using only wind and tidal currents. "We're not Amazon," says its captain, Sam Merrett. "We're not guaranteeing this thing in six hours. We're guaranteeing you a responsibly delivered good." Adds one of his collaborators, Andrew Willner, executive director of the Center for Post Carbon Logistics, "We are really just one or two generations away from people who still know how to do this stuff."

I had every intention to dig deeper into the green potential of shipping while aboard the *Edna A* but am lulled sluggish by the warmth and vibrations. I hang my wet gear in the engine room, where it will be dried in the heat pumped out by a pair of 800-horsepower engines.

When he's not showing a tenderfoot around the tug — a bedroom with two bunk beds, a bathroom with a shower, "all the amenities you need to live comfortably" — Chris's job is to keep these puppies humming. "It's like owning a home: there's always something to do."

Chris served as a medic in the Navy during Operation Desert Shield, but when he got back from Iraq, none of the "learnings" from his military service translated into employment-ready credentials. Growing up poor, he had learned how to do household repairs with his father, so he reckoned familiarity with motors would give him a smooth landing in marine engineering. That was 30 years ago.

A tall young man wearing a hoodie and sweatpants steps into the galley. Kevin Klerk is the first mate, a jack of all trades, doing everything from deckhand duties and standing watch to steering. "A lot of my friends in the city have jobs they don't like," he says. "I wake up on the boat and look at the water and I'm happy."

Kevin is also the cook. "Meatloaf or cheeseburgers?" he asks me, pulling a bag of onions out of a cupboard.

"Either! Or both!"

Chris's and Kevin's jobs seem to fit well-worn coveralls. I would be woefully inept in their boots, but at least one journalist was capable of ditching her desk in the city for the engine room of a tugboat on the Hudson.

In *My River Chronicles*, Jessica DuLong brings to life her journey from Manhattan office tower to volunteering aboard a restored New York City fireboat, becoming a licensed marine engineer and joining a crew that purchases an old tug. Beyond her blazing a trail in a masculine realm, the book is an ode to hands-on work in a part of the world where it has largely been forgotten.

The average North American has a nostalgic fondness for tugboats and the metallic ringing of gears at lock stations — an audible reminder, as one veteran tug captain tells DuLong, that "while most of the world is sleeping, there are people out there moving things back and forth that are absolutely necessary for you to go on with your life." But as our society becomes more virtual, most of us are blithely disconnected from the hands-on labor underpinning white-collar lives. Even on the Hudson, we seldom think about the factories and foundries where much of the heavy lifting that begat the U.S. took place, especially since their output was outsourced, their crumbling shells abandoned.

DuLong began to view the transformation of her country through a "Hudson River lens," through days defined by physical work: shifting levers, turning wrenches, welding steel. "As the United States faces economic upheaval that challenges us to rethink who we want to be as a nation," she writes, "I have discovered that it pays to take stock of who we have been: a country of innovators and doers, of people who make things, of workers who toil, sweat, and labor with their hands."

After the September 11 terrorist attacks, the 1931-built fireboat *John J. Harvey* was pressed back into service. Supporting emergency responders at Ground Zero, DuLong witnessed "the dichotomy between hands-on and hands-off work played out in stark relief. As blue-collar tradespeople swarmed over the pile, the earth seemed to have shifted on its axis.... Suddenly an Ivy League education seemed far less useful than knowing how to use a cutting torch."

The collapse of the Twin Towers, the slow-moving train wreck of climate change: any disaster provides an opportunity for introspection. For examining how we live, or how we've been told to live, and wondering what we might do differently.

"Want to meet the captain?" asks Chris, snapping me back to the present.

Ascending the metal stairs, I'm a little apprehensive, unsure how the man at the helm will respond to an interloper.

"Every time I see a paddleboarder, I shake my head," Earl Wedemeyer says when I poke my nose into the wheelhouse. "Know what we call paddleboards? Flotsam." Chuckling, he reaches for a handshake.

In his other hand, he holds a joystick-like controller. A click and the barge angles left. Another click and it angles right.

"It's like driving a car," says Earl, who is wearing a burgundy short-sleeved button-up and looks more like a friendly small-town accountant than a guy responsible for 900 tons of granite. "After you've been on the same road for a while, you don't even think about it. You get in your car, drive somewhere and get out. It becomes second nature. I'm basically driving a Winnebago."

The *Edna A* is 64 feet long and 23 feet wide, with 7.5-foot draw and a 15.5-foot air draft when the wheelhouse is raised. "Because of all the bridges we go under, the air draft is the most important thing I know," says Earl, who has worked on the water for nearly 50 years, piloting everything from shrimp boats and freighters to treasure-hunting boats in the South China Sea. Other than basic specs, he shies away from discussing the technical aspects of his job and would rather talk about learning how to read the water and wind, about the path of least resistance and the efficiency of moving things by water. This barge trip is keeping a lot of trucks off the highway, he says, speculating about the possibility of small cold-fusion generators powering tugs in the future. "Everything is waves and cycles. Waves and cycles. Time, gravity, energy, water, history. I've got a lot of time to think up here. I like to think."

The rain stops and streaks of light break through gray clouds as we glide through parallel curtains of green.

Approaching lock C4, a large house with manicured gardens is perched on a point beside the water.

"What would you say if you crashed into it?" I ask Earl.

"Dunno."

"I didn't mean to barge in."

"I'm surprised I didn't think of that."

"Me too. I'd be spending all my time up here thinking of barge puns."

We enter lock C2, at Mechanicville, and Earl points to the oldest continuously operating hydroelectric plant on the continent, which has been producing power since 1898. "How cool is this?" he says as we descend. "I can't believe they pay us to do this. Don't put that in your book."

In his spare time, Earl is a glassblower. Among other objects, he makes marbles. There's one of his creations atop a knob on the console. Deep blue with whorls of green, it looks like a miniature Earth.

Every day on my expedition, an entire universe unfolds, a sine graph of highs and lows, waves and cycles. Barging into the wheelhouse of a tug, I'm on top of the world. When the wind rears up or the rain pours down, when I'm exhausted and empty, I question my motivation for leaving home and doubt my ability to finish. But in the moment — enwrapped in a physical trial, as Zac Crouse said, and tackling basic, immediate problems — I don't wallow in the trough. The emotional weight lands and then lifts. Because unfailingly, at some point, all that water triggers an inkling of sanguinity. And whenever I get lonely, a little bit of human touch, whether sought-out or impromptu, gives me an even more nourishing boost.

Chris comes up the stairs and tells us dinner is ready.

"You should eat," Earl says to me. "When you get told to eat, eat!"

I pile a plate with meatloaf, mac and cheese, green beans, salad.

As we lock through C1, I pack my bags and put them beside my SUP. Chris and Kevin untie the *Edna A* from the barge. They're heading back north for another load of granite. A smaller tug slides into position behind the barge to continue the trek south. Half an hour later the captain kills the engine, and the first mate helps me get onto the water. We're a few hundred feet offshore from Waterford. I paddle to the visitor center and dock among a group of cruisers tied up for the night.

I'm rushing to set up my tent before the rain resumes when Bill, a boater from South Carolina, stops by for a welcoming chat and hands me a cold can of beer. Later, I call my wife and almost make the mistake of telling her that this has been the greatest day of my life.

The Erie Canal meets the Hudson River at Waterford, the oldest continually incorporated village in the U.S., dating back to 1794. I can see the gates of the Erie's lock E2 from my campsite, the start of a flight of five locks that raise westbound boats 169 feet over 1.5 miles, past a series of waterfalls on the Mohawk River, the highest set of lift locks in the world. The de facto first lock, meanwhile, is five miles south at Troy, where the Hudson drops to sea level.

Bill Sweitzer, the New York State Canal Corp.'s director of marketing, meets me at the Waterford visitor center midmorning.

The state and federal governments invested in this handsome brick building, which went up in 2000; there's a sign about eight feet up the front wall marking where the floodwaters from Hurricane Irene crested in 2011. But the building was designed to handle such inundations, and boaters provide a boon to the local economy. Staff at a supermarket across the Hudson disengage the geofencing on shopping carts so people can wheel groceries back to their boats. With about $100,000 cobbled together from various grants, Bill says, communities can set up a kayak launch and build a gazebo. These features bring visitors whose business could support a café or diner. Piece by piece, places like Waterford — or Schuylerville or Whitehall — can build a foundation.

I've been talking and texting for weeks with Bill and his colleague Shane Mahar from the New York Power Authority, the canal system's parent agency. They've given me indispensable information and support. Going into our first call, I figured a pair of government PR guys would be guided by risk management and liability (the norm in Canada). Instead, they whooped about how *fun* my plan was. That excitement is evident today as Bill drives me back up to lock C2 for a visit to the historic hydroelectric plant I passed yesterday. "Edison, Tesla and Westinghouse have been there!" he says with a big smile. "You can't miss it!"

Construction keeps us out of the main facility, whose turbines and generators have powered nearby towns and factories and, more recently, bitcoin mining. But we're allowed inside a smaller hydro plant, a steampunk paradise with gleaming circuit boards and copper pipes, preposterously large levers and gauges. Many of the lock stations still have boxy white buildings like this, creating electricity to open and close the gates and supplying a few kilowatts to the local grid — an old-fashioned decentralized system. "This is a two-century-old piece of infrastructure," Bill beams, "and it's still kicking!"

On our way back to Waterford, Bill makes two calls on my behalf. First, to the lock at Troy, which is run by the U.S. Army Corps of Engineers, to ask whether they'll let a paddleboard through. "Fine with me," says the man who answers. "I'm the maintenance guy, but we're short-staffed, so I'm the only one here today." Then Bill calls a fishing buddy whose relatives own the riverside Best Western in Troy and secures me a very generous friends-and-family rate.

Thunderstorms are brewing as I'm swallowed up by the Troy lock's 520-foot-by-45-foot chamber. The air is heavy, stifling.

The maintenance guy, armed with a clipboard, peers down at me. "How long is your, uh . . . your vessel?" he asks.

"Fourteen feet."

"And what's your . . . oh, never mind."

He jots down a few notes, and just like that, I have appeased another branch of the American government.

A short portage across River Street brings me to my downtown hotel. I stash my SUP behind some bushes in the parking lot, drape my sodden camping gear over every piece of furniture in the room, hang my sink-scrubbed underwear and socks in the bathroom and run some errands under a dark sky pierced with lightning. Stop one: buy a belt. No matter how much I eat, I'm shedding weight, and my shorts — the good ones, the pair I wear on land — are slipping. So I source a cheap vinyl belt via the outernet, asking a clerk at a chain drugstore, who directs me to a rack in the corner of a nearby convenience store.

Inner-city Troy is a jumble of gentrification (funky bars and shops, pricey restaurants, ornate 19th-century facades) and subsidized apartments whose tenants sit outside, waiting for the storm. They're not far from the river, but chain-link fences and private property block access.

July 4. Happy birthday, America. What better way to celebrate than with a paddle down your great river?

I gorge myself at the sleepy Best Western breakfast buffet and accept a clamshell stuffed with fresh fruit from the prescient man in the kitchen. "Not many guests today. Maybe you're gonna want this later." A roundup of yesterday's mass shootings scrolls on the TV news: five killed in Philadelphia, three in Fort Worth, a mother and two children in Missouri. Outside the automatic doors, my luggage cart loaded with dry bags, a nurse on her way to an early shift smokes a cigarette and stares at a deer walking along the deserted riverside promenade. She looks at me and shrugs. And then I'm on the water.

Just 315 miles from its source in the Adirondacks to its mouth in Manhattan, the Hudson barely cracks the top 100 longest rivers in the U.S. But its impact has vastly exceeded its size, Frances F. Dunwell shows in *The Hudson: America's River*, not only shaping New York City and the state but also global trade, politics and the modern environmental movement. Although she doesn't delve too deeply into colonial violence — "Native people, of course, had a different idea about what it meant to possess land" — Dunwell's book presents a concise summary of the waterway's original inhabitants. From the Lenape people in what is now the New York City area to the Mohicans up the valley and the Mohawks to the north and west, the Indigenous presence dates back more than 11,000 years. The brackish lower estuary provided oysters and other shellfish; shad, herring and sturgeon swam upstream to spawn in tributaries; turkey, grouse, quail and deer roamed the forest; corn, beans and squash were grown plentifully along its banks. Indigenous Peoples moved from villages to seasonal camps to hunt ducks that were migrating south and gather nuts and berries to prepare for winter. They felled trees, hollowed them out with sharpened rocks and paddled from shore to shore.

"They roamed large territories, which generally conformed to the boundaries of a watershed or stream drainage basin," Dunwell writes. "Water, used as a dividing line for property by many European settlers, was a uniting feature for native people of the Hudson Valley."

Before Henry Hudson showed up in 1609 — an Englishman hired by the Dutch to scope out a route to China — the Mohicans called it Mahicantuck. Loose translation: "river that flows two ways."

Below Troy, the Hudson is a 153-mile-long estuary. Twice a day, a push from the Atlantic reaches this city, although the ocean's power and salinity are more pronounced farther south. It's advisable, if possible, to paddle *with* the tide, adhering to the two-six-two rule: if traveling southbound, start two hours before the ebb begins, ride the tide for six, and then two more hours before the flow builds. Paddle smart, not hard. As luck has it, the best time for me to start today is early morning.

Beneath a misty drizzle, with the subtle oceangoing ebb augmented by yesterday's rain, I make it seven miles to Albany, the state capital, in about 90 minutes. A man in a yellow slicker is waiting beside the river. Scott Keller is executive director of the Hudson River Valley Greenway, a state-sponsored program to preserve and develop the valley's natural, historic, cultural and recreational resources. Part of his job involves getting people onto the water, Scott says, although few phrases put more fear into the hearts of conservationists than when somebody in state government says, "I'm here to help." But this program appears to be working. In 1991, when the Greenway was established, there was just one paddling outfitter on the river. Today there are at least 20, plus more than 200 put-in sites, scores of information kiosks and a detailed guidebook for self-propelled travelers.

"The more people we bring to the Hudson," Scott says, "the more people see how great the river is, the more people have a stake in making sure the Hudson gets cleaner and stays cleaner."

For a decade, Scott led annual group kayak trips from Albany to Manhattan. Over 11 or so days, four dozen people paddled the length of the estuary. "The second I pushed away from shore, I had a sense of peace. I'd spend months preparing, and it was stressful. As soon as we launched, even though I was responsible for everybody, my stress level dropped.

"I knew people better after 10 days on the water than I know my neighbors," he adds. "That's partially because the tents were so thin."

I could talk to Scott for hours, but the outgoing tide beckons.

"See any floaters yet?" he asks as I step onto my board. "On days like this, when we've had a couple inches of rain, you'll get a combined sewer overflow throughout the capital district, and that means raw sewage is going into the river. Don't go swimming for the next 10 miles. This can be the worst stretch on the river outside Manhattan."

The drizzle stops, the clouds part, the sun beats down. Holding off on submerging myself, I stop at a boat club, chug a couple of $1 cans of icy cola and crumple onto a bench in the shade. A small taste of a world of water, water everywhere, but not a drop to cool off in.

"Mind if I stay awhile?" I ask the merciful woman who had let me into the member's-only commissary.

"You can sit all day if you want."

The Hudson here is lined by rolling hills, green forests and lawns popping against the suddenly bright blue sky. I had secured permission in advance to camp at two different marinas on this part of the predominantly private riverside, but boosted by the tidal current and figuring the water is now clean enough for dunking every half hour, I muster the momentum to keep going. Boat traffic swells, families out for Independence Day cruises, smiles and waves as they pass. After quiet days farther north, it's nice to have some company.

The tide turns, but by sticking close to shore, I minimize drag. Also, as Scott Keller had recommended, it keeps me well outside the shipping channel, which is demarked by red and green buoys and is prowled by tankers like the 600-foot-long TRF *Mongstad*, steaming north to the oil terminals on the outskirts of Albany and displacing a disproportionately small wake.

By late afternoon, after a conveyer belt of energy bars and protein shakes, I'm hankering for real food. I stop at a newly renovated riverside park in Coxsackie. On the pristine grass, beside a pristine pavilion and playground, a family is tucking into a holiday feast: hot dogs and corn and potato salad. It takes all of my resolve not to ask for a handout. Down a sunblasted street lined by restored buildings, I get a take-out burger from the only open restaurant, an upscale tavern adjacent to a brand-new boutique hotel. Coxsackie is one of those gentrifying Hudson Valley towns; at the oyster bar atop the hotel, the seafood platter will set you back $160, though you can get the caviar for a mere $99.

"The Hudson Valley has changed," Gary, a local retiree out for his daily walk, tells me when I get back to the park. "It used to be a place to make money. Now it's a place to bring money."

The burger fuels me up for an 11-mile evening paddle to the village of Catskill, where the owner of the Hop-O-Nose Marina had indifferently acquiesced over the phone to my camping request. ("What? Um, sure, I guess.") But laggardly leaving Coxsackie, I worry I may have bitten off more than I can chew. Three or four more hours of paddling after a dozen hours of paddling is a lot of paddling. Plodding by the village of Athens, I'm tempted to pull over at another boutique hotel (until my phone informs me that rooms start at $350). Eventually, I see the cantilevered frame of the Rip Van Winkle Bridge. Fittingly, it feels like 20 years before I finally pass beneath.

It's dark and I'm dragging my ass by the time I spot the creek that leads to the Hop-O-Nose. Fireworks burst overhead. People are partying on patios. Why didn't I slow down and celebrate the holiday with locals? Is it too late to sidle up to a dock and cadge a cold one? Might this be my journalistic duty? Then I realize that some of these explosions are in fact lightning bolts, rapidly gaining on me from the north.

I hang a right onto Catskill Creek, squeezing a bit more juice from my muscles for the 41st mile of my day, the most I have ever paddled in one outing — and now the *hardest* I've ever sprinted on a SUP as a swirling wind begins to batter my board. I'm not panicking, at least not yet, just castigating myself for making another questionable choice and tensely waiting for the crack and flash that will send me scrambling for cover. It feels like a hurricane by the time I'm at the marina. Leaving my bags bungeed atop the SUP so it doesn't blow away, I pry my fingers off the paddle and dash into a building.

Turns out it's the bar.

"We're closed," a woman counting cash says without looking up.

I eye three men who must be regulars, sitting on stools, half-full drinks in front of them.

"Can I just get a beer and wait out the storm?" I ask.

"Whadya want?"

A plastic cup of IPA in hand, I can't stop shaking, a 50-50 cocktail of exhaustion and elation. Sam, Link and Mike pepper me with questions, then backslaps and high fives. Before I crossed the border, I wasn't sure how Americans would respond to me bursting in. In Catskill, on Independence Day, they treat me like an old friend.

CHAPTER 13

"Global warming and rising water levels are changing everything about this river. The chemistry of the river. The temperature of the water. The wildlife in and around the river. The communities around the river. This is maritime history that we have to document as it happens. It opens the door to a discussion about industry. Many of the industries that burgeoned here and were so successful, they contributed to the way things are now. We need to make sure we share this story, so people get insight into cause and consequences."

— Lisa Cline, executive director of
Hudson River Maritime Museum

CATSKILL CREEK IS SOCKED IN BY THICK FOG WHEN I SHOVE OFF FROM THE dock, the sky just starting to brighten. I can't see more than a few feet in front of me but, with questionable logic, doubt anybody else is foolhardy enough to be out here. Besides, it's 5 a.m. on July 5 — people are probably sleeping off yesterday's revelry.

Within the hour, starting from the west, the fog begins to dissipate and I can make out the spindly legs of herons peering into the water for their breakfast. Straining my ears for engines as I hug the marshy western shoreline of the Hudson, I start to hear the calls, coos and chirps of waterfowl and songbirds stirring. A quack and honk here, a whistle and trill there. Tall grasses rustle in the breeze, ripples wash into the shore and a duck takes flight, each flap of its wings crisp and distinct. I'm listening to nature's ablutions, to biomass breathing. Acoustic ecologist Gordon Hempton would call a dawn chorus like this the "music of place." On a reporting trip several years ago, he told me that such soundscapes inspire him to be a better neighbor because they make him feel part of something much bigger.

It takes me two hours to reach the Saugerties Lighthouse, a red-brick beacon built in 1869 on a tiny island — not much larger than the tower and two-story keepers' quarters — to replace an 1835 predecessor wrecked by ice floes. The lighthouse is attached by a wooden walkway to an even smaller islet, just a deck and some picnic tables and trees. The site is now a B&B and museum, and after a short swim, I sit and listen to the songbirds. A post with arrows pointing toward various New York landmarks informs me that the Statue of Liberty is 103 miles away.

The rest of the day follows a similar pattern. Paddle, swim, shade, birdsong, sunscreen, paddle, shade, paddle, swim, sunscreen, birds, paddle, shade, paddle, paddle, paddle. Time quivers out of focus, and I do my best to ward off heatstroke and sunstroke and a cumulative corporeal fatigue. Late afternoon, nearly 25 miles downstream from Catskill, I lie down on the ground in a park just north of the small city of Kingston. After closing my eyes for a few minutes, I sit up to sip some lukewarm water and eat the last of my pepperoni sticks. There's a grandmotherly woman with short gray hair sitting on a bench doing crossword puzzles. I say hello, and she nods curtly. Eventually she walks over to my SUP, studies it for a few minutes, then approaches me and asks the usual questions. Where are you going? Why?

Ruth lives nearby and comes to this park to look at swans and ships on the Hudson. "It's clean. You can thank Pete for that!" she says — the first of many shout-outs I hear to folk singer and activist Pete Seeger, who might be more responsible than anybody for the ecological turnaround in this valley.

There's something familiar about Ruth. In my discombobulated state, I can't figure it out. Then: she looks and sounds like my grandmother! I tell her and find out we're both secular Jews with relatives who emigrated from Poland. Suddenly, she feels like a distant cousin. "It's not far to Kingston," she says. "You'll get there."

Even with her encouragement, today's last five miles are a slog. I feel faint, dizzy. Why didn't I repose longer or ask Ruth for a ride? Is it irrational, or stupid, to stick to a self-imposed schedule? A sandy beach mobbed by boisterous teens announces that town is close and that there are multitudinous ways one could have spent this afternoon. I pass another historic lighthouse without giving it much of a glance; so much for soaking up the local attractions. Finally, I round a point and head up Rondout Creek, which used to be a busy thoroughfare when Kingston was a bustling port. On my right, a cluster of boats and brick buildings: I'm spending a night at the museum.

Inside the main hall of the Hudson River Maritime Museum, I give the exhibits a cursory, last-ounce-of-energy walkabout. Amid artifacts and photographs documenting the region's shipping and industrial past, there's an emphasis on climate change, environmentalism, the future of sail freight. In a cluttered upstairs office, I find executive director Lisa Cline wrapping a computer power cord with electrical tape as a tradesman fiddles with a fuse box.

"These cords are so fucking expensive," sighs Lisa, who has spikey short gray hair and rimless glasses, "and I shouldn't fucking swear so much."

I collapse into a chair across from her desk, and Lisa tells me about the nonprofit's overarching mission: an uphill battle to get people to slow down and, if I may paraphrase, give a shit. (I can relate.)

Founded in 1979 by tugboat and steamboat veterans, the museum's original goal was to preserve and celebrate the area's rich maritime history. Rondout Creek was the terminus of the 19th-century Delaware and Hudson Canal, built to bring coal from northeastern Pennsylvania to the Hudson and down to New York City. This made Kingston a shipping hotbed. "There were times in the 1800s," Lisa says, "when you could probably walk across the creek on boats." But like the Lake Champlain Maritime Museum, the vision here has widened. On top of eco-focused exhibits and collaborations with Indigenous communities, there's a boat school that teaches woodworking and other hands-on skills, a sailing school that gets people onto the water, and a solar-powered tour boat, the *Solaris*, that serves as a floating classroom, demonstrating that we don't always need to burn fossil fuels.

"We realized a few years ago that we had to touch on different aspects of the river and how things are changing," says Lisa. "Not just climate change, but also how industry brought waves of people up here to the traditional territory of the Lenape, and how gentrification is bringing waves of people to Kingston today.

"People are so busy. We're so disconnected from where our feet are. We're always looking at our phones and rushing around in our cars. A sense of place is easy to ignore — but it's much harder to ignore when you're on the water. Water slows everybody down, especially kids. We notice when we take kids out, whether it's on the *Solaris* or rowboats or tiny sailboats the size of a bathtub, the difference between giving them facts and figures when they're sitting in a classroom versus giving them facts and figures on a boat, it's night and day. They absorb information in a different way. A hatch opens up and you get more access to their brains."

The hatch to my brain is rapidly closing and I can't formulate any questions, but thankfully Lisa is on a roll and her insights keep me rapt.

"I think water can be a unifying force, as long as we fight to make it accessible. One of the things we really like about our museum is the yard is always open. People can eat at our picnic tables; they can launch kayaks from our docks. It's all free, and that's the way we want to keep it. When a waterfront is taken over by condos and restaurants and high-rises, public spaces become few and far between. We want this to be not only public but also a working waterfront again. To have solar-powered freight and sail freight, to see people loading and unloading boats."

Lisa leads me to the boat school, where I will sleep on the floor of an air-conditioned classroom — a reprieve from my sweaty tent. I eat a large pizza and an entire basket of garlic bread at a restaurant on the dense downtown street around the corner and wander back to the water. In the dying light, surrounded by masts and repurposed factories and warehouses, this looks like it could be a working wharf.

A triple-decker tour boat motors up the creek. I hear music and singing and brace myself for a drunken party cruise. Every passenger is on the open top floor, dozens of young men with side curls and yarmulkes: orthodox Jews belting out a ballad in Hebrew. I can't understand the words but imagine they're singing about some kind of deliverance.

My night at the museum is without incident. The ghosts of Henry Hudson and Benedict Arnold do not come alive to cause mayhem. With a premade battalion of peanut butter wraps and a mug of iced instant coffee awaiting in the boat school kitchen and no dewy tent to stow, I'm quickly out into another foggy no-viz reveille.

My day is a blurry copy of the last couple, with its share of singular occurrences. Fog gives way to sun and sapping humidity. Sympathetic boat club member gives me icy sports beverage. Buoyant waterside stranger with his cat on a leash in Poughkeepsie gives poetic soliloquy about carpe diem: "I like to come down here in the morning to meditate, to reflect, to breathe, to set an intention for the day, to pick a direction, to capture what I can and keep it moving. Know what I mean?"

River left, I paddle past a trio of Gilded Age estates: financier Ogden Mills's 65-room Beaux-Arts mansion at Staatsburgh; the 54-room Beaux-Arts Vanderbilt Mansion, built by the railroad tycoon in the late 1800s on a high bluff overlooking the river; and a relatively modest 49-room Colonial Revival villa, Springwood, home to Franklin Delano Roosevelt, the only American president to serve more than two terms. Even back then, the Hudson was sometimes a place where people brought money.

At Chelsea, late afternoon, I pick my way through parallel lines of moored sailboats to the yacht club. Commodore Mark Maxam is letting me camp on the club's lawn. He arrives in the evening bearing a six-pack and stories that are interrupted every 20 minutes by a commuter train blasting past just 80 feet away. "We call it the Chelsea pause," says Mark — goatee, crisp yet affable manner — after yet another midsentence break.

The train means I'm getting close to NYC. This blip of land we're on, between the tracks and the Hudson, was made with landfill from digging the city's subway lines. A boat club was established in Chelsea in 1821; 60 years later, it became an ice sailing club, a popular pastime featuring light-frame craft atop cast-iron runners, carving across a river that regularly froze over. (Circa 2023, ice yachting is no longer a plausible sport around here; you'd best choose a boat that floats.) Back then, wealthy property owners such as President FDR hired crews to build and race boats, competing against teams like the lads here in Chelsea. These ice yachts were the "fastest vehicles on earth at the time," according to the National Park Service, "regularly beating the trains racing up and down the shores of the Hudson. Even in modest breeze, these boats could reach speeds of 75 miles per hour."

The sun is sinking into the hills on the other side of the river, spotlighting the fleet of sailboats. "Check this out," says Mark. The tide is turning, from ebb to flood, and the bows of the boats swing north, row by row, starting in the shallow water closest to shore. He puts on a pair of protective earmuffs, rings a bell on the flagpole twice and fires a tiny ceremonial cannon before solemnly lowering and folding the Stars and Stripes.

Morning marks two weeks since I left Canada. You'll have to excuse me, I'm due for a rest.

First, in a fierce headwind, I struggle past Pollepel Island and the crenulated shell of Bannerman Castle, a simulated Scottish stronghold built by a scrap metal and munitions dealer in 1901 (and abandoned after a gunpowder explosion in 1951).

I skirt the remnants of an old breakwater poking out of the surface and gape at the round green bulk of Storm King Mountain, whose 1,350-foot summit looms over the river. Storm King kicked off one of the Hudson's foundational environmental fights: it took 17 years in court, but activists stopped Consolidated Edison's federally approved plan to carve away the mountain's face to build a pumped storage hydroelectric plant. The reverberations from that victory still echo.

Downstream from Storm King, the valley resembles a fjord. I beach my board at a state park to picnic and swim, defying the first two rules on a sign beside the garbage can. (The latter, sure, there are dangers, but *picnicking*?) Afterward, dropping to my knees to dig through a battering-ram wind in a notoriously treacherous notch, I round Constitution Island and see, on high ground river right, an imposing mass of gray-brown battlements and buildings: the West Point military academy. George Washington considered this perch "the most important strategic location in America." The Brits never captured it, even though in 1780 our old buddy Benedict tried to *sell* it to them. When the West Point commander's backstabbing scheme was discovered, he defected.

I pull into a small park on the other side of the Hudson in the tidy hamlet of Garrison, living to paddle another day. Just not tomorrow or the next one. Because while well-heeled parents pick up their children from a summer camp in the adjacent arts center, I'm deflating my board and trying not to look too much like a vagabond. Remember Ralph and Bunny Schiller, whose parents/in-laws brought my mother's family from Montreal to Brooklyn? One of their daughters, Laura, owns a country house in the hills above Garrison with her husband, David, and they're on their way down to the river to get me.

I am not fleeing hardship; my weariness is self-induced. But 60 years later, the Schillers are once again giving my mother's side of the family safe harbor.

Good timing. The break is necessary. I sleep in and eat like a teenager: leisurely family meals around a long, bountiful table with Laura and her sister and brother, Janet and Kenneth, who are visiting for the weekend.

My third cousins don't recall much about my mother moving into their home in Hoboken as a young woman. Laura, the eldest, was just eight at the time. But she remembers Iren babysitting and reading to them at night, picking up English vocabulary at the same time as the children. They'd come across unfamiliar words (*surface*) and erroneously sound them out together ("sure face").

"I don't remember her arriving," says Laura. "It felt like she was just there. She always seemed so loving."

"It was part of the immigrant experience," says Janet. "Jenny, our grandmother, was taken in by relatives in the city when she arrived."

"It's how people lived back then," says Kenneth. "It was often life or death. People had seen where the world can take us."

I don't see my cousins often, usually only at weddings. But we're conjoined through the stories of our parents, and this visit is a tacit reminder of the importance of sticking together in any situation.

My two days off the water in Garrison are also good timing because on Sunday the lower Hudson Valley is hammered with an unprecedented deluge. Nine inches of rain fall in three hours, causing flash floods. Highways and train tracks are washed out. A woman is killed when she's swept off the road while trying to escape a swamped house near West Point.

Windshield wipers at max, David is driving me back north to the city of Beacon on Sunday afternoon. Water gushes down the rocky hillside and pools on the highway. Sodden hikers trudge back to their cars from trails-turned-torrents, and state troopers stop traffic from entering impassible roads. It doesn't feel *post*apocalyptic, maybe *early* apocalyptic?

In a parking lot beside the Hudson, I transfer my gear into the back of Patricia Finnerty's beat-up electric sedan. We haven't met until this moment, but Patricia — 60-something, curly hair, muscular arms — is letting me crash in her spare room for a couple nights.

"It's what Pete would have wanted," she says as I splosh into the passenger seat. "He wanted people to have a home in every port."

Patricia is a member of the Beacon Sloop Club, which since 1978 has taken tens of thousands of people on free sailings aboard the *Woody Guthrie* — a scaled-down replica of a traditional Hudson cargo vessel. And Pete, of course, is Pete Seeger, who started the club to instill a sense of wonder and stewardship for the imperiled river that he loved.

CHAPTER 14

"The Hudson is my life. The country has problems with drugs and crimes and racial hatred. But the way I figure it, clean water and clean air and a clean earth is the most important issue of all. If we lose our rivers, the other social problems will be dwarfed. Black or white, hawk or dove, we'll all drown in garbage up to our eyeballs."

— Richie Garrett, inaugural president of the
Hudson River Fishermen's Association,
at the first Earth Day, April 22, 1970

IN THE 1960S, THE HUDSON WAS UNDER ATTACK. HAZARDOUS CONTAMINANTS from run-down factories — some derelict, others still in business — were poisoning aquatic life and threatening drinking water supplies. Even though the river is flushed twice a day by tides, this industrial influx, plus the 1.5 billion gallons of raw sewage being dumped into the Hudson daily in New York City, was killing it. Paint from a GM plant at Tarrytown, oil from the Penn Central railyard at Croton-Harmon and solvents from the Anaconda Wire and Cable yard in Hastings-on-Hudson were flowing directly into the waterway. Wetlands were being filled in, destroying habitat. Power plants were discharging warm wastewater, cooking the eggs and larvae of dozens of species. The risk of radioactive leaks from the Indian Point nuclear power plant hung in the air. The river was neither healthy nor safe for swimmers or fishers, and the latter weren't going to take it anymore.

A fly fisherman, ex-Marine and *Sports Illustrated* outdoor writer named Robert Boyle helped spark the resistance. At a meeting in a legion hall in 1966, Boyle told a small group of recreational and commercial fishers — many of them also ex-Marines and factory workers — about a pair of obscure pieces of legislation. The 1888 Rivers and Harbors Act and 1899 Refuse Act outlawed the pollution of American waters and put a bounty on perpetrators.

The group organized itself into the Hudson River Fishermen's Association, which evolved into the Hudson Riverkeeper — the first of more than 270 waterkeeper organizations now operating around the world. Within two years, the HRFA had shut down the Penn Central oil pipe and collected a $2,000 payment for reporting the violation, the first bounty ever awarded under the Refuse Act. Anaconda Wire and Cable was fined $200,000 in 1971, the stiffest penalty for any American polluter at the time, a case bolstered by a whistleblowing former employee. Emboldened, the HRFA and similar groups born in its wake around the continent have used the courts to target offenders large and small.

Triumphs on the Hudson included the protracted campaign to stop the hydroelectric facility on Storm King Mountain, which would have destroyed critical striped bass spawning grounds, and pushback against a proposal to build a $2-billion highway atop pilings on the river in New York City. The HRFA also contributed to efforts to stop General Electric from dumping PCBs and to instead clean up its mess, as well as to the passage of the Clean Water Act in 1972.

Half a century later, although it's still vulnerable, the Hudson supports more fish per acre and biomass per gallon than any major estuary on the North Atlantic coast. People catch their dinner in the river and, most of the time, can jump in without worry. And although groups such as the HRFA and Hudson Riverkeeper drummed up media coverage and filed legal challenges, they were the tip of a spear borne by leagues of working-class Americans.

The most important legacy of Robert Boyle was "conceiving the link between the environment and ordinary people," John Cronin and

Robert F. Kennedy Jr. write in *The Riverkeepers*. "He broke the conservation tradition that saw protecting the environment as a pursuit of the wealthy, and made it a blue-collar issue of protecting ecology, communities, and livelihoods." (Cronin became the first full-time Hudson Riverkeeper in 1970; Kennedy became the organization's first chief prosecuting attorney a year later and, more recently, an anti-vax conspiracy theorist and Trump cabinet appointee who gives Benedict Arnold a run for his money in the turncoat department.)

All of which brings us back to Pete Seeger.

Known by his first name up and down the valley, Pete wrote the anti-war anthem "Where Have All the Flowers Gone?" and labor-rallying cry "If I Had a Hammer," shared the stage with Woody Guthrie and was blacklisted during the McCarthy era for his leftist leanings. He and his wife, Toshi, lived in a log cabin they built with their own hands in 1950 in the hills above Beacon. Dismayed by the smell of diesel on the river and the democratic failure that allowed large corporations to use it as a toilet, he dove headfirst into grassroots organizing. Pete wrote a song called "My Dirty Stream" and walked along the shore, sometimes armed with his signature banjo, telling people they'd be able to swim in the Hudson someday. "He didn't go to Albany and lobby. He didn't go to Washington, and he didn't go to court," Robert F. Kennedy Jr., when he was still a crusading environmental lawyer, said about Pete. "He used his guitar and his voice and his joyful manner to summon people."

In 1996, after reading Rachel Carson's seminal book *Silent Spring*, which sounded an alarm about the devastating impacts of chemical pesticides, Pete had an outlandish idea: build a replica of the historic cargo sloops that once sailed the Hudson and get people onto the river so they would be struck by its beauty and join a collective cleanup. "Some people might think it's the most frivolous thing in the world to raise money for a sailboat," he said, knowing that much of the country's critical attention was focused on the Vietnam War and civil rights movement. "But we want people to love the Hudson, not think of it as a convenient sewer.

"If there's hope for the human race, there's hope for the Hudson."

With a cadre of musician and activist friends, and donors as diverse as the Rockefeller family and Newport Folk Festival, Pete and Toshi raised about $100,000 and commissioned the construction of the *Clearwater*. The 106-foot sloop was launched in 1969 in Maine, sailed to New York City and up the Hudson. Since then, it has taken thousands of people onto the river and served as a floating concert hall and classroom, inspiring dozens of nautical education programs across the country. The *Clearwater* sailed to Washington, D.C., for the inaugural Earth Day celebration in 1970, circulated petitions in support of the Clean Water Act and joined protests on the water at the Indian Point nuclear power plant and in the shadow of Storm King Mountain. But because the boat is so big, it's expensive to maintain and operate, so Pete asked its naval architect to draw up a smaller version. In 1978, the *Woody Guthrie* was launched, and the Beacon Sloop Club was born.

"The wind may be blowing against you, but if you use your sails right, you can sail into the wind, into the wind, into the wind, and you make slow progress using the very power of the wind that is against you," Pete once said. "This is a great analogy in life. If you can use the forces against you to push ahead, you're winning."

With more thunderstorms in the forecast, there's no guarantee the *Woody* will sail this evening, so I'm getting the tea from Steve Schwartz, one of the boat's rotating volunteer captains, outside the sloop club on the Beacon harborfront. To the north of where we're sitting, accessed via a gangway from Pete & Toshi Seeger Riverfront Park, there's a rainbow-colored circular in-river pool. A local community organization installs it every summer, giving kids a safe, free way to get into the water.

Steve — bushy white beard, Brooklyn accent, gnarled hands that know their way around an engine room — was recovering from a leg injury in 1978 when a friend at the local food co-op said, "Hey, do you want to go sailing on Pete's new boat?" He thought, "You can't really walk around on a sailboat. You probably sit in a deck chair with a piña colada. You know, with the little umbrella. 'Sure, I'm in for that.'" After majoring in "sex, drugs and revolution" at college, Steve had just moved to the area from the city to start a family ("I came upriver to spawn") and was looking for a little direction.

The 47-foot sloop had no motor back then. When the wind died, you rowed. Steve stood beside Pete at the oars, talking for three hours. That was 45 years ago, and while "America's tuning fork" passed away in 2014, Steve is still part of the crew.

"The boat is a two-step thing," he says. "The first is creating easy access to the river. All of Pete's environmental ideology was about getting people to see how fantastic this place is, no matter how bad the water quality was." The sloop stopped in a string of ports and was the centerpiece of roving music festivals. "All these towns on the Hudson have waterfronts that used to be the front door but had become the back door, the garage, the sewer." The second step was building camaraderie on the sloop. "That was Pete's big message: people who learn to work together can tackle insurmountable problems.

"What I learned from the elders," Steve continues, "is that you can't look at the end goal. You just have to be moving in the right direction. It's the struggle. If you're doing the right thing, you've just got to plug away." You need to celebrate your wins, Pete told him, and when you lose, go home and lick your wounds — "go home, get drunk, kick the dog."

"Pete actually said that!" says Steve. "He was not a saint, though he was saintly. I don't think he really got drunk and kicked the dog, but he cursed like a sailor. He put together swear words in an astounding way. He totally lost it one day and called me names that still make me blush thinking about them. And I grew up in Brooklyn!"

If the *Clearwater* hadn't been launched, Steve says, neither he nor I would be on the Hudson today. "It'd be a dead river. It'd be full of shit."

Not long ago, Quassaick Creek, across the river from Beacon, was full of shit. Hidden at the bottom of a lush green ravine on the city of Newburgh's southern boundary, the creek tumbles into the Hudson and suffered many of the same industrial indignities. In 1984, at the behest of a relentless local tipster, Robert F. Kennedy Jr. waded through the lower seven miles of the tributary, searching for the source of the poop. What he saw — and documented with photographs and water samples — was disturbing.

There was naphthalene in the creek, a chemical that causes mutations in animals, discharged by a textile factory that was pouring its unfiltered waste into the defective sewer system — one of two dozen illegal pipes and stacks spewing liquid and chemical fumes from the company's compound. Fifteen thousand gallons of contaminated groundwater from an oil storage facility were being pumped into the creek every day. Shredded filter paper was being "vomited" out of a pipe at a felt factory; concrete rubble spilled into the ravine from a block manufacturer, obstructing the flow; the grounds of a candlemaker were covered in wax. Seining the water near the Hudson, RFK Jr. netted long strings of toilet paper and human fecal matter.

Yet despite these Dantean discoveries, and a series of dams built to power a gauntlet of mills, nature was finding a way. Turtles, snakes, frogs and salamanders swam, slithered and splashed along the banks of the Quassaick. Female sunfish guarded their nests on the creek bed. Carp congregated in pools below bridges. Herring spawned where it met the Hudson. Kennedy met Latino fishermen who descended twisting paths to the water's edge and, standing atop jagged metal perches at a junkyard, cast for catfish for their kitchen tables.

Much of the Newburgh waterfront was just as fetid. Heaps of rusted, wrecked cars. Burned-out barges. The tanneries and foundries that had built the city were gone, leaving a wasteland along the Hudson, Kennedy writes, "where truckers come for illicit sex and drug dealers sell their wares." A destructive urban renewal program in the 1960s had uprooted the city's Black community and demolished 1,300 buildings for a promised rebuild that never happened. Poverty, racism and crime were rampant. In 2021, Newburgh was called the 36th most dangerous city in the U.S.

Kennedy and John Cronin investigated the curiously discounted sale of a public boat ramp and three acres of adjacent parkland to a friend of the mayor for a floating restaurant. The ramp was popular among low-income and minority residents, who used it to fish and wade into the river. Cronin asked whether public access would be maintained. A business partner of the developer buyer replied, "We are not going to have [Blacks] drinking and screwing and swimming around our new boat ramp, if that's what you mean by the public."

How does a place like this heal?

Access to housing, education, employment and health care are essential to well-being. But for Duane Martinez, the solution also involves Quassaick Creek, which, like the Hudson, thanks to determined citizens and legal action, has rebounded.

Duane and I slip through a gap in the fence behind the former candle factory and walk down an old roadway half reclaimed by nature. We stop beside a set of rapids, an unusually high flow for July after last weekend's cataclysmic rain. Sheltered by the canopy of a dense mixed forest, it's probably 10 degrees Celsius, or 20 degrees Fahrenheit, cooler down here than the blast furnace at street level, and the tarry scent of melting asphalt above has been replaced by an herbal, woody aroma.

Fortyish, wearing purple rimmed sunglasses, his long dark hair in a ponytail, Duane is the director of Scenic Hudson's River Cities program — the nonprofit's effort, in collaboration with local residents and officials, to help connect people to the outdoors and redress historical wrongs in three cities with large marginalized communities. In Newburgh, in addition to developing parks, gardens and farm plots, the goal is to create a new trail along Quassaick Creek.

"You don't feel like you're in a city when you're in this wild ravine," says Duane, raising his voice above the roar of the whitewater. "It feels really removed. Even though there's a smokestack right there, something else dominates. In my mind, there's no higher and better use of this land than for it to be remediated and used for both human and more-than-human life to flourish."

Established in 1963, Scenic Hudson led the fight against the Storm King power plant, helped hold General Electric accountable for PCB pollution and advises communities on how to prepare for rising sea levels. Its main thrust, however, is acquiring and protecting parcels of land. Since its inception, it has conserved more than 48,000 acres and created more than 40 parks. River Cities, launched in 2017 in Newburgh, Poughkeepsie and Kingston, marks a new direction. A Coloradan with a background in urban planning, Duane moved up-valley from Brooklyn to join the program, which he describes as "a turn toward more intentional work in urban areas, with a clear understanding that there's a disparity between access to nature and the benefits of nature."

Almost half of Newburgh's 28,500 residents identified as Latino or Hispanic in the 2022 census; 25.7 percent were Black. The city's poverty rate was 26.5 percent, more than double the state average. Residents often don't have the free time or vehicle required to travel to parks elsewhere on the Hudson, Duane tells me. By asking various communities how they interact with nature and what they want to see in the ravine, Scenic Hudson hopes to help people tap into the benefits of blue space. Which, as Pete would say, is a long-term mission.

"There's a protracted element to community-based planning that's new to a lot of organizations and government, to really understand how long it takes to build something that's actually owned by a community," says Duane. It can be efficient to concentrate on the technical aspects of an eco-infrastructure project: Does it pencil out financially? Does it adhere to conventional aesthetics? "But if we want something holistic, both culturally and ecologically, it's probably going to take more time. Once people say what they want and that input is digested by a project team and designers, it has to go back to a community and be vetted."

Duane says there could be a trail along the Quassaick within about five years, even though, when community engagement began, he and his colleagues realized that a lot of locals didn't know there was a creek at the bottom of the ravine. They had to back up, introduce people to the watershed and then get into deeper conversations about how children and adults might use the rejuvenated space. He shows me a map of the preferred route: 6.5 miles of paths connecting the lower creek with a pair of headwater lakes, spur trails providing access from more than a dozen streets and parks, 350 acres of tree canopy.

Duane and I return to the road and walk to the middle of a bridge over the ravine on a crumbling sidewalk that's blocked at both ends. There's a public housing community with 70 townhouse-style units a few minutes away. Duane pictures a dramatic staircase down to the water. We continue upstream to Muchattoes Lake, where, on a patch of dirt behind a strip mall with both a Honduran and Mexican restaurant, there are makeshift chairs and a bin of empty beer cans. People fish, have a drink and watch the sunset here, some from the nearby subsidized seniors' housing complex. This spot, a corner of the parking lot, could be a trailhead, with benches and picnic tables.

"Envisioning the greenway as a complex, multilevel landscape with different places where people can hang out is what excites me most," says Duane. "The creek is inaccessible and probably a little scary now to some folks, but it's in their backyard, and if we do this right, it holds a lot of potential."

There are no manuals for this type of project, he adds. But Scenic Hudson staff and their partners have a passion for urban environments, ecology and biodiversity, and an understanding of how these systems are related to human health. "We're trying to learn from locals and piece all these elements together into a compelling strategy for socio-ecological well-being. We're not putting a line between habitat and community health — it's just one thing."

While Duane lauds initiatives such as 30x30, a plan adopted by nearly 200 countries to protect 30 percent of the planet's land and ocean area by 2030, that incredible scale necessitates a focus on places where few people live. "Our connection to nature is not being improved by these big moves. That's not to say they're bad, but they don't repair the relationship we have to biodiversity.

"I don't think there's room on the planet, especially in industrialized areas, for people to be disconnected from nature anymore," he continues. "The biodiversity crisis is largely driven by the limited relationships we have with more-than-human life. Having more natural spaces that are diverse and complex is really important in terms of city planning, conservation and global systems. Because global systems are shaped by human action, and some of that action has to start with local experiences."

When embarking on projects, some of which support food security, manage storm runoff or host pop-up events, the River Cities team has many factors to consider. There are questions about allocating resources toward conservation in cities where the need for housing is acute; and there are concerns about "green gentrification," when the creation of parks and resurrection of waterways displaces the people they were meant to support. But Duane thinks they can find the right mix.

"Nature can support social justice for a community if there are regenerative spaces for people to gather and find joy and delight in being together," he says. "This doesn't have to be at odds with ecological restoration or habitat preservation. It's capital *I* inclusion, a multispecies richness.

"Water might be one of the most universally understood concepts in the world. It can be an equalizer," he adds. "When you think about racial disparities around access to health and ecosystem services, water provides so much. But the disparity around who has access to benefits cuts along racial and economic lines. So, it's not just about providing more blue space — it's providing blue space that's activated by people who live there."

We make one more stop upstream from Muchattoes at Crystal Lake, which is more of an algae-stained pond. In the 1940s, this was an oasis with a sandy beach, a boardwalk, a nightclub with dining and dancing. Illegal dumping soiled the lake, but Scenic Hudson and other groups organized volunteer cleanups. Mattresses, rusty barrels and dozens of tires were pulled out of the water. Now it's once again the heart of a park. Cottonwood branches sway in the breeze, fat bumblebees buzz around a community farm and a 1.5-mile trail leads up to Snake Hill, the highest point in Newburgh. I'm tempted to hike to the rocky summit, which overlooks the city, creek and Hudson River, but am already late for my next appointment.

Duane drops me off back at Patricia's bungalow in a quiet neighborhood on the outskirts of Newburgh. Even though she had a busy workday as a home care therapist, driving around the county for sessions with newborns and toddlers, she had time to bake a stack of Peruvian empanadas. They're packed in a bag, and we're quickly in her car, racing toward Beacon. The sky is clear and the *Woody Guthrie* is launching.

With Captain Patrick at the helm, we motor away from the dock. He kills the engine, and Patricia and her crewmates raise the sails. One of a dozen passengers this evening, I sit back on a wooden bench and relish the rare feeling of moving upriver without a paddle. A woman with a guitar strums and sings "If I Had a Hammer" and "This Land Is Your Land." The sky turns amber, then pink, then purple. The stars emerge. Lulled by the breeze and gentle rolling, I'm closing my eyes when Patrick taps me on the shoulder.

"Want a turn at the tiller?" he asks.

I put my hand on the wooden lever. The steering is supersensitive, the *Woody* altering course with every twitch of my arm. But soon I get the feel and settle into a relaxed stance, making small adjustments, listening to the bow slicing through the river and a song about a magic dragon who lived by the sea. Until realizing that we're bearing down on a cluster of boats moored in the Beacon harbor. At the captain's prompt, I pull the tiller and we tack hard into the wind.

CHAPTER 15

"It is increasingly clear that when it comes to mental health and wellbeing at a city level, considerations extend far beyond the hospital ward and responsibility extends far beyond any psychiatrist or clinical psychologist. Urban planning and design decisions affect people's lives in many ways. Such decisions sit at the heart of whether a city will support and promote the mental health and wellbeing of its population or, conversely, whether it will contribute to the development and maintenance of mental health problems. It is time for this impact — and for the role and opportunities of the urban environment — to be formally recognized. This is restorative urbanism."

— *Jenny Roe and Layla McCay,* Restorative Cities

LANDSCAPE ARCHITECT SIMON BELL WOULD CALL THE QUASSAICK CREEK greenway an example of urban blue acupuncture. Bell, a professor at the University of Edinburgh, is a regular collaborator of blue space researcher Mat White, and urban acupuncture is a design tactic through which small infrastructural interventions have a regenerative impact out of proportion to the cost. The term is derived from the practice, in traditional Chinese medicine, of penetrating the skin with a needle and improving the health of a patient by stimulating their central nervous system. In blue space parlance, *aquapuncture* means introducing or reintroducing a splash of water to a community — projects that are quick and adjustable — and hopefully, as design critic Justin McGuirk says, triggering a "catalytic effect on the organism as a whole."

To recap, spending time in blue space is good for us because it can reduce stress, encourage physical activity and kindle social engagement. This is why, for example, when researchers assessed the impact of the new open-air theater, playground and slipway in the low-income Teats Hill neighborhood in Plymouth, U.K., they saw that the well-being of area residents had improved. A trail along Quassaick Creek could have similar results.

"We know from our data that poorer communities access blue spaces like this for recreation because they can't afford to go to the posh places," says Mat White. "So, with polluted creeks, step number one, make them pleasant, because we don't want to be encouraging people to go to shitty places that are bad for their health.

"You can waste a lot of money doing things you *think* will work but don't. Simon Bell's idea is to use small amounts of resources exactly where they need to go. You work with local communities and then you implement, and the return on investment is high. That's the kind of thing that local communities can afford."

Since moving from England to the birthplace of Freud, Mat has remained immersed in blue space, shifting his gaze from the coastal environments that ring the U.K. to inland lakes and rivers. When we spoke after my paddling journey, he told me that our understanding of the mechanisms of blue space hasn't changed over the past few years, but several focused projects have allowed academics like him to make more conclusive statements about its benefits and more finely tuned recommendations about its tactical deployment. One study, looking at visits to 12 swimming spots on the Danube River in Austria, reaffirmed the findings of earlier U.K. research: lower-income respondents were 15 percent happier after going for a dip in the river. "What that's showing us, quite clearly, is that while we need to give people access to green and blue spaces, more important is that we need to ensure they *want* to use them." (The positive impacts of blue space for any individual should not be overstated, Mat told *Time* magazine, but because they "apply to millions of people . . . the overall public health benefit is huge.")

An array of projects like the research on Austria's rivers are informing Mat's role in the international High Level Panel for a Sustainable Ocean Economy, an initiative corralling 18 countries (among them the U.S. and Canada) to work together on marine protection, sustainable production and "equitable prosperity." The panel's 2024 report — "How Can a Healthy Ocean Improve Human Health and Enhance Wellbeing on a Rapidly Changing Planet?" — represents a breakthrough, Mat says, as the first high-level acknowledgment that active time in blue space can have a profound impact on health at a global scale. The team he was part of collated case studies from around the world: stress levels dropped among Indonesians who swam in the sea during the COVID-19 pandemic; every £1 invested in community activities on Morecambe Bay in North West England returned £2.16 "in terms of reduced costs of treating mental health-related conditions." A Spanish paper published in 2023 evaluated the impact of walking, hanging out at the beach and snorkeling on cancer patients. Monitoring changes in blood pressure, heart rate, sleep quality and mental health, the research team concluded that "exposure to blue spaces contributes to tension and anger reduction and improves the vigour mood state," making these activities "suitable for patients with similar characteristics to those enrolled in the study." Mat says, "There are very clear actions and opportunities identified for policymakers, looking in particular at physical activity."

Mat has also been busy as a principal investigator on Resonate, a European project that aims to build individual and community resilience through nature-based therapies. Researchers from nine countries are hoping to collect more proof that nature can help us physically, mentally and socially; to work with different sectors — including health, environment and economy — to propagate nature-based therapies that are suitable for large populations; and to encourage more use of low-cost approaches in cities, towns and coastal areas. Nature-based therapies, or NbTs, are a spectrum unto themselves. They include broad programs targeting groups or whole populations, like encouraging citizens to visit natural spaces close to home during early COVID-19 lockdowns, which was shown to have alleviated symptoms of anxiety and depression. NbTs can also be more targeted interventions designed to get at-risk populations moving to reduce the risks of cardiovascular and other diseases. Or they can be the type of outings that recreational therapists like Zac Crouse did in Nova Scotia with clients, an attempt to help individuals manage symptoms as part of a longer healing journey.

During our video call, Mat shares his screen and jumps from graphs to charts, from study to study, from country to country — a reflection of all the research he's juggling. He keeps apologizing that he has to leave in a minute to join another virtual meeting. Then he thinks of another project to show me and searches for the right document. "I've got so many tabs open it's bonkers. Deep breath. I'm sorry, I get so excited talking about this stuff."

I run a theory by Mat before I let him go — that blue spaces seem to help strangers connect with one another.

"I think there are elements of truth there," he says, "but I'd also challenge it to some extent, because there are also points of conflict." Poor older men often go to the water to fish, he says, and paddlers don't like it when somebody is casting a sharp barbed hook toward them.

Mat White is right, of course. I may be reconnoitering through rose-colored glasses, but life on the water is not always idyllic. There is death, destruction and an ongoing tug of war between public access and privatization. And yet how does one explain the parabolic travels of Dick Conant, who rarely experienced conflict and almost universally elicited delight during the couple decades he spent crisscrossing America in a canoe?

A gregarious, rumpled, extremely well-read and self-declared homeless Navy vet, six-foot-one and 300 pounds, Dick paddled and camped where he pleased, telling stories and making pals just about every time he pulled ashore in search of a grocery store, a library, a church, a bar. Even police officers fell under his charm; one state trooper on Lake Champlain, following up on a suspicious person complaint, was so impressed by the trespassing camper's wanderlust and courage that he tried to track him down again with a parting gift. "This stuff about 'finding oneself' is a bunch of baloney," Dick wrote in one of his journals. "I repeat that I am not out here 'finding myself.' I was never lost. What I am doing is paddling around finding geography I have not seen, observing various industry and transport, experiencing wildlife, meeting new people, most of whom are worth meeting, and having a jolly good time before I die."

In September 2014, on a trip from Plattsburgh to Florida, Dick took a break for a few days on the Lower Hudson. Less than three months later, his overturned red canoe was spotted in a North Carolinian swamp. His body has not been found.

My next stop, after leaving Newburgh and Beacon, is a residential seawall that Dick tied onto about 10 miles shy of New York City. A pilgrimage site, of sorts. But first I have to make it to the water.

Patricia is trying to drop me off back at Garrison landing so I can resume where I left off, but the main road leading down to the water remains closed two days after the storm. She finds a detour, then dashes off to work, and I pump up my board under an already scorching sun.

The commuter train that plies the eastern riverbank is still not running — maybe tomorrow, one of the men working on the railbed tells me. At the Canadian border, the tracks were too hot; here they got washed out. But I don't mind the reprieve from 90 decibels blasting past every 20 minutes and contemplate a world where, when rail and roads are kaput, the river is still running.

Our communication systems, for now, are also fine. I spend an hour on my phone while bobbing around the muddy shallows, trying to sort out the university tuition paperwork for one of my daughters while keeping an eye out for ships. ("I'm sorry, I don't have access to that form. I'm on a river outside New York City and am about to be swamped by an oil tanker.") Then I'm bombarded with texts from people I've met on the Hudson (and, of course, my mother): they're warning me that a sewer pipe has burst at Tarrytown, just downstream, and recreational activities on the river are not advised.

It's 33 degrees Celsius (91 Fahrenheit) with the humidity, and I paddle for hours without swimming. Woozy, I stumble off my SUP at a state park beneath the rocky summit of Hook Mountain and make a beeline for a drink machine. Just like my morning amid the "floaters" upriver near Albany, it's unsettling when cooling off is not an option.

As I chug a bottle of Gatorade, I realize two Orthodox Jewish men are staring at me. Duv and David are sitting at a picnic table in the shade, studying the Torah. They conduct the standard interview: Do you ever fall in? Where do you sleep? What do you eat? And then after I share my surname, the usual pious interrogation: Did you have a bar mitzvah? Do you go to synagogue? Is your wife Jewish? Do you know it's not too late to have a bar mitzvah?

Normally, I would be annoyed by this line of inquiry. But on this trip, embracing spontaneous interactions, their curiosity seems genuine and I respond with good humor. Nah, the Torah's not for me, but I'm seriously interested in progressive Mennonitism.

Invigorated by electrolytes and Talmudic tenacity, I paddle under the Tappan Zee Bridge, where the Hudson broadens to three miles, one of its widest points. Crabs scuttle below docks, and I smell the first hint of oceanic brine. And then, skimming the western shore, 25 miles south of Garrison, amid a string of boathouses, there's a man waving to me from a small square of grass.

Ben McGrath — tall, tussled hair, thoughtful — introduced me and thousands of other readers to Dick Conant. The itinerant 63-year-old canoeist had stopped at the home next door in September 2014, and the neighbor summoned Ben. Sitting at a table spread with sausage, caviar and vodka, Dick was wearing bib overalls and muddy boots; he had "a rust-colored beard, with patches of white, and his face was as red as a boiled lobster shell — a riparian Santa," Ben wrote in the *New Yorker*, where he is a staff writer. He would go on to publish a feature about Dick after the empty canoe was discovered and, in 2022, the book *Riverman*, an evocative account of a troubled man "who traveled alone and yet thrived on connection."

Spellbound by Dick's story and Ben's prose, I began corresponding with the writer. As my SUP approached Piermont, he invited me to camp on his lawn. This sliver of riverfront, a 20 foot by 20 foot annex down the hill from Ben's house, is grandfathered into the property. It's why he and his wife moved here from Brooklyn, after their home in low-lying Red Hook was flooded by Hurricane Sandy. "My goal was to get onto the water in as many ways as possible," Ben says, "and to raise our kids on the river."

In a village where many locals rarely venture onto the Hudson, a windsurfing board became his unlikely vessel of choice. He's not particularly good at it, but the rush of water beneath his feet feels like flying. After a good session, he's radiating for hours: "You're reliving the thing in your mind, you're useless for the rest of the day."

Dick's pit stop in Piermont not only piqued Ben's literary instincts, it also validated his fantasy about living on the water. "People saw this disheveled man in a filthy canoe overloaded with tarps and trash bags, yet they were drawn to him," he tells me, sitting on the deck of a restaurant down the street from his house, Jimmy Cliff crooning "Many Rivers to Cross" from the speakers. "His life might be hard, but for 10 hours of his day, you want to be doing what he's doing. You want to be on the water, moving through space and time, participating in the grandeur."

Ben was accustomed to writing long-form magazine pieces about professionals "who are determined not to let you into their lives." Now here was a man who was guileless about his aquatic adventures, whether holding court on a barstool or in the journals and unpublished books he left behind. People gave him dinner, drives, plane tickets. Portaging through Trenton, New Jersey, Dick bought beers and beans for a man who had just been released from prison and spent a restful night in a stranger's garage.

Some readers saw traces of *Into the Wild* in Dick's travels, a turn away from society, but Ben was captivated by the stories his "willing narrator" told about people. "He was getting into nature and away from the nine-to-five, for sure, but what he was doing allowed him to meet people all along the way. Unlike oceans and lakes, rivers are the basis of civilization itself. Rivers are urban places. If you travel along a river, you'll find people. If you're on a river in the middle of nowhere and you follow it, you will find yourself in a settlement at some point. Which is not true if you get on a trail.

"For a person who craved but couldn't sustain friendship, it was an amazing way to have a social life."

Throughout history, there have always been vagabonds. The freight-hopping railroad tramp, the backpacker, the hitchhiker. We're generally leery of drifters. "If you saw Dick trudging through town with his pack, most people, for better or for worse, would look the other way," says Ben. "Something about him getting on the water made lawyers, scientists and other 'refined' people interested in him. I don't know why exactly, but on the river, a hobo and a cigarette boat driver and a kayak racer, they'll all kind of equals and they're willing to talk to one another in a way that you wouldn't see on land."

"Why?" I ask.

"That's a good question. What do you think?"

I'm not sure, either, but it might have something to do with the way water alters our perspective and slows us down. The way, as Ben writes, "aggregated raindrops" serve as a conduit between anonymous strangers.

Because of his love for ice skating, Ben used to think of himself as a pond person. "You find the most pristine pond in the woods, with nobody around, and you create this perfect experience, making virgin marks on black ice." But now he finds that vision limiting, an illusion of perfectibility masking an inward experience. "You're looking into the mirror of the lake to see the reflection of yourself," he says "What I think makes life interesting is turning the lens onto other people. So a river is sort of an anti-xenophobic phenomenon, because it comes from somewhere and is going somewhere else. You can't close ranks around it, and there's something about it that orients your mindset toward elsewhere and not toward perfecting your own little realm."

In *Riverman*, Ben describes the American river-trip canon as a three-act saga. First, there were Lewis and Clark, whose journals of exploration in an "unknown" western frontier at the start of the 19th century "tell a story of economic destiny obscured by scientific observation." Next up, *Adventures of Huckleberry Finn*, in which the river "no longer represented a frontier but a world onto its own, offering freedom from an imperfect society." By the time it was published in the 1880s, Mark Twain knew his Great American Novel was already an anachronism, Ben writes; river towns were turning to the railroad for "wealth and upbringing." Finally, there is *Deliverance*, the 1970 novel by James Dickey, turned into a landmark film two years later, in which middle-aged urbanites embark on a canoe trip down a primordial river and mayhem ensues. "Paranoia begets violence begets more paranoia. Or is it the other way around?" asks Ben, adding the writer John McPhee's observation that *Deliverance*'s "thought-wave effects seem to have reached wherever canoes may float."

Might I suggest a present-day paddleboarding postscript? A very minor fourth act, a smidge of *Heart of Darkness*, Wes Anderson–style?

Departing Piermont, a night of DWD (drinking while dehydrated) has left my bowels in rough shape. South of the village, river right, one of the first mansions you see high above the water — an artsy enclave whose residents reportedly include Angelina Jolie, Al Pacino and Björk — belongs to Bill Murray. I need to go number two and nose into a marshy beach, grab my toilet paper, slink inland and dig a hole in the sand. I picture the actor taking in the sunrise from the precipice, wearing a robe, smoking a cigar, bemused.

CHAPTER 16

"Some of the older white paddlers were afraid of me because they thought I was going to take something from them, but that's as far from the truth as possible. That's their fear. If you're a rich white guy, you've probably got more insecurities than the guy who's suffering on the streets, because you have more to lose and you think a Black guy coming into your space is going to take it from you. Hence why you try to hold onto power the way you do, hence why you try to put people in their place the way you do. You've based your life on trying to hold onto material things — and it's not yours. The river is not yours."

— Chev Dixon, kayak instructor, athlete and activist

PAST BILL MURRAY'S HOUSE, PAST THE BASALT RAMPARTS OF THE PALISADES, I angle across to the eastern side of the Hudson. The suspended double decks of the George Washington Bridge hang over the river in the distance: the gateway to New York City. When it opened in 1931, the first crossing between New Jersey and New York that didn't tunnel through the ground, the George Washington was the longest span in the world. It remains the busiest motor vehicle bridge anywhere.

Nearing the mouth of the Hudson, the tidal current is stronger, pulling me seaward. But before getting subsumed by the spires of Gotham, I pause at another pilgrimage site: the Yonkers Paddling and Rowing Club, just upstream from the Bronx, where a teenaged Chev

Dixon looked through the fence at a rack of kayaks and thought, "Dude, if we can get a couple of those things, we can make it across!"

Chev — dreadlocks, effervescent, boundless energy — was 18 at the time. Born in Kingston, Jamaica, he had moved to Yonkers with his family five years earlier and loved playing basketball. But after a kid pulled a knife on him during a pickup game, he and his friends wandered down to the waterfront. Gerry Blackstone, a coach at the club, saw the teens, opened the gate, showed them the boathouse and encouraged them to come back if they wanted to try kayaking. "I was hungry," recalls Chev, "for something different."

He returned the next day and hasn't left. Now in his early 30s, Chev is a barrier-breaking kayak coach and athlete, one of the first Black instructors to achieve the top level of American Canoe Association certification. Two weeks before I reached Yonkers, he completed a 685-mile expedition dubbed the Hudson Valley Challenge. Accompanied by revolving groups of supporters, he ran, cycled and hiked to the source of the river in the Adirondacks and to the top of the highest peak, then paddled back down to the city. "I want to show Black and Brown people that they can be adventurers," says Chev, "and that the great outdoors is right here."

One of Chev's gigs these days is working as director of the Hudson River Riders, a free program, started at the Yonkers club by Blackstone, to develop paddling skills among underprivileged youth and awaken a sense of environmental stewardship. "Paddling is a gateway for introducing youth to so many possibilities," Chev tells me. "It gives you confidence, and not just the confidence to be a good kayaker, but to be a good person — to learn how to move through society by learning how to move on rivers, to learn about risk management and how to look ahead and plan for the next step, how to put others first, how to be a leader. That's what it really teaches. Learning how to access the river can be a challenge, but it helps you tap into who you are."

Kids who grow up in Yonkers — or the Bronx or Harlem — might see the Hudson every day but never have an opportunity to get onto the water. They might look at the cliffs on the far shore but never venture across for a hike. There were no field trips at Chev's high school, no outdoor education program. There's only one public pool in the community, so a lot of local kids don't learn how to swim. The Hudson River Riders provides a dose of aquapuncture. In concert with other free paddling programs in the New York City area, Chev estimates they get around 65,000 people onto the water every summer.

"Whenever I bring a kid onto the river, it's the best feeling," he says. "It's a warm burst of joy to be with somebody who wants to explore. It's about nature, it's about the human family, it's about trying to empower people to get moving and take some ownership around protecting the planet and all its waterways. Helping people understand themselves and the Earth is the most godly work you can do."

When Chev started splashing around the Hudson, the kayaking world, in Yonkers and elsewhere, was predominantly white. He was an anomaly and confronted stereotypical perceptions of troublesome young Black men. Steadily gaining skills and experience in the cockpit, he pushed back. "I gave them another perspective. 'No, I'm not a hoodlum, and I'm going to call you out on your shit. This is a mostly Black neighborhood, so why is everybody here white?' I got into some arguments, but most of the people I said were racist have come around."

The paddling scene in North America, like other outdoor pursuits, is now more diverse than ever. There's a thriving Black cycling community in New York City; Blacks are twice as likely to ride as whites. Encouraged by groups such as the Hood Hikers and Hiking While Black, there's a lively local hiking culture. But Chev often feels tokenized by media coverage and sponsorships, especially because there are others — like his friend Devin Brown, aiming to become the first Black woman to kayak the length of the Mississippi River — just as deserving of the attention.

The Hudson Valley Challenge did not receive much press, but two months after Chev reached the end of the river, a British endurance athlete made headlines. Lewis Pugh swam the length of the waterway, from the Adirondacks to Battery Park, to raise awareness about the importance of clean rivers. He completed the 30-day journey "unassisted," meaning he wore only a Speedo, cap and googles, but had a well-equipped support crew in tow. "A guy comes from England and gets the media spotlight, but a local guy doing something to get local people outside is ignored?" says Chev. "What the fuck is that about? Why do we have to highlight people coming from another country and act like they're heroes who are coming to save us?"

Chev had a similarly troubling experience with a paddleboarder from the U.K. five years earlier. She had SUPed to New York City from Albany to draw attention to plastic pollution; he joined her on the Hudson one day. But when he started to pick up pieces of plastic, she asked him to stop, because they needed the video footage. "They wanted pictures of the garbage," Chev says. "They didn't want to clean it up.

"We clean the river every day! The kids in Hudson River Riders never paddle past garbage. That's against our rules. I pull shit out of the Hudson every day! Excuse my fucking language, but these things fire me up! Why are you coming here to tell us to clean our river? The river is already pretty clean because of our efforts. We don't need anybody from England telling us what to do."

What riles Chev most about the white savior narrative is a lack of representation that, tacitly, dissuades some kids from picking up a paddle. If they don't see themselves on the water, how will they find it? "Nature is there and she welcomes you," he says, "no matter your race, religion, sexual orientation — none of that. It's about unity. We all have to get along. None of us own this great river."

Catching a seam of current, I burst south from Yonkers, under the George Washington Bridge. Traffic has picked up: freighters, tugs and barges, sailboats, speedboats, Jet Skis, yachts. Wakes and waves ricochet off the concrete embankment, and I bronco up and down on my board.

Parks and paths on the Harlem shoreline are packed on another hot July afternoon. Yet even these jaded New Yorkers, accomplished in the art of nonchalance, are curious.

"Where you comin' from?"

"Canada."

"Fucking awesome!"

The buildings get taller and taller as I speed down the Upper West Side, the water choppier and choppier. I pass the bottom end of Central Park and a series of piers that jut out into the river. Cruise ship terminals, parking lots, barren postindustrial rectangles awaiting their next iteration. Slipping past the gray bulk of the USS *Intrepid*, a Second World War aircraft carrier turned museum, I stop at a floating dock below the Manhattan Kayak Co. boathouse. A long-distance paddleboarder who gave me intel on the Hudson, Paris Montoya, has hooked me up.

In a city where space is at a premium, paddlers pay to sardine their kayaks and SUPs here. Jay, the manager, is letting me leave my board for a few days. My cousin Laura and her husband David are back from Garrison and are letting me bunk in the spare room of their Manhattan apartment. I rinse off the grime of the river in an outdoor shower and, with a dry bag on my back and another over my shoulder, start walking toward the subway.

Wasted by weeks of heat, I sleep so late the next morning Laura and David are worried. But after one rest day, I'm jonesing to be back on my board.

Paris is beside me on his SUP. His partner, Eva, and their friend E.C. are in kayaks. Eva and Paris have radios clipped to their PFDs and conduct a brief safety meeting before we leave the protected cove between the boathouse and *Intrepid*. Our objective: the Statue of Liberty.

We paddle out and turn south, tight to the shore. The towers of Midtown Manhattan rise to my left. I can make out the Empire State Building, its upper floors disappearing into clouds. Tour boats and ferries cannon along the shipping channel in the middle of the river, displacing three-foot rolling wakes which bounce off the hardened waterfront. Police boats and coast guard cutters zip around; a slow tug pushes a barge. It's rush hour on the Hudson, and remaining upright is challenging. So, too, is making forward progress. But whenever we reach one of the piers where boats dock and depart, we need to race across; ferries have schedules to keep and their captains don't like slowing down, even if they see us. Eva radios in our whereabouts and intended line each time we cross, and we raft up and wait for a large window before bolting through the middle of the river to the New Jersey side. It's harrowing, and my heart pulses with a blend of adrenaline and defiance. We need to defer to big fast boats to remain safe and lawful, but nobody owns this great river.

And lo, as we paddle out of the Hudson atop the last push of ebb: Lady Liberty, her torch held high. It doesn't look *that* big from water level yet makes me feel so incredibly small.

We begin circumnavigating the statue and Ellis Island in a clockwise direction. I want to stop for pictures, to reflect on the immigrant processing station where millions first set foot in America, to savor the end of this leg of my jour—

"Let's go!" barks Paris. "Pick up the pace."

Like sharks, enormous tour boats are circling the main attraction, and apparently they have the right of way.

Heading back up along the Jersey shore, we pull into a long narrow inlet. Amid a couple marinas and a ferry landing, there's a surf-themed patio restaurant — a perfect place to wait for the tide to turn and see what a thunderstorm moving toward us might do.

"The number of paddlers in the city exploded during the pandemic," Paris says, insisting that I grab a chunk of deep-fried cod from his comically large platter of fish and chips.

"If we had any time to go anywhere," says Eva, "we went to the boathouse."

"It's so crowded in New York," he adds. "It's quiet on the water. Except for all the boats."

Looking at the weather radar and tide charts on their phones, Eva and Paris squabble about our optimal departure time — a cute couple's quarrel, I tell them, which fails to diffuse the situation. I duck away to the bathroom, and when I return, they announce that we have a decent window for crossing the river.

Boat traffic has intensified — it's always rush hour on the Hudson — and wakes ricochet off one another. But there are patterns within this chaos, and though the ride is bumpy, and there are flashes of lightning above New Jersey, we bisect the shipping lane and are swiftly nestled amongst the sturdy piers of Manhattan.

Teasing aside, I'm grateful for Eva's and Paris's guidance, and armed with as much advice as I can badger out of them, but without a radio, I set off for New Jersey on my own the following afternoon.

I zip past the midtown ferry terminal without delaying commuter traffic and, as instructed, make a hard right toward the middle of the river once I reach Chelsea Piers, so I'm perpendicular to traffic. "Ships in the channel move quickly," Scott Keller had told me in Albany. "If you see one two miles away, you've got 15 minutes to cross. It's usually better to wait. Let the big boys go first."

On the edge of the channel, I look both ways. Nobody coming. I look again, then bust across.

I'm aiming for a compact beach in Hoboken, New Jersey, and am not sure how easy it will be to get my bearings. But there it is: dozens of people are on the Hudson in brightly colored kayaks.

With wonderous serendipity, today is City of Water Day, an annual event to champion a climate-resilient and equitably shared waterfront here at the bottom of the Hudson. And this beach is the home turf of the Hoboken Cove Community Boathouse, an all-volunteer nonprofit whose mission is to provide free water-sport programs and access to local waterways.

Activities today include angling lessons, kayaking or paddleboarding around the sheltered cove, or hopping into an outrigger canoe for a foray on the river. There are presentations about water quality and other environmental issues and later a cardboard kayak race. This program mirrors what the boathouse does all summer. It gets about 300 people onto the water every week. And most of them are not white.

"If you want to see diversity, come to the boathouse," says Oscar Hernandez, one of the volunteers on the nonprofit's board of directors. "People who live in Hoboken have money. It's totally gentrified. But people who come to our programs — a lot of Black and Brown and

Asian people, from teenagers to 70-year-olds, about two-thirds of them women — they come from inland areas in Jersey, and they wouldn't have access to the river otherwise. They don't have much money; they probably don't have a car. People around here use half their income just to pay rent, so you have families and kids who've never been on the water, and that's not OK."

Wearing a bright yellow shirt and ballcap, Oscar would normally be running around helping with today's activities, but he twisted his ankle earlier and is sitting on the ground with an ice pack. Which makes him a captive interviewee.

In Uruguay, where he grew up, he biked to the beach frequently. Getting to the water was calming. "During the pandemic, we really learned how important outdoor activities are," says Oscar, whose day job is with a nonprofit that helps people who are having trouble with their mortgages. "We knew that before, but we really saw it during COVID. Even if you can't be on it, it's good to be near it. To sit on a bench with a coffee and a book, to bring your kids to a playground. And it's free, which is huge in a place that's so expensive. This is a place that everybody should be able to enjoy."

It's also a place where public space can be precarious. NY Waterway, which operates the largest ferry and excursion fleet in New York Harbor, wanted to build the city's biggest ferry repair and refueling station at a former shipyard immediately adjacent to Hoboken Cove. "That's when the fight started," says Oscar. "We organized, did rallies, sent postcards to the governor, were busy on social media. It was nonstop. We have nothing against ferries. We love public transportation. But there are so many better places to put this."

The city of Hoboken said it would use imminent domain to take the land from NY Waterway to prevent the development. The New Jersey government said it would use imminent domain to take it from the city so the ferry company could build. Eventually the governor helped broker an agreement. A temporary dry dock will be set up next to the beach for three years while an existing facility a mile and a half to the north is upgraded. "The fight is over, but we are a little afraid," says Oscar. "Because once there is a full operating ferry facility here, they're not going to want to give it up."

This is yet another of those long-term struggles. But hopping to the railing of a terrace, looking out at all the people on the water, arms akimbo, Oscar has all the motivation he needs. "It's not about just getting somebody into a kayak for half an hour. It's getting them *excited* about it. People get excited about little things, and then they want to learn more, and then they'll teach other people. That's what we want. We create stewards, and they go on to inspire others."

There's another reason I came to Hoboken today.

I walk five minutes from the beach through a shaded park where kids splash in a fountain to Castle Point Terrace, a short street that tees into the campus of the Stevens Institute of Technology. This is Oscar's favorite block in Hoboken. If he wins the lottery, he wants to buy one of the $3.5-million houses.

Sixty years ago, these substantial brick homes, on a cobblestone roadway canopied by hardwoods, didn't cost nearly as much. I stop at a corner across from the university and look though a cast-iron fence at a frat house with a leaded-glass door. Laura, Janet and Kenneth lived on the second and third floors of this house for a few years with my mother and their parents, Bunny and Ralph, when Ralph was a Stevens prof. Bunny hosted a post-Thanksgiving dinner party in 1963. She invited a physics grad student who was being supervised by one of Ralph's friends, thinking that the young single cousin living with her family might be sweet on another recently landed scientist. And then Bunny, quite coincidently, had tickets to a concert that she could no longer attend, sending the pair on a date.

On their second date, they went for coffee and watched the ice skaters at the Rockefeller Center rink. It was a cold day in mid-December, but my father wore only a thin raincoat, beneath which he had concealed a single red rose. He asked my mother to marry him. She thought he was joking and laughed.

Standing outside the house on Castle Point Terrace, I think about the journeys that brought my parents to this part of the world and my own path to this particular place and time, about the colossal geopolitical and personal challenges they faced during the Second World War and the 1960s, about the calculus of intergenerational decision-making versus the impenetrable prism of factors far beyond our control. If not for that dinner party, I might not be here.

How can we live purposefully in our random world? How does one know when to tread water and when to swim?

I text my mother to tell her where I am.

"Go to the deli at the bottom of the hill," she replies, "and get a pastrami sandwich."

PART III

ALBANY TO TORONTO

~~~~~~

"That one could now savor fresh oysters so far from the sea symbolized the single greatest triumph of the Erie Canal: it compressed distance and time in ways that had previously seemed impossible."

— Carol Sheriff, The Artificial River

"At first I was simply curious whether one could accomplish such a voyage without coming out of the water repeatedly, and for many miles, but later I grew interested in the notion of what America would look like from the rivers, and I wanted to see those secret parts hidden from road travelers."

— William Least Heat-Moon, River-Horse

PART III

ALBANY TO TORONTO

CHAPTER 17

"It was as if America's rivers, far from delivering the future, had continued vacuuming up ambition as they slid, preserving along the water's edge a snaking time capsule."

— Ben McGrath, Riverman

"IT WAS BIZARRE. IT WAS ONE OF THE WEIRDEST EXPERIENCES OF MY LIFE." Len Tantillo — white hair, white mustache, late 70s — straddles the double yellow line in the middle of Broadway. We're in downtown Albany on a scorching Monday afternoon in mid-July, and there are no cars driving along one of the main roads in the New York State capital, an attractive streetscape of century-old mid-rises. Nor any people on the sidewalk. Sky: hazy, pallid, fumée du Quebec. Vibe: desolate adjacent. A plastic bag catches a thermal above the baking asphalt and whips past.

"The day the story broke, there was nobody home," continues Len, an acclaimed and prolific artist whose oeuvre consists primarily of historical and marine paintings. He's also my ferryman today, shuttling me to the Erie Canal from the bus station, where I had arrived via Greyhound from Manhattan, so I can begin paddling west, and along the way showing me how Albany can return to its roots and make a bold move at the same time. "When I got back to the house, there were television trucks in our driveway and reporters with cameras trying to take pictures through the windows of my studio. That night on the news, the governor commented on it, the mayor commented on it, and the city offered $15,000 so we could put this on paper and provide a little more detail."

This, he says, arms spread wide, still on Broadway, still no cars, is where the water will be.

To paint historical scenes, Len studies old maps to see what places looked like in the 17th and 18th centuries. Albany evolved out of a fur trade settlement along a section of the Hudson River that used to be twice as wide; it was narrowed by infilling tidal mudflats and other development over the last couple hundred years. The shoreline was once more or less where we're standing, and the Erie Canal used to flow into the Hudson less than a mile north of this spot. Now a tangle of elevated highways and access ramps shimmers in the heat between us and the river, and the Hudson is linked to the canal about 10 miles away, in Waterford.

There is increasing talk about "interstate removal" in Albany, restoring the urban core's connection to the Hudson and reawakening the area's economic, ecological and cultural potential. It's happening in other cities, including nearby Syracuse, and could work here. But one morning, driving down Broadway, Len wondered, "Instead of trying to bring the city to the water, what happens if you bring the water back into the city?"

Len's idea leapfrogged from a friend's appointment book, where he'd sketched it out on a random page over lunch, to a friend of his friend, who happened to see it on that random date a couple months later and happened to be married to a journalist. It became front-page news; TV stations picked up the story. An architect as well as an artist, Len had mapped out a plan to construct a brand-new canal right in the heart of downtown Albany. An oasis to gather around.

That brief media flurry took place in 1996, with regular follow-up coverage since then. Collaborating with a trio of friends — a landscape designer, an urban planner and a civil engineer — Len developed a comprehensive schematic. The other three men have passed away, and their blueprint needs a wholesale update. But the outrageously ambitious and even more outrageously expensive idea seems to be gaining momentum, with a nonprofit group at the helm and a growing community of well-connected backers. (The first act of the city's transformation into "Upstate Venice," according to the group, was the recently completed $15-million Albany Skyway, an interstate-ramp-turned-linear-park that has made the waterfront more accessible to pedestrians and cyclists. New York governor Kathy Hochul called the Skyway an "infrastructure project that promotes equity and connectivity," one rooted in "improving quality of life and righting the wrongs of the past.")

We drive down the block to a plaza in front of the historic D&H Building and peel ourselves off the seats of Len's hatchback. The grand gothic complex, a tower flanked by a pair of five-story wings, is the State University of New York's main administrative headquarters, but it used to be HQ for the Delaware and Hudson Railway. Train tracks ran between the building and the river, with streetcar lines on the city side. There's a small park here now, dry and tumbleweed-rolling-past empty. Len thinks it could become a boat basin, a wide spot on the new canal's short splash through downtown: a public space ringed by restaurants and patios and greenery and people who would finally have a goddamn reason to come downtown. He shows me an enchanting painted rendering on his phone. In the lee of the D&H, windows lit up at dusk, a couple walks along a wooden dock as a water taxi approaches.

"You saw what this city looks like today," Len says, conceding that the frayed, utilitarian bus terminal and surrounding desert of empty parking lots don't create the most favorable first impression. "This isn't the city that I moved into 50 years ago. The city that I moved into was a *city*. It had stores and businesses right here; it had pedestrian traffic. But since then, it's been in a slow and constant decline.

"We need to think of our waterways in a different way," he adds, inspired by how other places — Buffalo, Chicago, San Antonio — have enlivened their canals and riverfronts, blue acupuncture interventions. "If you have water to begin with, you've already overcome the greatest obstacle. The resource has been handed to you. So how do you use it?"

Len makes one last stop on our way to the Erie (well, one last stop before a brewpub). A few minutes north of the D&H Building, in an industrial pocket beside Interstate 787, he envisages a smaller park and boat basin — this one on the site of the Erie's original first lock. Although this end of the canal was rerouted to Waterford when it was enlarged, Albany was the original easternmost terminus. During a 2001 dig, an archaeology team from a nearby college unearthed limestone blocks that formed a portion of the lock chamber and the red-brick foundation of a toll collector's building. This part of the Albany canal project could be low-hanging fruit: rewatering the place where "America's river" was first connected to the interior of the continent.

Sitting at the bar inside Wolff's Biergarten, savoring the dark coolness of this former fire department engine house (and the coolness of a crisp pilsner), Len gets philosophical. When he started painting, he wanted his pictures to convey a grassroots history of the country. Of the place he called home and the people, Indigenous and settler, who had lived there in the past. "Always with the sense in the back of my mind that if people were aware of where they came from, they could do a better job of figuring out where they're going. That was pretty naive on my part, but I still can't give that up."

Len's canal plan may sound like a pipe dream, and he doesn't expect to see any shovels in the ground during his lifetime. But maybe there will be water flowing down Broadway for his grandchildren. Sometimes a Hail Mary gets you a touchdown.

"It's very depressing to not see a clear path to survival," he says. "We've been told over and over again that the Earth is getting warmer, that it's going to affect everybody, everywhere, and that it will be more and more difficult year after year to change things. And we're there now. We have the hottest day on the planet on a Monday, we beat Monday's record on a Tuesday, and then we beat Tuesday's record on a Wednesday. What more will it take? This is why I find solace in painting that past. If I'm in world that existed in 1720, it immerses me for a while, at least for as long as I'm sitting in front of that canvas. I try to figure out who's there, what they're doing, what their life was about.

"Art is a way of seeing things. It can broaden your perspective. The world gets bigger and ideas can expand. But it doesn't make solutions any easier."

We finish our beers and I clean a plate of fries topped with cheese, bacon and sour cream, loading up on carbs and fats and forgetting that bar food doesn't make paddling any easier. Len drives 20 minutes to a boat launch just above lock E6 on the Erie Canal. The first set of locks are clumped together in a 1.5-mile stretch leading up from Waterford, but with nearly 30 more to go on the Erie, I've decided to skip that protracted procedure.

With an artist's eye for detail, Len asks about the minutia of my trip as I pump up my board. It's already early evening and I've got 11 miles to cover to reach lock E7, where I want to camp, so I don't linger, thanking him profusely and belching prodigiously while propelling myself away from shore.

To its boosters, the Erie Canal embodied progress when it was carved out of the wilds of Upstate New York and opened to traffic in 1825. Motivated by both economic and ideological imperatives, the canal played a major role in the transformation of the young nation's geography and economy, historian Carol Sheriff writes in *The Artificial River*. Championed by New York governor DeWitt Clinton — a former state legislator, former U.S. senator, the former mayor of New York City and a failed presidential candidate — it was an end run around Washington's concentration on financing roads. Called both "Clinton's Folly" and "Clinton's Ditch" during various stages of its development, the Erie ignited an industrial revolution and altered the daily habits and values of ordinary citizens. It sparked widespread mobility, rapid environmental change, market expansion and moral reform. It convinced middle-class women and men, writes Sheriff, that they "were taking an active role in realizing a divinely sanctioned movement toward the perfectibility of the natural and human worlds."

That folly aside, I wonder, after paddling away from Len and baptizing myself with a quick swim, why not look to the waterway again for some clues about our next steps?

The first 92 miles of the westbound Erie Canal are cojoined with the Mohawk River, which flows east through the Mohawk Valley — one of the only gaps in the mountains that protected the American West from the increasingly crowded East Coast in early 19th century. A gap, according to Sheriff, where Americans believed God intended them to build a river.

This curvy section of the Mohawk — marshy edges, green hills, oxbow corners — is peaceful, pretty. Ducks and small islands and a sea of trees. It's not the industrial image one conjures when thinking about the Erie. On a quiet summer evening, released from the asphalt furnace of Albany, it feels barely touched by human hands.

Now it's getting dark, well past nine o'clock. Nautical twilight: both the horizon and bright stars visible, an overlap that allows mariners to take reliable readings. Digging around in a dry bag for my headlamp, I don't know whether there will be a low dock or a high ladder at the lock station. Then I remember: E7 is open late tonight! Maybe I can get a lift to the upstream side and have a faster start in the morning.

I phone the number on my laminated map.

"Lock seven," a man answers. "Sean here."

"Hi. I'm paddling westbound and will be at E7 in five minutes. Would you be able to lock me through? My friend Bill from the Canal Corp. might have told you I was coming."

"Pardon?"

I repeat my request. The same line I used heading down the Champlain Canal, never a problem.

There's a pause.

"Oh, you're *that* guy. Come on in! I can't wait to meet you."

I hurry ahead under a black sky, and a set of enormous metal doors begins to swing open with a whir. An enigmatic gateway, borrowing the title from one of J. B. MacKinnon's transcendent books, to the once and future world.

CHAPTER 18

"And this was the way we ascended: the big portals closing us into a near dark, thousands of pounds of flowing river pushing against the forward gates, leaking out a pattern in splatter and spray of a liquid angel, wings spread out as if to fly out of the Stygian tank . . ."

— William Least Heat-Moon, River-Horse

MOST SCHOOLCHILDREN IN NEW YORK ARE INTRODUCED TO THE ERIE Canal in fourth grade as part of the social studies curriculum. They learn the classic song — "I've got an old mule and her name is Sal / Fifteen years on the Erie Canal" — and about the series of engineering breakthroughs that transformed their state and country, from the original 40-foot-wide, four-foot-deep waterway to today's third iteration, the so-called barge canal, which ranges from 120 to 200 feet in width and 12 to 23 feet in depth.

Before the canal opened, it took two weeks to travel from Albany to Buffalo by stagecoach over rough trails. With 83 locks overcoming 571 feet of elevation over more than 350 miles, the trip was shortened to five days. The cost of transporting cargo from swelling coastal communities to the sparsely populated interior was cut by 90 percent, thanks to the efficiency of horse- or mule-pulled boats versus ox-drawn wagons. In 1800, moving a ton of goods 30 miles inland had cost the same as shipping the load to England.

Beyond financial incentives and payoffs, teachers emphasize the social movements that the canal bolstered — suffrage, abolitionism, religious revival. It was the internet of its day: newspapers, speakers and ideas traveled from Albany to Buffalo and back, converging and pinballing off one another. Elizabeth Cady Stanton and Susan B. Anthony, two of the leaders of the women's rights movement in 19th-century America, lived in the Erie's catchment and were both active in antislavery campaigns before focusing their energy on the vote. Suffragettes reached audiences across the state via the canal: rallies, marches, pickets. These efforts bore fruit when the 19th Amendment recognized the right of women to vote (though it was many years before that right included women of color).

Like the Champlain Canal, the Erie was also a mainline on the Underground Railroad, with Blacks and white abolitionist supporters settling in canal towns and setting up safe houses near the water. It helped thousands of enslaved people escape to Canada via Niagara Falls, and Black men and women found employment on the canal, funding their journeys to freedom.

Now that the pendulum has started to swing away from a one-sided recitation of the past, teachers no longer ignore the Erie's profound impact on Indigenous Peoples. The "building boom and the urban explosion that it triggered," reads one lesson plan, "dramatically accelerated the dispossession and disruption of traditional life ways of the region's Native Americans."

The Erie spans the ancestral homelands of the Mohican Nation, who lived in the upper Hudson Valley, and the Haudenosaunee, or Iroquois, Confederacy, whose six Nations — Seneca, Cayuga, Oneida, Onondaga, Mohawk and Tuscarora — occupied all of Upstate New York and a swath of land from Southwestern Ontario to the southwestern corner of Quebec. Driven out of North Carolina by colonial violence, the Tuscarora had moved north in the early 1700s and joined their linguistic and cultural relatives. Subsisting on fish, game and cultivated grains, the confederacy flourished. Its 17th-century population "may have been denser than the diverse population of modern times," according to *Bond of Union* by historian Gerard Koeppel.

First the water giveth. Then . . . you know the rest.

As historian Laurence M. Hauptman writes in *Conspiracy of Interests*, "transportation interests combined with land speculation" dramatically and irrevocably transformed the region. Not only were the Oneida on the central section of the canal and the Senecas farther west pushed from their traditional territory, but for every Haudenosaunee Nation the "sudden appearance of hundreds of thousands of non-Indian taxpaying citizens . . . added fuel to attempts to Christianize, educate, concentrate, or remove Indians from the state." (Hauptman's book was published in 1999, apparently before the term *Indian* was dispossessed by *Aboriginal*, let alone *Indigenous*. I've kept his original language here and want to pass along a footnote shared with me by Tuscarora scholar Joe Stahlman, whom you'll meet later: "Larry's books look at history from a white perspective, but because he's good at the record, he at least tells that half of the story with brutal honesty.")

The idea for this audacious canal is credited to flour merchant Jesse Hawley, who went bankrupt trying to export his product to market from the Rochester area and couldn't shake this timeless impulse while locked up in debtor's prison. (Koeppel: "A child clawing a channel through sand at water's edge or flicking a stick to link sidewalk puddles indulges the human instinct to create waterways. Canals are as old of the ingenuity of humans trying to move themselves or their things more quickly and cheaply.") Penned under the pseudonym Hercules in 1807 and 1808, Hawley wrote a series of essays for a local newspaper detailing the route and benefits of a canal from Albany to Buffalo — "a burlesque on civilization and the useful arts," he exalted, "for the inventive and enterprising genius of European Americans."

New York assemblyman Joshua Forman relayed Hawley's vision to the state legislature and called for surveys to examine its practicality. Rebuffed by President Thomas Jefferson, the idea gained support within New York, with state senator DeWitt Clinton coming aboard in 1810, in between stints as mayor of New York City, and becoming its most influential advocate. The War of 1812 threw a wrench into planning, but the project was approved in 1817 by the New York State Legislature, which authorized $7 million for construction. Digging commenced on July 4 of that year near Rome, New York, a central section chosen because, without many natural obstacles to overcome, the miles would come fast and steady, shutting down detractors.

If they're paying attention, students in New York will learn, as per the National Park Service's official narrative, that building the Erie took eight years of felling and excavating trees, blasting rocks and pouring an innovative new kind of hydraulic cement that hardened under water; that it sliced through fields, forests, cliffs and swamps; that teams of horses and mules pulled barges carrying wheat, flour, lumber and whiskey eastward, while people and manufactured goods went west (including the heavy furniture and fragile houseware of settlers, who didn't want to move to the interior without the comforts of home); that it was the longest artificial waterway on the continent; and that if the canal had not been constructed, Midwestern business would've instead looked down the Mississippi to New Orleans for markets. Which meant that in the decades leading up to the Civil War, in a region that leaned toward union over secession, "political sympathies might have taken a different form."

So, it was kind of a thing.

In Canada, we don't hear much about the Erie. Most us don't even know that it remains a navigable route — a string of natural rivers, engineered channels and lakes that sees way more pleasure boats than barges these day; more cyclists and hikers on the parallel Empire State Trail than paddlers; and, more to the point, is a daunting prospect for a guy on a SUP to size up in the midst of what will go down as the hottest summer on record.

After a sleepless sweat in my tent beside the E7 lock tender's office — cars come and go throughout the night, headlights sweeping across nylon — I pack up and leave early. Before departing home, I had talked to a steward who watches over this section of the Erie, part of a program that sees volunteers spruce up the waterway, report issues and serve as friendly ambassadors. Molly Brown works with a summer school program in which students with disabilities spend time at the canal — youth who live in the area, she told me over the phone, but rarely come to the water. "There are lots of have-nots around here," she said, "and this is one way we can help create a more connected community." On these regular field trips, children learn about things like the importance of clean water and the impact of invasive species. They help cut plants and do cleanups. And one of their classes is going to be at E8, a dozen miles and approximately 4,800 paddle strokes away, at 10 a.m.

I huff it so I can meet with the teacher and students and arrive just a little late, but the lock station is quiet. Checking my phone, I see a message: there are air quality warnings today, more smoke drifting down from Canada, and schools have canceled outdoor activities. Wildfires further disconnecting children from the natural world, another example of our propensity for self-propelling cycles.

Deflated, the rest of the morning is a downer. I feel soft after five nights on a bed in Manhattan and am uneasy about the lengthy (and potentially smoky) canal unspooling ahead. I'm well aware that a long journey begins with a single step, but a few hours into this third leg of my trip, I'm dispirited by how many miles remain. Thankfully the low doesn't last. Before my fears can fester for too long, I'm at E9, where Clay, the lock tender, lets me fill my water bottles from the cooler in his office, dispenses intel on camping options ahead and calls his colleague at the next lock — "to make sure he has eyes on you." Better yet, he doesn't bat an eye when I clumsily drop a water bottle in the office and make a mess.

A few miles upstream, I chat about the weather and the river with a man sitting on a staircase that descends into the water, feet submerged, below his Trump-flag-adorned RV. We debate whether the dark clouds gathering to the northeast will blow this way. He thinks I'm good and points out the rock-encircled pool he has constructed in the shallows. "Think I might take a dip," he says.

Soon, I'm out of sight upriver and it's pouring, but there's no thunder and the rain feels like the best kind of shower. Had lightning struck, my new friend would probably have granted me refuge, regardless of any partisan differences.

I'm spooked about camping at scrubby E11 in the small city of Amsterdam — "It's a city," Clay had cautioned — and decide to keep going in search of a better spot. Lugging my board around the lock because I arrived after operating hours, I encounter a guy sitting in a red sports car in the parking lot who points out that a rig with wheels would make portaging easier. The next lock station is pretty far and I won't make it before dark. Fretting about where I'm going to sleep, I'm lumbering past the sports car again with my bags when the outernet kicks into gear. Unsolicited, the driver recommends a park, river left, a couple miles yonder, if I need a place to camp.

The old Yankee Hill Lock, spread around a vestigial channel from the mid-1800s second canal, is perfect: dock, picnic table, porta potty. There's a No Camping sign, of course, this one specifying that no canoe or kayak camping is permitted — yet saying nothing about SUP. When I query a man walking toward the water with his fishing gear, he figures I'm fine.

"You're the guy from Canada going to Buffalo, right?" he says. "My buddy in Amsterdam said you'd be coming."

Back in Ottawa, my wife and I had wondered whether sharing granular details about my itinerary on social media could invite trouble. In real life, revealing your plan on the Erie means people pass you along to the next folks down the line.

Psychologists and sociologists would call these weak-tie interactions. Bantering with a barista, exchanging greetings with a bus driver, conversing about cumulonimbus with a Trump fan. We missed these interactions during the COVID-19 pandemic. They boost our mood and, according to psychologist Gillian Sandstrom from the University of Sussex, confer a sense of belonging that's "essential to thriving."

In an essay she wrote for CBC Radio, Canadian writer Kyo Maclear describes her morning with a singing group that her partner hosts for unhoused men facing addiction challenges. A handful of participants settle awkwardly into chairs, seemingly uneager for a bonding experience. But there are moments when the voices grow closer and closer, and she feels a swell in her chest that others seem to catch too.

"In a culture built on individualism, there is something to be said for communality even if it's not second nature or, frankly, 100 percent enjoyable," Maclear observes. "To persist and let yourself be lifted. To refuse relation-lessness. To show up for something bigger than yourself and, for an hour, ride with a wild and off-key ensemble . . . sometimes it's important to walk around like a weird wild duck and sometimes it's important to aim for collective lift off, however wobbly that might be."

Daybreak is cloaked in dense fog. The remnant of the old canal — masonry block walls chinked with moss, overhanging branches reflected in still water — evokes, like my first lock on the Erie, another ancient portal. One I nearly tumble into while shuffling to the porta potty.

The sun quickly burns off the fog, and it's even hotter than yesterday. By midmorning, I'm knackered. Craving real food, a cold drink. Enter Swamp Thing.

To recap, in as close to haiku form as I can manage:

Fultonville, fast food.

Steep overgrown riverbank.

Smelly disheveled me.

Sustained by my aforementioned bushwhacking Dunkin' Donuts smorgasbord and frequent swims in questionable water, I'm at E14 by midafternoon. Usually by myself when I'm getting locked through, this time I'm sharing the chamber with a small white yacht. The captain and I get to talking while water flows in through underground tunnels and we begin to slowly rise. After telling him my story, I pop the question: got room for a passenger?

"Sure!"

When the water tops out, Larry LaBrier helps me drag my SUP across the swim platform at the stern and throws my dry bags into a dinghy hanging off a pair of davits. Also aboard *Living the Dream* are his wife and sister- and brother-in-law. They're doing part of the Great Loop, a popular months-long boating circuit around the eastern half of the continent. Sitting in the bridge beneath an awning, relishing the breeze and stretching my cramped fingers as we cruise between forested shorelines under a crisp blue sky, I'm living the dream.

Ensign Petey, a black-and-white "suitcase" poodle, tries to lick the Dunkin' Donuts residue off my face as Larry, a retired accountant with a white goatee, dips into his catalog of marine travels. He has sailed across the Atlantic before but already, at the outset of this maiden heartland voyage, prefers the Erie. "When you're on the ocean, the scenery never changes. *This* is gorgeous. You see parts of the country you'd probably never see otherwise."

Larry pulls up to the pier at a marina and campground in St. Johnsville. He needs gas and, with his crew, decides to spend the night. Begrudgingly, I disembark and carry my gear to the end of a large rectangular lawn beside the water. A scattering of hardwood trees provides shade. The campground manager points out the showers and for dinner suggests a Yemeni-owned deli a half mile walk into town. I am still living the dream.

I'm lazing on the grass, drying my dew-soaked camping gear in the sun and wind, when a beat-up pickup truck crunches into the parking lot. A grizzled man with a fishing rod walks my way and stands beside the canal wall. Wearing a plaid shirt and jeans, hair poking out beneath his ballcap, he looks to be in his 70s. A woman follows carrying a patio chair and bottle of water. He sits, she leaves, he sighs as the pickup drives away. Then he turns toward me and, ever so slightly, nods.

I ask if the fish are biting, and he looks at me quizzically.

"I'd probably have to put my line in the water for them to take an interest," he says. "Reckon they don't want to meet me halfway."

We exchange names, and I ask Joe if this a lucky spot. "I don't like fishing here," he says. "Prefer the reservoirs with the good clean water. You can eat the fish here though. I throw most of 'em back, but some I can't resist. My old lady's got a way of cooking up pickerel."

Tonight, he adds, she's cooking dinner for a friend and dumped him here.

Joe lights a joint and offers me a toke. I decline but, wanting to show solidarity, remark that recreational weed is now legal in New York.

"I thought it was legal in the '70s," he replies.

A Vietnam War vet, Joe lives a few miles away. He starts spinning stories. About a kid who drowned trying to swim across the river here. About some of the locals who have overdosed and died. About how pervasive and destructive hard drugs are in this area. About his son, in prison for selling meth, whom he's going to visit tomorrow. "Thought he was gonna be a gangster. Now look at him."

Interstate 90 cuts across the landscape on the far side of the canal, and Joe tells me that townsfolk in St. Johnsville voted against a freeway exit when the thruway was built. "They thought it'd bring AIDS and immigrants and people getting off the highway to rob them. I'd rather have the traffic and noise. At least something would be moving."

Another man ambles over: heavyset, round face, fishing rod. Chewing on a cigar, he casts, then tells us that he and his wife are retired and driving around the country in their RV. "We've got people in just about every state. Figured we'd go see 'em and say our hellos and goodbyes."

His words hang in the air. "Goodbyes." Not "See you next time."

The sun slants, shadows lengthen.

This campground is underrated by his guidebook, our new friend says. "People want things to be just so, and then you get somewhere like this and it's *nice*."

When the man heads back toward his RV, Joe worries aloud that his old lady won't be coming back. "I think she's leaving me here." I can't tell if he's joking or if serial abandonment is part of their matrimonial yin-yang.

"She brought you a chair and a bottle of water," I say. "She must care about you. She's going to come back."

"Yeah," he grumbles. "For her chair."

When I return from town with a lamb wrap and tabouli salad, Joe and the chair are gone.

It's a rare night with no rain in the forecast, so I leave the fly off my tent and am sliding into sleep when I hear voices getting closer and closer. The unmistakable edge of a couple bickering while attempting to keep their voices low.

Then a flashlight beam alights on my face.

"It's OK," I hear a man stage-whisper. "We were talking earlier."

Joe.

"Hey bud," he says from a few feet away. "Did you see my phone?"

"Sorry, Joe. I was back before dark, and it wasn't where you were sitting. Maybe check the truck?"

When in a tent by yourself at night, getting interrogated with a light shining in your eyes is at best unpleasant and possibly dangerous. But tonight in St. Johnsville, it's just Joe.

"OK, man," he says after a beat. "Good night."

CHAPTER 19

"What do we do with glorious things that have outlived their original intent? When we're wise, we preserve them. When we're brilliant, we preserve and repurpose them."

— Nick Yetto, "A Brief History of the Erie Canal"

ANOTHER MUGGY MORNING. ANOTHER PLASTIC BOWL OF INSTANT OATMEAL and enamel steel mug of instant coffee. Another half-marathon paddle in the rising mercury to make it to a meeting on time.

Little Falls, my rendezvous point, is snuggled into a rocky gorge where the Mohawk River drops 40 feet and where, after I pass under a 150-ton steel guillotine gate menacingly poised above my head, lock E17 lifts me 40.5 feet, the largest vertical on New York's canal system. Hemmed in by high cliffs, this was one of the biggest impasses for Erie engineers to crack. Their solution, a 170-foot hand-cut limestone aqueduct connecting the canal to town, built in an astonishing eight weeks, was a tourist draw from day one (and puts modern-era infrastructure deficits into perspective).

"Here the smooth waters of the Canal wind round this tumultuous current, producing a pleasant association of the beauties of nature with the works of art," remarked one visitor in 1835, her phrase "works of art" standard lingo at the time for the Erie's human-made structures.

Although the main business was cargo, millions of passengers boarded long narrow canal boats in the waterway's first few decades.

Among the settlers, salesmen and evangelical preachers were streams of tourists, many on their way to Niagara Falls, a wonder of the world now within reach. Forty travelers could sardine themselves into a 78-by-14-foot canal packet. During the day, they enjoyed a carpeted sitting room with comfortable chairs and mahogany tables stocked with newspapers and books. For meals, crew members converted the cabin into an elegant dining room. At night, a curtain divided the hold into separate quarters for women and men, with berths pulled down from the walls and cots strung from hooks in the ceiling.

The biggest concern during these voyages was not nocturnal hijinks belowdecks, but the countless low bridges that boats slipped beneath. Farmers, whose land had been severed by the canal, needed access to their fields on both sides of the channel; in some stretches, there was a bridge every quarter mile. These could be fatal for topside passengers who, transfixed by the scenery, had to drop to the deck or hastily retreat to the cabin to dodge the wooden spans. "Newspapers carried reports," Sheriff writes, "of unwary (or intoxicated) passengers smashed to death against bridges."

In those early years there was tension around the technology that made these journeys possible. Although the canal was seen as a righteous enterprise — as an instrument for spreading civilization westward, a notion that by the 1840s would be known as Manifest Destiny — boats pulled by animals represented a mechanical imposition upon the bucolic countryside. Even the frequently used descriptor "artificial river" was a contradiction: the adjective speaking to human mastery over the landscape, the noun a link to an eroding past.

To critics such as Nathaniel Hawthorne, the "works of art" represented a "too-rapid, unthinking advance." Constructing the Erie necessitated draining swamps — which caused "vibrant forests to decay," Hawthorne complained, into "ghostlike" cemeteries — and begat "ill-developed towns where the extremes of wealth and poverty stand in stark contrast to each other." (Hawthorne's contemporary Herman Melville tried to secure a job on the canal. Unsuccessful, he shipped out for England in 1839, a dozen years later in *Moby-Dick* describing the average canal worker as a "terror to the smiling innocence of the villages through which he floats; his swarthy visage and bold swagger are not unshunned in cities.")

Little Falls had just a few hundred residents when the Erie was completed. But surrounded by dairy farms, it became the largest cheese maker in the United States by the time the Civil War started. A dramatic waterfall above today's lock E17 powered its textile, paper, flour and lumber mills. The canal connected them to markets. Almost all of these mills have closed over the past century, but I see the next iteration of this industrial heritage when I paddle past colossal brick buildings that now house an art center, inn, restaurant and shops, part of the city's downtown revitalization, and tie up at a dock beside a 19th-century warehouse that has been converted into a visitor center.

Tom Ryan is waiting for me on the shaded veranda. Wearing a blue New York State Canals golf shirt, gray hair parted to the left, Tom used to be the harbormaster here and ran a tour boat. He also worked for the federal and state governments, serving as chief of staff at the New York Thruway Authority from 2009 to 2012. In that role, he oversaw the New York State Canal Corp., whose management, in 2016, was transferred to the New York Power Authority — a better administrative fit, by most accounts I heard.

Canal politics have always been tumultuous, Tom tells me as I climb into his SUV for a tour of Little Falls. A consultant's report on the future of the Erie that was leaked after he left the Thruway Authority mapped out what he calls "moments of activity," not a fully navigable waterway. "They were going to segment the canal," he says, "to save money." Tom and others pushed back and, with the emotional hook of the 2025 bicentennial in sight, won a reprieve. "Once the Erie Canal goes away, you lose it forever," he says. "We don't want to be the generation that loses it forever."

Economically, the canal was a resounding success out of the gate. Boat traffic was so heavy and the backlog at locks so long that work to widen and reroute it started in 1836. Communities on the water boomed. Buffalo, population 2,000 when construction began on the Erie, became the biggest grain port in the world by 1900. Rochester grew from 1,000 to 80,000 residents in 50 years and, for a while, was the country's largest flour producer. Syracuse surged from a swampy crossroads of 250 to a city of 10,000 within a decade; those briny wetlands allowed it to dominate the American salt market for half a century. And settlers kept streaming west, "securing the territory," writes Hauptman, "against any and all threats from the British Lion in Canada."

"At stake was control — political, territorial, and commercial — of what now seems so inevitably to have become the United States," Koeppel asserts in *Bond of Union*. Yet without the Erie, "there would have been no penetration of the Appalachian range before interests inimical to the United States — French, English, Spanish, Russian and native or discontented American — laid permanent claim to pieces of the continental interior."

The thing about progress, however, is that it keeps progressing. Short rail lines started to spider throughout New York in the 1830s, often serving as links to the Erie and usurping the role of lateral canals. At first, the state legislature kept rail freight in check, imposing tolls and only permitting trains to carry cargo in winter when the canal was frozen. Ultimately, railroads took over more and more passenger and freight traffic, and small outfits consolidated into larger ventures running longer lines. The first train in the state, the ironically named *DeWitt Clinton*, linked Albany and Schenectady in 1831, a bypass around the 27 locks on that leg of the original canal. Although steamboats began to replace horses and mules on the Erie in the 1860s and the canal's biggest tonnage year was in the 1880s, the efficiency of rail — followed by highways, followed by the St. Lawrence Seaway and a wider water route to the Great Lakes — meant that the canal's evolution into a primarily recreational ribbon was inevitable.

Yet those railways were rolled out alongside the canal, and later, highways were bulldozed beside train tracks. And for places like Little Falls, economic and cultural vitality is still tied to the canal. From job creation and a viable central business district to quality of life for locals, the water remains a prime resource.

~

The leaked report that Tom Ryan mentioned was produced by a firm hired by the state as part of its Reimagine the Canals initiative. Tasked with suggesting options to stop the spread of invasive species such as the foot-slicing water chestnut, the consultants called for the permanent closure of several locks, plus a dewatered section west of Utica. When the press got hold of these confidential recommendations, the Canal Corp. quickly said it would not be closing any of the waterway, while a mayor from one canal town pointed out that invasive species were already moving back and forth between the Great Lakes and Atlantic via the St. Lawrence.

The full Reimagine the Canals report was released in 2020. With input from a big tent of state government departments, nonprofits, community leaders, business groups and academics, it probed issues such as ecological restoration and economic regeneration. Acknowledging the decline in manufacturing along the route and the related, almost complete disappearance of commercial shipping, plus the threat of "extreme, unpredictable weather" due to climate change, from drought in western New York to flooding in the Mohawk Valley, the task force had a dizzying assortment of factors to balance. (Resulting from both summer storms and winter ice jams, floods have been recorded in the Mohawk Valley since the 1600s, but four of the six most disastrous inundations took place between 2010 and 2020.)

From east to west, task force recommendations focused on mitigating floods, restoring wetlands and expanding irrigation to support farmers. The report also noted opportunities for more water-based activities, such as swimming and paddleboarding, and a need for a broader transformation of the acres upon acres of vacant or underused formerly industrial canal-side property — think marinas, hotels, retail, offices and homes, an adaptive-reuse aquapunctural vision in part of the state where 80 percent of the population lives within 25 miles of the Erie.

"Successfully ushering in the 'third coming' of the iconic Erie Canal," the Reimagine the Canals report concludes, "will provide a global example of how the past can once again be put towards the service of the future."

In concert with the Champlain and several shorter canals, the Erie is the centerpiece of a 500-plus-mile network of connective waterways and parallel multiuse paths in New York State. In 2020, the annual economic impact of tourism on and around this system was estimated at $1.3 billion. The most recent figure for non-tourism economic activity, in 2014, was $6.2 billion. The same year, New York's canals were reported to support more than 26,000 jobs and provide more than $700 million in tax revenue for the state.

These are some big numbers. This is a solid foundation. All of which was swirling around my head during my tour with Tom.

We drive past a stone block fragment from the Little Falls Canal, opened in 1795 to bypass the same waterfall that the Erie later circumvented. Past an upscale inn in a former textile mill where Civil War uniforms were made. Past impeccably maintained Victorian houses on leafy streets. Past a discordant main street — on one side, historic facades and a canopied sidewalk, supported by decorated columns and topped with the Stars and Stripes, to shield shoppers from the elements; on the other, sunbaked parking lots and box stores, the outcome of a not-fully-realized 1960s urban renewal scheme that displaced thousands of residents and more than 100 businesses.

I spy a chain drugstore on the new side of the street and blurt out, "Can we stop?"

The cheap sunglasses I purchased at a bodega in New York City — my fifth pair of the trip so far — are already broken.

Like mismatched partners in a buddy cop movie, Tom and I each select shades from the rotating rack, and he takes me back to the visitor center.

"I find myself down here most days, watching the water go by," he says while walking me to the dock. "This is a town that's endured a lot of the ups and downs of modern society. I've spent a lot of my years having basic conversations about the canal with people who don't think we should keep it going, but they have never been on it. That's one of the reasons it hasn't flourished. But as a society, we spend all kinds of money on all kinds of things."

I could camp in this park for free. There's an air-conditioned lounge inside, a food truck across the street and a vintage car show tonight. But I've only made it 80 miles up the Erie so far and want to get some distance behind me.

This is the day, you may recall from my introduction, all those pairs of sunglasses ago, that I will go on to forsake several potential campsites, including a marina in the village of Ilion, where, beside some leather-clad bikers and snarling pit bulls, I wolf down a burger. The day that I opt not to camp at lock E18, where a shirtless man with a gargantuan white beard bellows, unprompted, "God bless you, brother!" The day my deliberations swing wildly back and forth from "Sleep right here?" to "Maybe I'll just paddle forever."

It's the day of my long, lonely, smoky, sweaty entrée into Utica, where Swamp Thing hauls himself out of the water and slithers to a motel.

After that glorious dead-to-the-world slumber at the Rest Inn, after I meet Sam and Jared and am reminded yet again how fortunate I am to be spending the whole day, every day, on the water, an equilibrium sets in. A blurring of the cosmic boundaries between my clammy skin and the surroundings. A recognition that it doesn't really matter if I make it to my daily destination on time or at all. Because regardless of where I put down my paddle, *somebody* will be there, and maybe this elusive serendipity holds a message or two.

Dr. Seuss might not have been picturing a budget motel when he wrote about the places we'll go, but really his classic isn't about geography. It's about the entire phantasmagoria of mysteries within and ahead. Five days into the Erie Canal, as the wear seeps deeper into my bones, I feel my resolve welling. Halfway through my four-month circuit, I feel myself carried along an everlasting current. Even if I'm paddling against said current.

In Utica, I buy breakfast at the gas station where I purchased dinner last night. The clerk, a young woman with half a dozen eye piercings, lets me fill up my water bottles with ice.

"You should see all the things I give away," she says. "We sell toothbrushes here for like $8. That's fucking crazy. But my mom's a dental hygienist, so I bring in toothbrushes and let people have them for free."

The Empire State Trail traces the shoreline in Utica. Walkers, runners and cyclists glide by, most greeting me with a cheery good morning. I cross paths with a canoeist who, like me, isn't deterred by the sulfurous post-storm runoff. "I haven't seen many other paddlers out here," I say as we approach one another.

"Seldom do," he replies without breaking pace.

In Erie Canal communities like this, the third iteration of the waterway skirts downtown. That made it "more barrier than boulevard," William Least Heat-Moon writes in *River-Horse*, his book about a cross-continent boat trip on America's inland waterways, "and the traveler no longer glides right through the nub of gaiety and commerce."

I had been warned about spending the night at lock E20 on the far side of Utica ("illegal activity, drugs"), but in the light of day it's a pleasant park, more gaiety than illicit commerce. It's also the high point of this part of the Erie. There's a plateau from E20 to E21, beyond which the locks descend and the canal drains into Lake Ontario, not the Hudson. The water is clearer here, more blue-green than brown. The concrete slab walls are covered with zebra mussels, whose filtering prowess explains the clarity, and I see a pair of pizza-sized snapping turtles swimming beneath my SUP. A jet-black mink scampers along the shore, stopping to watch me before slipping into the shrubbery. A couple of families are camping in a small clearing on the water's edge. Two women prepare a meal, and half a dozen kids splash atop floating mattresses in the middle of the channel.

In Rome, where the first shovel went into the ground in 1817, I say hi to three guys fishing under a bridge. They glare back harshly. I chalk it up to the withering temperature, but the region's economic struggles — job loss and population decline since the 1990s — could have something to do with their disposition. They might be fishing for dinner.

Just before Rome, the canal's trajectory bends from northwest to due west and I'm paddling straight into a whistling headwind. Crossing back and forth between the north and south shore, I can't evade the gusts, so I put my head down and snail forward.

Craving conversation after four quiet nights, I'm aiming for the resort village of Sylvan Beach, at the eastern end of Oneida Lake, about 15 miles from Rome. It's a Friday and the prospect of dinner at a pub has me hankering for greasy food and camaraderie. Alas, none of the campgrounds I phone have any sites available and the marinas don't allow tenting. Coupled with my painfully slow progress, oscillating haphazardly from shore to shore, this means lock E22 will be my stopover.

When I arrive, I discover an attractive expanse of emerald-green grass dotted with trees. The tidy lock tender's office is surrounded by bird feeders and flower beds, but other than the bees buzzing around this pollinator paradise, there is no movement.

In an instant, I am bounding about with glee. If I'm going to be by myself, at least I'm in this dreamy place. There are a handful of great possibilities for pitching my tent, including a copse of evergreens overlooking the lock chamber, but I opt for a quiet cluster of picnic tables at the far, downstream end of the property.

I set up and walk back up to the office, where I wedge the nozzle of a hose into the crook of a tree so I can guerilla shower and do some laundry. Later, I'm jury-rigging a clothesline near my tent when I hear a car pull into the parking lot behind me. Alone in an isolated place, my spidey sense tingles.

Turning around, I see that it's a shiny white BMW sedan and relax. A physiological response I'm ashamed to admit — that somebody who can afford a car like that probably doesn't represent a threat.

A young man, early 20s, steps out of the vehicle, pops the trunk and emerges with a tackle box and rod. Rob, who lives in Rome, tells me that he loves being away from the noise and stress of the city. "This is the place I come," he says, "to get away from all that." He's here to fish for walleye. He doesn't eat them, but his neighbor does, supplying worms in exchange for a share of the catch.

Thirsty, I ask Rob if he happens to have a beer he can spare.

"Sorry. Just this bottle of Mountain Dew. Want it?"

I'm tempted but decline, not desperate enough to take his only drink.

"Do you have a cup?" he asks. "I could pour you some."

Tempted again. Decline again.

Then I remember the donuts I bought in Utica: a little squished, but still grist for the barter system.

"Sure," he says, selecting a chocolate glazed from the crumpled box and filling my mug.

A family of five from Utica arrives to fish: grandfather, dad and three kids, members of the Oneida Nation. We chat affably as they set up beside the water a few feet from my tent.

We're a bit of a motley crew: Rob jigging for walleye; kids waiting patiently as their grandfather readies their lines; me doing downward dog on the grass, butt in the air, as my teriyaki chicken and rice rehydrates. But the weak-tie bonds are holding. I wanted to stay in a town tonight so I wouldn't be lonesome. Turns out, as Ben McGrath had reminded me on the Hudson, I just had to follow the water.

The sun is drooping; puffy clouds drift past beneath a watercolor fade from purple to amber. After I eat, a sudden rain shower sends everybody scrambling to their cars and me scrambling to shove clothes into dry bags and seal up the tent.

CHAPTER 20

> "A unique feeling envelops you when you voyage across Oneida Lake, a sensation of immersion within a pulsating biosphere that teems with life. Odors of algae, vegetation, and fish mix together, saturating the air with a rich blending. Midges and related aquatic insects rise from the lake's depths and clouds of them hover above you while their body casings, discarded in the hatching process, punctuate the surface of the water below."
>
> — Oneida Lake Association

SUNLIGHT DANCES ACROSS THE GRAY NYLON ABOVE MY HEAD IN THE morning. Much more gentle than headlights.

Outside my tent, a large man with a large moustache is drinking a steaming cup of coffee. Lock tender Dan is inspecting the picnic tables to ensure wasps are not constructing nests. He's planning to spend the day mowing lawns, pruning trees and cutting back brush and affirms my observation that this is one of the nicest locks on the Erie. He also confirms that many of his Canal Corp. colleagues are part of an influx of Russians to the area ("There's Big Sergei, who is small, and Little Sergei, who is big"), because Americans don't seem to want these jobs, even though you're outside all day and the master of your own domain.

"I don't care what happens 100 yards down or up from the lock," Dan says. "Just here."

Eight thousand yards downstream, I paddle into Sylvan Beach, bustling with boaters and cottagers. I tie up at the mouth of the canal, protected from the open lake by a breakwater, and walk past an amusement park and beachside bars to a pancake house. Despite the long line of families waiting for tables, I'm seated right away at an old-school lunch counter. My plate of eggs, bacon and potatoes arrives quickly. As one does, I take a selfie and see that my face and shirt are filthy, my beard and hair bedraggled. Sniffing said shirt, laundered last night at the lock, I realize why nobody is sitting beside me. Swamp Thing's holiday-town persona: the begrimed visage of Brunch Thing!

Sylvan Beach is at the eastern end of Oneida Lake, which is 21 miles long — the largest lake fully inside New York State — and shaped like a chubby trout. It's also quite shallow, an average depth of just 22 feet. So when a strong wind is blowing from the west, as it is today, with speeds reaching 24 miles per hour, it whips up waves that will make paddling westward an ordeal. The Oneida name for the lake, Tsioqui, means "white water."

I stop at the beach on the walk back to my board. Ocean-like breakers pound the sand. My mission is to paddle 10 miles to the Cornell Biological Field Station, which pokes out from the south side of the lake at Shackelton Point. Kneeling on my SUP and lashing down my dry bags, I'm planning to fight southwest across a small bay and then work my way west along the exposed southern shore.

"Where ya heading?" a voice inquires from the boat docked next to me.

I share my float plan with the stout tanned man.

He shakes his head. "This lake gets really snotty in a westerly wind. There's more than 20 miles of fetch. Want a ride?"

Chris and his wife, Kristen, offer to shuttle me to a marina about half of the way to Shackelton Point. I don't mind a grind but know to never look gift horsepower in the mouth.

We load my board into the back of their boat and roar past the breakwater into the chop. "I love it when it's rough!" Chris shouts, beaming, as we bounce up and down with bone-rattling thumps. "It's freedom!"

It's also fast. Frightening, but fast. Until about halfway to my halfway point, when the motor conks out.

Kristen lowers the anchor while Chris studies the console. We're still bouncing, just quietly and a little more softly. Something has clogged the fuel line, Chris suspects, and he doesn't appear even slightly worried. A 30-year Navy veteran, he's going to call one of their sons and tell him to come with the other boat and a tow rope. Could take a couple hours.

I feel terrible. They're out here in the middle of the lake because of me. But Kristen and Chris are fine with hanging out in the waves while waiting for their tow. "We're just going to fish," he says as they help me lower my SUP back into the water.

I battle my way to the marina where they were going to drop me off, stop to rest and guzzle some water, then inch west. All left-side paddling, often dropping to my knees to give the wind less surface to pummel. Lots of cursing, lots of curious looks from people at lakeside cottages. Lots of spillage while attempting to pour electrolyte powder into my Nalgene. Lots of regret about one's reach exceeding one's grasp.

On the open lake, today's wind makes yesterday's lurching on the narrow canal seem like a breeze. But obstinance can be a virtue, right? It's the struggle that matters, no? Especially if progress is agonizingly slow. Gulping down lime-flavored water periodically, it takes me three hours to make seven miles.

Finally in the lee of Shackelton Point, I spot the tiny pincer-shaped inlet where Cornell University keeps its research vessels.

Ashore, shaking, I gather my belongings and stagger up a path through a thicket. My directions are to follow the road until I reach a white house. But there's a white columned gazebo overlooking the lake, and inside sit two women and two men, sipping wine and eating whitefish canapés with sliced apricots and peaches.

"You," one of men says, "must be our visitor."

Somehow, apparently, I'm in a Jane Austen novel.

Lars Rudstam — Hawaiian shirt, round face, barefoot — is an aquatic ecology and fisheries researcher at Cornell and director of the field station. Hannah, his wife, is an emeritus education professor at the university. The other couple are their friends Lyuba Burlakova and Sasha Karatayev, professors at SUNY Buffalo and two of the world's leading mollusk experts.

Lars unfolds a lawn chair and pours me a glass of white.

My parents, two brothers and their wives are all scientists. Dinner-table conversations at family gatherings can bounce from physics to biology to chemistry, soaring high above my head. I take a sip of chardonnay and gird myself for a test. To paraphrase Matt Damon's character in *The Martian* — who realizes he'll need to uncork all his brain power to keep himself alive while marooned on Mars — I'm going to have to science the shit out of this conversation.

Lars and Hannah have lived for more than three decades on this 430-acre campus, a former maple farm, donated by an affluent alumnus in the mid-1950s, sprinkled with towering trees and whitewashed buildings, some of them nearly two centuries old. Among myriad projects, the field station has served as home base for a decades-long study of the Oneida Lake ecosystem, a database detailing the minutiae of its ever-changing aquatic food web and a model for freshwater research around the globe. "It gives us a long-term perspective," Lars says. "An opportunity to look at the impacts of climate change, of invasive species coming in, of management decisions."

This lake has always had a productive fishery, he tells me when I ask for the big picture. It's part of a vast watershed with a tremendous inflow of nutrients. For a long period, that included too much phosphorus and other pollutants. But around 40 years ago, when phosphates were removed from laundry detergent and sewage treatment plants were enhanced, water quality started to improve on Oneida and the Great Lakes. "That shows," he says, "that we can clean up our act."

Lars speaks about the delicate balance state officials are trying to maintain. The rapid rise of cormorant populations, for example, led to a decline in the number of walleye and yellow perch in the lake. Cormorants were "controlled" by oiling eggs and destroying nests, he says, and these two fish species rebounded. This approach to wildlife management was set in part by some of his research, a study that he's updating now. Ultimately, his models will help determine how many cormorants will live, although many anglers would simply say kill the birds, so it's a political issue as well as biological. "I fear I caused a lot of cormorant deaths in North America with that earlier study," says Lars, "so I really want to get the next one right."

Hannah — sunglasses, shoulder-length gray hair, kind smile — thinks about other changes on the lake. With Lars, she raised their two sons here and remembers a time when it was dangerous to swim or kayak because there were so many Jet Skis. "It was like a highway," she says. "When we first moved here, we'd sit on the porch and watch the barges go past. We saw them every day. It feels like I haven't seen one in years. Over 32 years, it's been really interesting to see both the long-term changes and seasonal changes. But the climate change differences are scary. We can remember when it froze."

"It still freezes," Lars interjects. "But not every winter, and not for as long."

"We used to sit here and look at the ice fisherman," Hannah says. "Now they can't go out anymore. It's often too dangerous."

Speaking of too dangerous, now well into my second glass of wine, I turn to Lyuba and Sasha, who are originally from Belarus and Georgia respectively, and ask about their mollusk research.

"What do you want to know?" asks Sasha, whose mannerisms remind me of my mother. "I can talk for hours and hours."

"Weeks!" says Lyuba.

"Have some more wine," says Lars.

Sasha launches into a crash course on the biology of the invasive quagga mussel, which is less famous than its cousin the zebra mussel but now 10 times more plentiful in the Great Lakes watershed. It's not uncommon to find a thousand quagga in a single square foot of sand or mud at the bottom of a lake. Voracious feeders, each mussel can filter a liter of water every day, consuming plankton from the water column — food that would otherwise be eaten by native fish species — while depositing feces and rejected toxins on the lakebed.

This leads to clearer water and allows more light to reach bottom-dwelling plants, which can stimulate the growth of weeds and blooms of cyanobacteria. But it also allows some organisms, such as the crayfish, to thrive. "This has a strong cascading effect on the whole system," says Sasha. "Everybody asks, 'What's the effect on fish?' That depends."

The butterfly effect, Oneida Lake edition, is making my head swim. Now the sun is starting to droop. Hannah walks me to a lawn at the tip of Shackelton Point where I pitch my tent beneath a colossal maple, then head to their house for dinner. She has prepared a feast — salmon, pasta, salad — and Sasha opens a bottle of Georgian wine.

The conversation meanders back to the decline in boat traffic on Oneida Lake. "We've done some work on the largest lake in Belarus," says Lyuba. "All motorboats are prohibited, except for biological station boats."

"Also lifeguards and police," adds Sasha.

I tell them about the *Apollonia* schooner, that sail freight experiment on the Hudson.

Lyuba: "That's how it was done, all the years before. Rivers were arteries for all the development."

Sasha: "But there's a reason we're not doing it anymore. One hour on the highway equals one day on the water."

Hannah: "And it's seasonal on the water."

Sasha: "But maybe with global climate change, we could do it all year round."

Lars: "They only ship things that are really big now."

Sasha: "On a truck, you can deliver to an exact spot."

Lars: "Time is money."

We're all quiet for a few seconds, then Lars tell me that after a month and a half of clockwise paddling from Ottawa, I'm only a three-hour drive from home.

Tipsy and tired, my ability to make small talk, let alone talk science, drops off a cliff. I thank my hosts and head back to my tent. When my headlamp illuminates the fly, I see that the unzipped doorway to the vestibule is thick with spiderwebs. I sweep off the webs and dozens of busy spiders with my towel, brush my teeth and return a few minutes later to see that the bugs are back and appear to have brought reinforcements.

Too sleepy to agonize about the universe conspiring against me, I rivet onto the task at hand. I don't want to pass through the spiders' sticky lair every time I exit the tent — say, to pee, after an evening involving a few glasses of wine — so I brush them off again, remove the pegs and drag my tent about 20 feet away. Then I wait, inspecting every couple minutes. No spiders. Must have been on a nest. I shudder and snuggle into my quilt.

The prevailing wind slackens and pivots and, at 6 a.m., is blowing ever so gently from the east. Oneida Lake is glass, an entirely different manifestation than yesterday's mess. For 10 miles, I'm transfixed by the web of plants and fish beneath my SUP, like I'm skimming across the surface of an immense aquarium. Forearm-sized fish dart beneath tangles of eelgrass and herbaceous whorled strands of elodea waterweeds. Schools of minnows murmur like starlings.

At the far end of the lake, the canal enters the westward-flowing Oneida River, a sinuous, thickly treed realm of wide curves and the occasional arrow-straight cut. The heat and humidity are climbing, and my tepid drinking water doesn't quench. Small shacks are tucked into the woods. Nobody appears to be home, but I can sense eyes upon me. Here hangs a Confederate flag, there blasts ZZ Top, there's a guy who looks like he could be *in* ZZ Top. Dripping sweat and half delirious, I jump in every half hour, hydration by osmosis. Pressing into the steamy jungle of afternoon, *Heart of Darkness* comes to mind again: "But his soul was mad. Being alone in the wilderness, it had looked within itself and, by heavens I tell you, it had gone mad."

Yet I'm not alone, nor in the wilderness. Just sapped and thirsty and progressively more loopy. I enter lock E23 at the same time as Michelle and Jim, taking a day trip in their pontoon boat. They toss me an icy can of lemon water before motoring off.

"The nature of this voyage," William Least Heat-Moon's copilot said as they passed through this lock, "is to encounter shit alternating with sugar so we keep getting sucked into continuing" — a remark, the author notes, that doubles as a metaphor for life.

Sheltering from the sun under a tree, I'm not sure how far I'll get today, then I round a corner and practically paddle into Joslyn and Kevin, the first two SUPers I've seen on Erie. An active, outdoorsy couple, they're using their boards as swim platforms this afternoon, drifting around with drinks. Kevin hands me a zero-proof beer from their cooler bag. Sugar!

I come to a tee where the Oneida meets the Seneca River. Their combined waters flow north as the Oswego River, emptying into Lake Ontario, just 25 miles distant. I hang a left and paddle up the Seneca, sights set on a park near the village of Baldwinsville, about four hours away. A boat approaches from behind, and I can feel it bearing down on me as I angle toward the shore. It roars past, then decelerates with a splash. I'm prepared to glower when the man at the wheel says, "I gotta know your story."

I hold onto the side of Scott and Kim's cruiser as they troll along. She proffers a bag of chips so I can grab a handful while being pulled slowly upstream. He scoops two bottles of water from the ice in their cooler, plus a baggie with some shrimps and a tiny Tupperware of cocktail sauce. A few minutes later, when we reach their gorgeous riverfront home, they offer their spare room for the night.

It's enticing, but the deluge of cold drinks and kind-heartedness has given me the juice to keep going. And going. And going. Until 30 miles into today's paddle, in the home stretch to Baldwinsville, the sun begins to sag and so do I. When a small aluminum outboard putters up behind me, I know my next move.

"Mind if I grab hold of the side?" I ask before looking closely.

"I don't mind if you don't mind," the man at the tiller replies. He's wearing jean shorts, nothing more, and his boat is full of empty beer cans. But he seems sober enough, and I'm tired enough, so I hold onto the boat as he put-puts ahead, waving to people on shore.

Shane is going home to feed his cat, Little Bastard, after spending the day at his camp.

"Fishing?" I ask.

"No! Drinking!"

Shane asks me the usual questions: "Where you going? Why?" Then he's quiet. "Are you a fugitive?"

"Are you a cop?" I parry.

"If you're on the run," he advises, "you should have picked something faster."

Shane has spent time in jail. He broke into a school and stole some flashlights. Then he broke into a business through the roof and cut a hole in the safe. "At least that was worth it."

The cabins and houses on the shoreline become denser as we approach Baldwinsville. Born and raised here, Shane points out who lives where, who married whom, who died and when and how. His wife passed away a year ago, and he recently sold their horse farm.

"I got nothing left," he says. "Except this river. I'll always have this river."

Shane drops me off at the park, insisting that I write down his phone number and call him if I run into any trouble. It's dusk and the mosquitoes are swarming. I cover myself in bug spray and share my canister with a young couple who are swatting wildly as they walk to the water. There's a No Camping sign, of course, and a police car in the parking lot, so I stick to the shadows. At 9 p.m. an officer steps out of her vehicle, locks the bathroom door and drives away. I figure I'm fine for the night. Still, I drag my board out of sight behind a stand of trees.

Heartened by the succession of people I met today, yet not ready for the cavalcade to end, I phone my wife to rhapsodize. Lisa is wrapped up in household chores and doesn't have time to listen. Instead, I deliver the roundup to my mother, naturally censoring some of the disquieting details (inebriated boatman, hiding from law enforcement, shrimp cocktail).

"Where are you?" she asks, quite possibly zooming in on a digital map.

I relay my coordinates. She's looking at a satellite view of the park.

"You're camping in strange places," Ma says. "The world is not safe these days."

As a toddler, my mother was ferried around Eastern Europe by her mother, an odyssey whose only goal was survival. They hitched rides on trucks and tanks; her tiny body was passed through windows into packed railcars. After my grandmother reunited with my grandfather, literally bumping into him on the street in Tbilisi after two and a half years apart, they eked out an existence through factory jobs and black-market food that Zaida scrounged. And she's worried about me?

"I know you're prepared," she says, "but there are a lot of things you can't control."

Ma is concerned about bad weather, treacherous waters and how the people of Upstate New York might react to an interloper turning up on a paddleboard. "It's the feeling a mother gets when their kid decides to do something . . . unusual."

My mother's reaction when I told her I was doing this trip? "I'm not ready for your midlife crisis."

"Isn't this better," I ask, "than buying a sports car?"

Long pause. "I would have been OK with a sports car."

After high school, not yet 18, I drove to California with my friend Rob and not much of a plan. Ma doesn't remember being worried. "I knew you had enough sense to not get into trouble. But now you're looking for trouble."

CHAPTER 21

"Like many of you, as I read the latest scientific warnings, I'm afraid. In particular, I feel deep anxiety for my children, and about the state of the world we are leaving to those who will live throughout most of this century and beyond. All of us who take seriously these scientific realities wrestle with despair. The truth is that we don't know if we will win this fight — if we will rise to the challenge in time. But it is worth appreciating that those who rallied in the face of fascism 80 years ago likewise didn't know if they would win. We often forget that there was a good chunk of the [Second World War's] early years during which the outcome was far from certain. Yet that generation rallied regardless, and in the process surprised themselves by what they were capable of achieving."

— *Seth Klein*, A Good War

LEERY ABOUT A COP ROUSING ME FROM MY MAKESHIFT CAMP, I'M PACKED up and paddling before breakfast.

Thankfully, it's just a mile into Baldwinsville and, after disembarking at a downtown dock, a 25-minute walk to a highway-side McDonald's. Visions of hotcakes dancing in my head, I hop a fence into a cemetery and set a brisk pace to the arterial road where abundance awaits. Mirage-like, a produce market materializes. I buy local peaches, cucumbers and freshly baked bread; eat two fast-food breakfasts; and at the supermarket next door fill a basket with nuts, dried fruit, beef jerky and, yes, more peanut butter and tortillas. Nothing else withstands the dry bag sauna.

It's nearly noon after all my provisioning, and I continue west on the Seneca River. Severe thunderstorms are in the forecast, so I check the radar frequently. Ominous dark clouds are blowing in from the west as I approach a mile-long slate cut channel, a deep trench with sheer walls straight-lining between the curves of an oxbow, not a good spot to get caught during lightning. Paddling hard, I emerge from the cut and reach Cross Lake, the south end of which is bisected by the canal. Open water is not a good place to be in a storm either.

The black clouds are just south of the lake and there's another, nastier front coming fast from the west, but I figure I can zip across and get off the water on the opposite side, rather than sit tight. Midlake, the edge of the first system catches me, and a feisty wind pushes me north. Alarmed, I abandon my line and try to get *anywhere* on the far shore before the storm hits, racking the crannies of my verging-on-panicked gray matter for lightning avoidance strategies. Stop, drop and roll? Make yourself look big? Flee? Flee!

Mercifully, mid-vamoose, the wind relents. I reset and bolt to the river mouth on the far shore. Cinching my leash to a log, I scurry into a high canopied hardwood forest seconds before the first spine-tingling crack of lightning. Trees shake, thunder roars. But it passes in minutes, and sunlight permeates the crowns of maple and birch, dappling the carpet of fuzzy new growth at my feet.

The rest of the day is dull by comparison, and I'm on autopilot, counting strokes and sprinting the final few hundred yards toward a campground when I hear somebody yell, "Take a break! Have a beer!"

Over my right shoulder, I see a group of people waving from the back of a boat moored at a marina. Body: "I'm zonked, let's set up camp and chill." Brain: "C'mon, why not?" (Lest you deem all of this drinking unbecoming, as far back as the 1840s, one Erie Canal traveler dutifully recorded, there were between three and six "groggeries" at almost every lock and stopping place: "rum, gin, brandy, wine, beer, cider . . . meet the eye every few miles.")

When I reach the boat, Matt Donahue — red ballcap, red T-shirt, big grin — reaches down and helps me climb aboard. He introduces his wife and son, as well as their friends who are visiting from England, and hands me a can of beer.

"Where the hell are you going?" he asks.

Matt and his gang are inquisitive, incredulous, impressed. They are *happy* for me. That somebody is doing something for no tangible reason other than really wanting to. There is high-fiving and rib-digging, teasing and laughing. Their joy makes me joyous. When it's my turn to ask questions, I learn that Matt and his wife grew up in Weedsport, a small village just south of the canal, a turning basin on the original Erie that was bypassed by the rerouted barge canal. That's the *port* part; *weed* comes from the surname of a pair of local merchant brothers, not a proliferation of undesired plants, nor a predilection for cannabis.

I lean back on a bench, ignoring the soft drizzle that has started to fall, enjoying the jovial conversation and padded cushion. Matt informs me that I'm just over halfway from Albany to Buffalo and, as if sensing my weariness, tells me that he used to be in the U.S. Navy Seabees, an elite construction battalion whose members swoop into perilous places to build roads, bridges, buildings, anything. "Our motto was 'The difficult takes time. The impossible, a little longer.'"

Then he hands me another cold beer for the road and we hug. Not an awkward, one-armed back-patting. A *real* hug.

"Where else," I ponder while paddling away, "do two middle-aged men who have just met hug like *that*?"

Several of the men I've met recently — Matt, Chris on Oneida Lake, Chris on the tugboat — served in the military. Their well-rounded capacity can't be a coincidence. In *The Good War*, Seth Klein calls for a wartime response to global warming. The Second World War, he writes, is a helpful, hopeful reminder "that *we have done this before. We have mobilized in common cause across society to confront an* existential threat . . . [retooling] our entire economy in the space of a few short years."

Climate change mitigation and adaptation is not the military's mandate, but Klein's idea is intriguing. Soldier-style operational savvy could help scale up smaller sustainability projects and bring national agencies into collaboration with local groups. In 2023, the U.S. government announced the launch of the American Climate Corps. Inspired by the Civilian Conservation Corps, which saw three million workers plant trees, build roads and expand national parks during the Great Depression, thousands of young people are being hired to prevent wildfires, restore wetlands and do pretty much anything that advances environmental justice and deploys clean energy. A similar program has been proposed in Canada. These types of efforts, suggests a think tank called Energy Innovation, "could help protect those most impacted by climate change."

Have you ever paddleboarded buck naked?

Uh, me neither.

Until now!

It's a languid afternoon, and I'm on the edge of the Montezuma National Wildlife Refuge, a nearly 10,000-acre tract of marshes, grasslands, shrublands and forests. It's been hours since I've seen a single person, just a few disused cabins. I usually swim wearing my shirt and shorts so the wet clothing keeps me a little cooler when I'm on the board, but I strip down and enjoy the solitude on one of my dips. And then, though I'm no exhibitionist, simply a fella going with the feral flow, remain starkers when I'm back upright.

There's a long thin mottled brownish-black thing in the murky water portside. Time for another round of one of my favorite pass-the-time-while-paddling games: stick or snake? This stick begins to wriggle and dives out of sight. Updated score: sticks 7,158, snakes 2. (It was a common watersnake, I deduce later. They can grow to more than four feet and, though they look like the venomous cottonmouth, are totally harmless.)

With the sun hitting hard from the west, I play another game: trying to stay as close as possible to the left bank to catch some shade and dodge the wind, edging around semi-submerged strainer trees and ducking under branches without getting tick stowaways in my undercarriage.

An iridescent blue damselfly lands on my neon green PFD, which is draped across my bow. Its wings are tucked together, and it appears to be staring at me with those huge, widely spaced eyes. My full frontal is surely a coincidence, but the insect's gaze is a little unnerving.

Bursts of birdsong erupt from trees that overhang this long straightaway. Fish leap out of the water to nip bugs. Herons stand statue-still, then whoosh into flight as I approach. Cicadas buzz. Montezuma's marshes, once a hideout for thieving highwaymen, were drained during canal and dam construction, and "area wildlife virtually went the way of the water — gone," according to the refuge website. Restoration work, including a series of new dikes, started in the 1930s. Today it's a thriving habit for waterfowl, shorebirds, raptors, warblers and woodpeckers, a throwback to the period when the Cayuga hunted and fished here and "the sunlight over the marshes was actually shut off by the clouds of ducks and geese." The state's inaugural bald eagle reintroduction program took place in Montezuma in the 1970s. More than 20 were released. Visitors come here to see these enormous white-headed national symbols, one of which — not a word of a lie — is gliding above the shoreline right now.

Scrutinizing me with its piercing gaze. Which is a sign. To put on my shorts. Just in time.

A trio of pleasure boaters pass me slowly, smiles and waves all around, as the pine and cedar give way to farmland. Soon: a canyon of cornstalks, their ten-foot-tall tassels reflected in the smooth green water. A little later: the village of Clyde.

I see the same three boats moored at the river landing, a former railyard that the community, cobbling together grants, has transformed into a park with trails, washrooms, a pavilion and playground. The project cost around $600,000, giving locals a place to congregate and visitors a reason to stop and spend a little money. I set up my tent and walk across a bridge to the small downtown and find El Canal Mexican Restaurant, where my boater neighbors have also decamped. Sitting beneath a tin ceiling on the ground floor of a heritage building, I eat all the tacos and beef and beans and rice and chips and salsa on my table, then a pair of ice-cream sandwiches from the gas station down the block and go to bed still a little hungry.

A long camera lens pokes out of the reeds. A burst of clicks as I pass. I am being stalked. Thankfully, I'm not naked.

The man shooting me — cargo shorts, square jaw, perfect TV-anchor hair — clambers down to the water's edge. He drove for an hour and tried to get me in Clyde, but I was gone before he arrived. He raced ahead to a bridge over the canal but again was too late. Now, nearing noon in the town of Lyons, there's no escaping John Kucko. Like a bloodhound hunting by instinct, he always gets the story.

Yesterday, while I was kneeling on my board in a lock chamber, my phone rang. I've been taking care of housekeeping while locking so I don't lose paddling time. With one elbow crooked around a slimy rope dangling beside the damp wall, I've got two free hands and about 15 minutes to have a snack, scribble some thoughts on a notepad, check the weather, send texts, make calls. But it's jarring when my phone rings — probably my mother — and I almost drop it into the water. This unknown caller is a network television sportscaster turned digital storyteller with more than half a million Facebook followers and a weekly show on CBS. Turns out there's been some online chatter about me among long-distance boaters, and John loves the Erie Canal.

Everybody knows "Kutch-coe" in western New York. His post about my trip, "Man on a Mission," nets thousands of likes and hundreds of encouraging comments. Although, for the record, I must note one fabrication: "Saw him on Tinder! He's making the most of his trip down the canal!" Swamp Thing don't play that game.

Swamp Thing would almost certainly have wallowed in the luscious peppermint fields of Lyons had I been here in the mid-1800s.

Peppermint grew bountifully in the surrounding wetlands when the Erie came through. Connected to global markets by the canal, farmers began cultivating the menthol-fragranced plant. They'd cut the two-foot-tall bushes with scythes, leave it in rows to dry and take wagonloads to distilleries, where it was boiled in vats to produce an essential oil that was deemed, in Hamburg, Germany, to be the purest, best-tasting peppermint oil in the world. Used for an array of medicinal purposes, to flavor candy and repel mice, peppermint oil put Lyons onto the map.

"When the wind blew a certain way, the whole town smelled like peppermint," Bob Stopper tells me. "That must have been something!"

Eighty-two years old, wearing blue jeans and hiking boots, Bob is a retired high school teacher and an Erie Canal über-volunteer. He picks me up at the dock, and we drive past fields where peppermint no longer grows, stopping to look at remnants of the original canal. Bob insists I step out of the car for a picture beside a block of stone the size of a coffin. Will future archaeologists puzzle over these strange ditches, trying to piece together who built them and why? Will aliens probe them for evidence of an intelligent civilization?

Bob points out a house that used to be a shop where salt fish was sold to boaters in the 1830s. A dusty rural crossroads that was once a village hub: post office, general store, hotel. A barn where mules for the towpath were kept. A factory where bricks were made, another where jars were made. Bob's wife is housebound and not well. Unable to stay away long, he uses his rare bits of free time to talk to travelers about the Erie Canal, to see if there's anything we need. (Sailors are often looking for cocktails, Bob reports, while power boaters crave steak and paddlers just want somewhere to stretch.)

"Why do you do this?" I ask.

"It's good for you to get a feeling for what we have here. If we don't promote the canal, I think it's going to be lost."

"Why does that matter?"

"This is an economically depressed county. It's struggling in many ways." We pass a school parking lot that's surprisingly busy for a summer day, and Bob tells me that free children's camps providing free meals are a big draw. "But it used to be different . . ."

He trails off, then gathers his thoughts.

"When the old-timers were on a job, they didn't leave it half finished at four o'clock because it was the end of the workday. I think we watch the clock a little bit too much these days. People today become easily frustrated. They give up on what could be wonderful contributions to the world. Had the people who built the canal given up, this community would not be here. You can't give up if something doesn't work today. Try something a little different tomorrow. And don't cuss and swear at people who are trying something a little bit different."

On the surface, this might sound like the "kids these days" ranting of a curmudgeonly senior. Today's generation doesn't respect the value of hard work, yadda yadda. But to me, Bob doesn't sound judgmental or dismissive; he's not complaining about youth. He's just saying that there are a few essential ingredients for any significant, conscious change: desire, effort, time.

CHAPTER 22

~~~~~

"In some of these Erie Canal cities, there is no meaningful interaction between people from different walks of life. Everybody is the same color in your neighborhood, the same socioeconomic status. That's not a dignified society."

— Lemir Teron, Howard University professor

PWW. PADDLING WHILE WHITE. OF THIS I AM UTTERLY GUILTY. WHICH IS patently obvious both when I'm on the water and a few months later during a video chat with Lemir Teron, a professor in the Department of Earth, Environment and Equity at Howard University, and Renée Barry, one of his former grad students. They coauthored a 2023 paper examining race and recreation along the Erie Canal, a "Rust Belt still reeling from the racialised environmental injustices of industrial development and decline."

Lemir, whose work focuses on issues such as health and urban forestry, tells me he was asked to help "democratize" the Erie as part of the Reimagine the Canals initiative. "What I've seen, for the most part, is that folks like you on a paddleboard have been privileged when we talk about who we're designing recreational opportunities for," he says. "There are a lot of recreational opportunities that marginalized communities should be invited to, but historically that hasn't been the state's push."

Beyond looking at the segregation baked into leisure activities and the need for some museums to stop marketing "heritage fantasies,"

Lemir and Renée started to think about the present-day intersection of environment and health on the Erie. The canal's bicentennial, a year before America's 250th birthday, is an opportune time to deconstruct this symbol of progress. "What needs to happen for the canal to be a more equalized space," Renée says, "is to talk about how it has always been a place of inequality and remains a place of inequality." Heritage tourism and outdoor recreation hold economic potential, she adds, but the former cannot ignore the canal's impact on the Haudenosaunee or on Black laborers, for instance, and the latter can't cater predominantly to affluent visitors like me.

"I'll go one step further," says Lemir. "In reimagining the canal, we're starting to look at who gets access to recreation — an economic elite and whiter crowd — but we also need to look at who gets access to the pain. Like, who's more prone to flooding? A lower-income population, Black folks who live on the canal. So, in addition to who gets to boat or paddleboard, we need to talk about who's getting the other side of the environmental coin. And who's getting hurt economically?"

Rust Belt cities have been "hemorrhaging" for decades, so if you want to have a real conversation about inequality, Lemir says, you need to target historically overlooked communities for workforce development. "So it's not just 'We want you to have a picnic beside the water,' but how people in these communities can get access to training and jobs that last decades into the future."

The interstate redevelopment projects that are at various stages across New York should include investments in Black communities, says Lemir. Investments around the Erie Canal bicentennial should do the same. "We need museums and recreation, but our people also need jobs." The poverty rate in some of these communities is more than 50 percent, he says, and household incomes in some places are $20,000. "You can't make it in this country in the 21st century on $20,000 per year."

Because the canal spans the entire Empire State, it can serve as a jumping-off point for a lot of conversations, says Renée. "It intersects with so many different communities in New York. It would be worthwhile for more people to spend time on the Erie Canal and use their experiences to help deconstruct some of the myths." That includes the myth of human hegemony over nature.

"When we improve ecology, we also improve public health," says Lemir. "So many things can start from this transformation. If you want to talk about something that's a needle mover politically, something that's a needle mover at a household level, people want to be healthy. People need access to less sedentary lifestyles. The Erie Canal alone isn't going to make people healthier, but providing access to recreation — so they can spend more time outside with their families — should be a critical part of the conversation about improving health.

"We can't overlook the fact that Black and Brown folks are already using these spaces for recreation, so when we talk about the future of these waterways, we need to pay attention to things that might not be in the pamphlets. They may not be paddleboarding, but there are vibrant things already going on, like fishing. I don't want to overstate the potential of the canal. It's not a panacea. But it can be one piece of the puzzle."

Recreation, he continues, has the ability to bring people together. Even in segregated Syracuse, where he used to work, the basketball court is different. "You see professors playing with 15-year-old kids, you see rich and poor together, Black and white and Brown. I think recreation generally offers a chance to do that. We may not be doing the same things, we may not be coming together as equals, but maybe the Erie Canal can be a new public square. We've got to make sure there's no crazy economic bar of entry. You need to make sure there are inexpensive or free things to do. But if you want to have a true cross section, which outdoor recreation generally allows, there's no better place than a 350-mile corridor."

The idea that a place with specific environmental attributes can reduce socioeconomic health inequalities is called equigenesis. Rich Mitchell, a population health researcher at the University of Glasgow, coined the word after publishing a paper in 2008 that suggested income-related health disparities were less pronounced in neighborhoods with better access to green space.

The most powerful way to reduce health inequalities, according to this research, would be to reduce economic inequality — an outlandish idea to politicians and power brokers. But Rich and his collaborators know that the places where we live also contribute hugely to our identity and behaviors. "Neighbourhoods are, in effect, like fields in which we grow lives, rather than crops," he writes. "Perhaps 'place' is one way we might think differently about health inequalities. . . . [Perhaps] some features of the social, physical or service environment could act to create health equality."

When I was working on my book about walking, I spent a wet morning with Rich in Glasgow trying to keep up with his long strides. Rich, whose studies helped steer Mat White toward blue space, saw how beneficial developing urban trails in disadvantaged communities could be. How more attractive pathways could reduce stress. How public walking groups could reduce the use of and expenditures on prescription drugs. And how, in an almost subversive way, urban acupuncture could slice through the status quo. "To narrow inequalities in health," Rich writes, "we need to affect the lived experiences of everyone, every day."

As governments around the world become more right-wing, they're even less likely to allocate resources to help address inequality than when I was in Glasgow a dozen years ago. But tapping into the power of nature in a strategic, evidence-backed way seems to provide a lot of ROI. And the biggest dividends might come from blue space.

What's more, as suggested by both Mat's research and the environmental resistance on the Erie and Hudson, people with less money and lower levels of education seem to care more about ecological issues. Mat frequently attends policy meetings where "experts" argue that poor people need to be taught about conservation. "They don't! We need to educate the rich," he says. "The poor care about their waterways. They care about biodiversity. They're more connected than the rich." Why? "My guess is that the rich often see these as places to be exploited. They might like them, but they don't necessarily derive the same benefits, because they're already well off, mentally and physically, whereas poor people know they're benefiting."

Every potential blue acupuncture intervention would be different because every place is different. Without community consultations, like the process Scenic Hudson is helming on Quassaick Creek in Newburgh, projects won't work. But even though they have to be "bottom-up," Mat says, there also needs to be "top-down" planning so interventions can be standardized and scaled up. "Otherwise, the resources required to do something different in every site would be overwhelming."

Urban Blue Spaces, a guidebook of sorts that Mat coedited with landscape acupuncturist Simon Bell and handful of collaborators, explores a constellation of solutions. A new cycling path along a city's riparian corridor, for instance, will encourage active transportation and curtail car use while providing a psychological glimmer. A stormwater pond will reduce flooding and localized temperatures and establish habitat for flora and fauna in addition to leisure space for nearby residents. Even though the designs deployed and materials used should befit the local environment, successful models can be adapted and applied elsewhere.

In Wroclaw, Poland, a wide staircase was constructed above the water's edge on a run-down stretch of river, encouraging people to sit and sunbathe. In Bruges, Belgium, a swimming dock was installed at the confluence of two canals, increasing access to the water for people without boats and drawing attention to the fact that the canals are now clean enough for swimming. In Paris, pop-up sandy beaches for lounging and socializing have replaced cars on the banks of the Seine. In Ljubljana, the capital of Slovenia, a pontooned wooden platform on the city's namesake river has created a place to fish in the heart of the downtown. How many of us live in communities where such measures would be a breath of fresh air?

"As we look to the future, there is no doubt that we will have to reinvigorate our efforts to avoid causing further damage to our aquatic environments and also take much greater care over the types of settings we build for people to live in," British researcher

Michael Depledge writes in the foreword to *Urban Blue Spaces*. "Unattractive, oppressive, lifeless urban ecosystems themselves continue to threaten physical and mental health. This . . . highlights the need to remember the unbreakable interconnections between nature, ecosystems, human health, and well-being."

Newark, the next village past Lyons, was once the rose capital of America. In 1901, a climbing rose bred at a local farm became one of the most widely planted varieties in the world. I'm not sure what varieties are growing outside the welcome center today, but the park where I pitch my tent is sprinkled with flowers and shade trees and catches a good wind off the water. There's also a café about 70 feet from my campsite, a social enterprise run by a nonprofit that supports people with special needs through employment and other programs. I buy an iced latte and brownie and sink into a chair swing beside my tent.

A young man carrying a bottle of soda approaches.

"Can I join you?" he asks.

"Of course," I reply, sliding to my left.

We introduce ourselves — I'll call him Steve — and he says that he comes here every day to look at the canal. Sometimes he goes fishing or kayaking, but mostly he sits and looks at the water. We shoot the breeze, and my read on Steve shifts from client of the agency that runs the café to friendly guy who enjoys telling strangers about his hometown.

The woman who greeted me at the welcome center wanders over.

"You all settled? Anybody bothering you?" she asks me with a wink.

"Well, Steve's been bothering me, but just a little bit."

His laughter begins immediately.

We clink coffee and cola.

An hour later, I dress up for dinner — i.e., put on the *other* shirt — and paddle across the canal to a restaurant to meet my high school best friend for the first time in nearly 30 years.

Rob, the guy I drove to California with when I was a teenager, is now a law and public policy professor at SUNY Brockport. We drifted apart after graduation and reconnected online during the pandemic. I found out he lives just south of the canal and threatened to drop by if I was ever in the neighborhood. Now here I am. And there he is, with Martha, his wife, at a high top in the corner.

After talking to so many new people over the past few weeks, it feels normal to catch up over food and drink with a guy I haven't seen in decades. There are traces of our shared history, coupled with the surge of curiosity I get when meeting somebody new. Martha and Rob look relaxed together. He's a Chinese-Canadian atheist; she's an ex-Mormon whose still-practicing family have embraced her husband. When they visit Martha's parents, they do a lot of kayaking. Maybe it's a frequency illusion — or the beer — but water seems like a conduit to contentment.

I babble something about the connective spirit of water and Rob reminds me, in that vein, that the Erie Canal was also a conduit for Mormonism. A heavy cast-iron printing press was barged up from New York City to Palmyra, one village west of here, where the Book of Mormon was produced and then shipped far and wide. Then he leans forward and tells me that a wave of settlers in this part of the state were among the world's first climate refugees.

Have you heard of the Tambora volcano eruption? I hadn't either.

One of the largest volcanic events ever documented — more powerful than Krakatoa, 10 times more powerful than Pinatubo — the 1815 explosion in what is now Indonesia sent enough ash and pollutants into the air to destabilize societies around the globe. Nearly 40,000 people near ground zero were killed; hundreds of thousands starved to death. Crops failed in Asia and Europe, spurring a mass migration from the U.K. to the U.S. In New England, however, where many landed, 1816 was known as "the year without a summer." Snow fell in several East Coast states and provinces that June and July. It was the worst harvest ever recorded on the continent, prompting tens of thousands of people from the northeast to move deeper into the interior, including Western New York and the fertile farmland here in Wayne County. That influx, according to historian Wolfgang Behringer, who wrote a book about Tambora, helped make the case for the Erie Canal. "President Thomas Jefferson had rejected the idea as pointless, since the canal only led to wilderness," he writes. "Thanks to the shock of the Tambora crisis... the project was able to go ahead."

That night, I dream about rivers of lava and plumes of ash and awake to thunder.

Storm clouds amass. Humidity builds. Big rain is coming. Fortuitously, echoing my uncannily timed respite with relatives on the Hudson, I've got a few days' rest ahead. It's less than 10 miles to Palmyra, where a couple I've never met are going to pack me into their van and take me home.

First, after de-SUPing at the village dock, I walk up to Main Street and duck out of the sticky morning into a small museum. This three-story red-brick building is where the first copies of the Book of Mormon were printed in 1829. Joseph Smith, the religion's founder, had a series of visions near Palmyra. He established the first Mormon church about 30 miles to the southeast. But here in the Grandin Building, where a teenaged docent in a long dress is showing visitors a restoration of the original printing press, thousands of copies of the book were typeset, printed and bound, then set loose on the Erie Canal. When the Mormons were run out of town, the canal helped Smith and his followers move farther west.

I accept a reproduced signature of pages from the first edition Book of Mormon — "and now if there be fault, it be the mistake of men" — and embark upon my own mission. Find a dollar store and purchase sunglasses, my seventh pair of the trip. (Yes, all of the broken sunglasses were the fault of Dan.)

Back at the dock, Beth and Rick Walker pull into the parking lot right on schedule. They live about 10 minutes away and, along with one of their four adult daughters, Sara, are volunteer canal stewards. Beth and Sara also kayaked the length of the canal in stages a couple years ago and agreed to share advice before my trip. "Just let us know,"

Beth had said during our call, "if you need anything when you're passing through."

There's a roof rack atop the van for my board and a menagerie of animals to meet at their farmhouse: tiny foster kittens rummaging around a mud room, a big old golden retriever, three more cats, two turtles. Outside in the chicken coop, Beth corrals a handful of fresh eggs. She's tall with short gray hair and an unflappable demeanor. Rick is short — my height — and has a gentle temperament that calls to mind my grandfather. Beth is a math professor, Rick a retired project manager who served on submarines in the Navy, and Sara — who joins us for dinner on the covered veranda as sheets of rain fall — is a palliative care social worker. Other than the canal, we don't have much in common, but they feel like family already.

Sara was 10 when they moved into this house, and she started walking and biking on the towpath with her parents and sisters. Even though they were canoe campers, it didn't occur to them to paddle on the Erie. When Sara got a kayak, she was drawn to wilder creeks. But after years of driving across and walking along the canal, they decided to get onto the water.

"It didn't feel exciting at first," Sara says as we sit at a round table, plates heaped with pasta and salad. "But then we started to think about the extent of it, as something that reaches across the whole state."

The end-to-end voyage with her mother started in spring 2018 and ended in fall 2020. They did day-long legs with two cars, or Rick would do drop-offs and pickups, plus a couple of multiday outings on stretches with waterside B&Bs.

"We didn't prepare, we didn't train," says Beth. "We just wanted to paddle together."

The trio became volunteer stewards in 2021 when the program was launched. They had fallen in love with the canal, and despite navigating a new mother/adult-daughter dynamic on their trip had not fallen out of love with each other, so they wanted to remain involved. The role entails tasks like collecting garbage and cutting back weeds at boat launches along a seven-mile stretch, from Lyons to Newark.

The women kayak for a few hours picking up trash, with Rick trailing in a canoe. "I'm the garbage barge," he sighs.

From the water they have removed chairs, duck decoys, fishing line, lures, bait containers, pieces of Styrofoam and so, so many plastic bottles. "There's something very satisfying about picking up random garbage," says Rick, "and realizing that the next boater or paddler who comes through isn't going to have to look at it."

They also leave cards with their names and phone numbers at lock stations and visitor centers, encouraging travelers to call if they need help. But what compelled them to provide a malodorous voyageur with room and board?

"What are the odds," Rick deadpans, "of having two serial killers around the same table?"

Beth: "It's just what you do."

Rick: "We've always been the types who if there's something we can do, we just do it. Extending hospitality to a stranger just feels right."

Beth: "It's not without risk on either part, but we've never been burned by it. And you have to give up control in a way. You can't get back to the water without us. There's no Uber out here. There's a lot of power you give up; that's hard for a lot of people. People tend to be much more willing to offer help than to accept it."

It's raining ever harder the next day, so, not shy about accepting help, I stay a third night. We leave my paddleboard on top of the van, deflating it slightly so the air pressure doesn't spike in the heat. When Beth runs some errands, the SUP begins to oscillate as she drives down a secondary highway, then rips the roof rack off the top of the vehicle, flying into a ditch. There's a small scratch on the nose of the board, but no other damage.

"That," Beth says, inspecting the SUP with relief and admiration, "is one bad fish."

CHAPTER 23

"Our story was born out of self-protection. The public's perception of the homeless immediately assumes drink, drugs and mental health issues, and prompts fear. The first few times we'd been asked how it was that we had time to walk so far and so long, we had answered truthfully: 'Because we're homeless, we lost our home, but it wasn't our fault. We're just going where the path takes us.' People recoiled and the wind was silenced by their sharp intake of breath. . . . So we had invented a lie that was more palatable. For them and us. We had sold our home, looking for a midlife adventure, going where the wind took us — at the moment it was blowing us west."

— Raynor Winn, The Salt Path

SUNDAY MORNING. THE LORD'S DAY. PADDLING AWAY FROM MY GUARDIAN angels, I'm moving like a creaky old man after 48-plus hours of repose. But as if by providence, the sky is clear and the air cool and I fall into a metronomic cadence, gliding through the epicenters of the polished, manicured towns of Fairport and Pittsford.

People jog, ride high-end bikes and walk purebred dogs on the towpath in these prosperous Rochester bedroom communities. The waterside homes are immaculate, the restaurants pricey. (Yesterday afternoon, at the packed Lock 32 Brewing Company, Pittsford's mayor told me that an article in luxe *Food & Wine* magazine dubbed this section of canal "upstate Europe" when the pandemic forced a best-selling author to slum it and vacay on domestic waters.) This feels like an Erie Canal theme park, complete with tour boats, but it gets people to the water, another glimpse of what could be.

A couple hours later, as the canal curls around southeastern Rochester, nobody else is on the water. Sheer walls, some overgrown with vegetation, the start of a shale ledge that was once an ancient seabed. Chain-link fences, highways and the hum of traffic overhead: it feels like I shouldn't be here. Although when I startle a woman fishing under a bridge and her container of bait tumbles into water, and I grab it and hold it up to her on a paddle, she proclaims, "You're a lifesaver!"

There are, however, plenty of people on the trails that parallel the canal through the city. And to the west, as the terrain morphs from built-up to suburban to linear park, there are throngs of people, many of whom are not white. Packs of Black cyclists on road bikes rip past, tires whirring atop fine gravel. Latino families barbecue and blast Spanish-language hip-hop, vocals and bass lines popping. A multiracial upstate utopia.

Then: alligators!

Hundreds of green creatures dead ahead, coming my way.

Also: police cars, flashing lights, cheering crowds and helmeted swimmers in survival suits thrashing toward me.

I paddle hard to the left bank, grab onto a railing and watch the finale of the Canaligator Race, a fixture at the Canal Days festival in Spencerport. Pay a few bucks to sponsor a small plastic gator; win a prize if your reptile performs well. The neon-green racers are dumped into the water off a bridge and ushered toward the finish line by volunteer firefighters.

The festival also features a carnival on a field just above the village dock, which is where Simon Devenish, who runs the local tourism bureau, has secured permission for me to camp.

Figuring that anywhere thousands of people line the canal to yell at plastic alligators is fairly safe, I stack my board and bags beside a tree and zigzag through the crowd to the Spencerport Depot & Canal Museum.

Simon, an Aussie transplant, shows me around the former trolley station and invites me to a bonfire he and his wife are hosting tonight.

In a compact community like this, everything is within walking distance, including a Texas-style barbecue joint that my mother directs me to after I tell her my whereabouts. There's also a convenient gas station with a swiveling rack of sunglasses, where I buy pair number eight, having already stepped on my Palmyra purchase.

I explain my Sisyphean predicament to the young dreadlocked clerk.

"Man, I know what you mean," he says. "I keep busting my headphones. I've had like five pairs in the last five years."

"Eight pairs in two months for me."

"Do better," he says, shaking his head.

There must be some magic in the air, because as of this writing I still have the same jaunty red sunglasses.

Logs crack and spit embers from the firepit in Simon's fenceless backyard. Lawn chairs, a beer fridge in the garage, neighbors coming and going, playful teasing and banter. Randy from next door tells me that his great-grandfather helped build the canal. "I've got just one question about what you're doing," he says. "Why?"

Why? The farther I get, the better I understand that I'll never fully know. But over the next few days, a veritable receiving line of strangers drum home the idea that my initial motivations for departing no longer matter.

While bunking with the Walkers, Rick drove me into Rochester so I could be the guest on an NPR radio call-in show. That coverage, plus John Kucko's social media, plus a few stories in small-town newspapers, mean I'm no longer a weird guy paddleboarding the wrong way up the Erie Canal. I'm a weird guy people are *expecting*, which ratchets up the string of affirmations, like Matt Donahue's hug on the back of his boat on repeat. Beneath bridges, on bits of weedy grass, amid rusted-out cars and train tracks, atop concrete blocks and soggy easy chairs, there are people — and most of them want to acknowledge that we are out here together on this resplendent strip of blue, a fleeting verbal thread that connects us both to something bigger than the sum of any one soul, every salutation a pinprick of hope.

"Dan the man!" a boater exclaims the next morning.

"You that Dan guy?" asks another.

"You got this," a woman with a fishing rod says, smiling. "Seventy-five miles to go."

"Are you traveling on *that*?" a teenaged cyclist inquires.

"Pedal boat guy!"

"I'm proud of you, pal!"

West of Spencerport, the canal is lined by a grass-covered earthen berm. Sit-down kayakers and canoers might feel confined by this vantage, but I can see over the berm and am floating above a countersunk pastoral patchwork of farms and fields. People on the towpath take pictures and holler encouragement, like spectators in a slo-mo ultramarathon. There are even aid stations: little free libraries, water jugs and welcoming benches where cute bungalows abut the towpath. Appraised on their individual merits, none of these ephemeral encounters carry much weight. But add up these vignettes and views and my emotional well is full. As Art Cohn said on Lake Champlain, it's poetry, it's as good as it gets.

At Brockport, I take a break at the welcome center, and Susan Smith introduces me to her "cleaning group," a trio of young adult volunteers with developmental disabilities who are part of a "day-hab without walls" program run by a nonprofit. They pepper me with questions as we walk to the water together. ("We became buddies," Susan says on the phone a few months later when I ask her about the program. "They shared their worries and joys with me. You really get to know somebody when you're scrubbing floors together.")

Susan tells some friends about me, and eight miles past Brockport, as I paddle toward one of the lift bridges common on this part of the canal, a 60-something couple are waving over the railing. Sue Starkweather and Doug Miller drove here from the next village, Albion, just to say hello.

I tell Sue and Doug that I'm planning to stay in Albion, and they offer to meet me at their hometown landing with some snacks. I hesitate, contemplating a quiet night after yesterday's bonfire, then accept.

When I reach Albion, despite the sensation that I've been camping in canal towns since time immemorial, something feels off. Perhaps it's the furtive drug deal I see right after hauling my board onto shore. Or the fact I have to get the code to the bathroom door from a cop sitting behind protective glass after I get buzzed into the police station, which has a tank-like armored SWAT vehicle parked outside. Or the unhoused man sleeping in the bushes (though there's a fine line between being on a paddling trip and looking unhoused). Or the two scruffy white guys sitting in the nearby gazebo, who don't return my smiling hello and are probably harmless but score near the top of the menacing scale. Other than those plundering racoons way back in Oka, I haven't had a single hostile encounter on this entire trip. Could tonight be the pot of coal at the end of the rainbow? Am I — or is my stuff — at risk?

Paralyzed, I'm perched atop a picnic table, unsure whether I've got the guts to set up my tent but also unsure where else I might go. Then Sue and Doug arrive bearing dried fruits, nuts, a baggie of homemade cookies and a six-pack. We eat, drink and talk as the sun dips. Sue, the village historian, says that Albion was the original home of the Charles W. Howard Santa School, where, starting in 1937, a local farmer taught hundreds of men (and a few women) how to properly portray Saint Nick.

Sue and Doug's companionship feels like a Christmas gift. Scanning the near-dark park, I realize they probably came here to check on me. My gear is still in a pile beside the canal wall, the first stop where I'm not comfortable leaving it unattended.

"Is it safe to camp here?" I ask.

"Do you feel safe?" Sue replies.

"I'm not sure."

"We're not sure either."

Sue phones her brother, a former tugboat captain who lives directly across the water, and he lets me tent in his yard.

The love parade continues the next day, an effervescent kinship, as if emanating from the depths of the canal itself.

A couple sitting on their dock give me sandwiches and juice they had packed in case they saw me. I pose for photos, and people tell me about their own aquatic adventures, about relatives whose lives and livelihoods revolved around the waterway.

John Kucko tracks me down to shoot more video at the Medina Culvert, the only place where the Erie Canal flows over a road. "I should've brought my drone," he says. Maybe he's in cahoots with my mother?

Three miles later, in the village of Medina, a man recommends a diner just up the hill from the harbor, and I make a beeline for Captain Kidz. When I ask for my bill, the server points toward the guy from the dock, sitting at a booth in the corner, and says it's been taken care of.

After lunch, back on my board, a middle-aged man with a gray brush cut leans over a bridge to take my picture.

"See you soon," he says.

"Pardon me?"

"I'm Tom."

"Uh, Tom?"

"Thomas Bruggman."

"Oh!"

Tom and I have been corresponding for a few days. He got in touch after seeing my story online, told me about the indie campground he runs beside the canal in Gasport and offered to pick me up at the neighboring marina. "See you soon," I say.

Now there's a guy in a kayak with a wide grin speeding directly toward me.

"I'm Gary. Tom's friend. Reckoned you might want some company."

Gary pivots his boat and falls into pace beside me. For five miles, the distraction of making conversation is a salve for my depleted muscles. We glide into the marina where Tom is waiting with his pickup truck, adorned with a logo he designed, the silhouette of a sasquatch walking betwixt a stand of evergreens. Five minutes later I'm cracking open a can of Yuengling outside his RV at Tomtuga, the trippiest campground I've ever seen (and committed, sight unseen, to spending a night at).

A 15-foot-tall skeleton hangs at the entrance to the two-acre property, wearing a T-shirt with the Tomtuga logo. There's another branded oversized skeleton sitting in a rowboat beside a small pond. Giant white plastic cubes are scattered around; they light up in a rainbow of colors after it gets dark. "It's like Tortuga, the pirate island off the coast of Haiti, except my name is Tom," my host says, decoding the nomenclature. "It's the pirate island of Gasport, even though we were landlocked until the Erie Canal came through."

When he bought the place three years ago, Tom removed dozens of abandoned vehicle carcasses, leveled the ground and installed electrical outlets. His plans include purchasing a few old cigarette boats to use as cabins for guests and a decommissioned tugboat to repurpose as a pirate-themed ice cream parlor on his canal frontage. (Staff will wear pirate shirts, of course, and carry pretend flintlock pistols.) A seldom-used train track, belonging to a regional short line railroad, crosses the back of the lot. "I'm an emergency backup Santa on the Polar Express," Tom says, telling me about a local Christmas tradition for kids that involves a train excursion from a museum in Medina to a stand-in for the North Pole here in Gasport.

He seems like a big kid, a dreamer, so it's no surprise when he reveals that he's an admirer of P. T. Barnum, the greatest showman. "You need some razzmatazz," Tom says, "to sell the canal to people."

Gary joins me on the water in the morning. We paddle half a dozen miles to a snack bar, where he buys me a hot dog and milkshake, hands me a bag of homemade beef jerky and turns back. (Yes, we hug. And yes, I can't stop eating.)

A mile ahead, at Lockport, a pair of massive concrete locks lift me 60 feet up the Niagara Escarpment. Replacing the original flight of five locks, this is the last set of locks on the Erie, and a melancholic feeling descends as I paddle on, alone again, into the hazy afternoon. When Gary joined me yesterday, my instinctive thought was that I didn't want to make small talk. Fleeting chin-wags are fine, but sustained conversation can be a chore when you're tuckered out. Now I miss the fellowship. I've generally stolen away on long trips solo. Maybe there's something to be said for having an accomplice.

West of Lockport, the engineered canal joins Tonawanda Creek, whose banks are heavily forested and devoid of people. Outside a half-finished house, one of the few folks I see tells me he recently moved back to this part of New York to live on the water. "The world is going to shit," he says, "so I might as well have some fun."

It's nearly dusk when I reach the marina whose owner gave me permission to camp. But I don't realize, walking up from the dock, that the mulleted man who looks like Joe Exotic from *Tiger King*, sitting in an open-sided party tent surrounded by a pile of empty Budweiser cans, is also one of the owners.

"Who the fuck are you?" he demands.

My glassy-eyed interlocutor — let's call him Fred — warms up when I tell him my story and insists that I join him for a Bud. "Before you set up your tent," he says, more command than request.

I'm tired and just want to shower and eat and sleep, but I'm on foreign turf and don't want to be provoke Fred, so I sit and listen to his increasingly slurred stories. About how this marina was going to shut down 30 years ago, so members pooled their money and bought it. Very cool. About living on his boat and all the weed he smokes. Less cool. About "witching hour" on the water, late afternoon on weekends, when boaters reach peak drunkenness. About how he winters in Florida but hates Miami. "It's a little too *dark* for my liking," he winces theatrically. "A little too *dark*."

The more he talks, the more indignant he gets. Fred keeps circling back to me being permitted to camp here without his blessing. "We'll figure out how you can pay. We'll figure something out."

"For sure," I reply, distressed by where Fred's incoherent thought-wave might lead. "We'll figure something out."

When he gets up to retrieve more beer from his boat, I blabber something about needing to make some calls and thank him for his hospitality. Then I walk briskly to the far corner of the property to camp, nervously glancing back toward Fred's boat. At this Bud-alcohol level, he seems like more of a fall-asleep-in-chair type than someone prone to aggressive outbursts. But a seafaring life doesn't always becalm, and he may be no stranger to the latter. I tiptoe toward the washroom to shower and hear snoring from the party tent. And leave promptly at dawn, before any accounting.

The run down the rest of Tonawanda Creek is quick, and there's a green-and-white highway sign on the water just before it spills out into the Niagara River: Buffalo and Lake Erie are written in block letters, with an arrow pointing left.

I head south, upstream on the Niagara, tight to the eastern side. The current is strong: the Niagara is one of the fastest flowing rivers in this part of the continent, racing toward the falls, about 10 miles to the northwest. It's a chore, but I make progress. When I reach the bottom of Grand Island, my wind buffer is gone and a fierce southwesterly hits me. My pace drops to about a mile an hour. My goal is the Black Rock Lock, which allows boats to skip the rapids under the international Peace Bridge; from there, I should have a more sheltered paddle into downtown Buffalo. But when I reach a park just north of the lock, I realize how pooched I am and decide, knowing that I'll be heading back down this river in a couple days, that there's no shame in calling an Uber.

CHAPTER 24

"I'm just one of those people who just doesn't want to be quiet anymore. It's not about ego. It's about saving what we have. Even if you can look out your window and see green trees and blue skies, it is diminishing. People need to realize that and look to the basic teachings. We need to think about what we're doing."

—*Joe Stahlman, cultural studies researcher and consultant*

DEPENDING ON WHO YOU ASK, THE ERIE CANAL EITHER STARTS OR ENDS IN Buffalo. Like so many things rooted in the past, it's a matter of perspective. Regardless, a historical plaque on the boardwalk overlooking the Buffalo River in the city's Canalside district marks the western terminus of the waterway.

A jumble of cranes, overpasses and gaping pits where skyscrapers will soon rise, Canalside is the heart of Buffalo's ongoing wholesale waterfront makeover. In recent decades, the confluence of the city's namesake river and Lake Erie was considered "the dark side of town where truckers went to refuel, grain scoopers grabbed a beer and street racers burned rubber on an empty stretch of highway," the local tourism bureau says with a splash of literary flair. Now it's "home to kayakers, paddleboarders, boaters, bikers and hikers — the site of a radical transformation from desolate to destination." And one of the best places to get a handle on this transformation is the

Longshed, a gabled-roof two-story wooden building modeled after the storehouse that stood at the start (or end) of the Erie Canal some 200 years ago.

Although the Longshed is destined to become a visitor center, when I arrive at Canalside in August 2023, it's home to the biggest project that the Buffalo Maritime Center has ever undertaken. The nonprofit, whose mission is to inspire meaningful connections through community boatbuilding and the preservation of maritime culture, is leading the construction of a full-sized replica of the *Seneca Chief*, the first vessel to transit the Erie Canal in 1825 as part of a celebratory four-boat flotilla that departed Buffalo that October. Taking shape in a welcoming public space, with barn doors rolled wide open and a viewing mezzanine above, the boat-to-be is scheduled to retrace that original journey in fall 2025.

Governor DeWitt Clinton was the guest of honor on the inaugural 10-day voyage. When the *Seneca Chief* reached New York Harbor, he poured a keg of Lake Erie's finest H_2O over the side of the boat, symbolically "wedding the waters" and linking the Great Lakes with the Atlantic.

Commemorating the bicentennial of such colonial bulldozery is inherently tricky. On one hand, despite overwhelming obstacles, the Erie Canal was a resounding success. To recap: it cut the cost of freight by 90 percent and shortened the trip for passengers traveling between Albany and Buffalo from two weeks to five days. It's the main reason New York City became the biggest metropolis and busiest port in the United States. It also carried ideas, as travelers conveyed news and disseminated movements. Many historians say the canal was key to the formation of an American identity. "Built with a combination of vision, determination, ingenuity and hard work," a typical account reads, "the Erie Canal solidified these central elements of our American character."

Then there's the other hand.

The attempted erasure of Indigenous Peoples, whose traditional territories the canal steamrolled through. The deaths of more than 1,000 of the roughly 50,000 workers who built the canal: enough trench collapses, drownings, accidental explosions and malaria to cement the canal a spot among the 10 most dangerous construction projects ever around the world. And the environmental consequences of wedding the waters, which continue to play out today.

When Buffalo Maritime Center executive director Brian Trzeciak rolled up his sleeves for the *Seneca Chief* replica, the former toy designer and teacher — tidy beard, tattoos peeking out from his golf shirt — knew that the project couldn't simply celebrate the canal. "We didn't want to just repeat the dominant narrative," he tells me. We're sitting on a bench near the Longshed on a sunny morning with the bustle of activity inside — a dozen or so volunteers measuring and trimming white oak planks around a whale-sized wooden skeleton — harkening back to an era when this shoreline was a hopping commercial strip. "New York State wasn't an empty wilderness when Europeans arrived. There were people here already. The Erie Canal was built on broken treaties. DeWitt Clinton wasn't a hero. There shouldn't be a hero. There should be a *story*."

One of Brian's early challenges was finding out why the first boat to travel the canal was given such an appropriative (or inappropriate) name. So he cold-called cultural studies researcher Joe Stahlman, a member of the Tuscarora Nation and, at the time, director of the Seneca-Iroquois National Museum.

"We're building a replica of the *Seneca Chief*," Brian said to Joe. "Do you have any idea why it was called that?"

Joe's reply, according to Brian: "Oh Jesus. Here we go."

But that phone call was a catalyst. Joe, who was born in Niagara Falls, New York, and grew up in Texas, had first read about the Erie Canal's impact on Indigenous Peoples as an undergraduate student. Most of what he first encountered came from white "experts," starting with the books of Laurence M. Hauptman. Relying on this official record, Joe saw the canal and the progress that it represented as part of a continuum driven by the hunger for more western lands, by Manifest Destiny and the Doctrine of Discovery. But he also saw that, despite the violence, lies and trickery forced upon them, Haudenosaunee

Nations had managed to hang onto some of their lands and keep alive their belief systems and cultural traditions.

Joe became a consultant to the replica project and dove into additional research. He wasn't able to find out conclusively why the name *Seneca Chief* had been chosen. But he learned more about Clinton's complicated involvement with Indigenous communities, including his acquisition of "choice lots" on Seneca Lake, a prominent geographical feature that could be connected to the boat's name (and may be one of the earliest examples of shady real estate speculation in the state). A lifelong politician with an underlying interest in anthropology, Clinton derided the Haudenosaunee as "roving barbarians and savage beasts," while at the same admiring their military prowess, oratory power and closeness to "the sublime scenery of nature." The governor believed the Haudenosaunee would one day vanish from the landscape — he saw this as an "inevitable tragic loss," Joe writes — and may have christened his boat the *Seneca Chief* "as a stinging honor towards the people pushed aside."

The *Noah's Ark*, which joined the *Seneca Chief* in the inaugural flotilla, was another sting. Among its cargo of animal pairs (two bear cubs, two eagles, two fawns and so on) were two Seneca boys. The boat was only partially named after the patriarch chosen by God to perpetuate the human race after the flood; it was also a nod to Mordecai Noah, a Jewish journalist and politician from New York City who wanted to establish a refuge for his people on Grand Island, on the Niagara River north of Buffalo, where the Erie-era ark was outfitted.

There is no record, Joe tells me, of what happened to the two boys.

After Brian leaves, Joe joins me outside the Longshed. He drives us to a coffee shop, which requires approximately 17 turns over three blocks to reach thanks to the maze of construction throughout Canalside. Then we get lost trying to find the underground café, requiring three stops to ask for directions while wandering around the plaza at the base of an office tower, including one exchange in Spanish with a construction worker from Nicaragua who shrugs a suggestion: "Internet?"

Upon finally securing our coffees, we sit on a downtown street where cars have been displaced by a light rail line. I admit that although I usually brag about my innate sense of direction, I'm having trouble finding my way around Buffalo after so much time on the canal. Our search for the café notwithstanding, Joe tells me that he has no problem navigating urban environments. "We're people of the city now," he says, long dark hair tucked behind his ears, a concise urgency in his words. "When you live in a place like this, you learn where the bus stops and subway lines are. You learn the grid."

Five years ago, when Joe moved back to New York, he had to get used to the Great Lakes. He had left as a kid and grew up near reservoirs and rivers in Texas, swimming and fishing and trekking through the scrublands. Returning east, looking out over Lake Erie, the power of the water was mesmerizing. "It's not a mystical thing," he says when I ask about the connection between Indigenous Peoples and blue space. "You understand it because you use it. You understand what the currents are like, when the fish come, how the winds behave. It's not being close to nature in some animalistic way. It's just having reverence and respect for where you live."

For too long, Joe says, we have believed that water washes away all the dirty things we do. "But actually, water holds all of our dysfunction. It shows when our behaviors are terrible and we need to change. If we can't even drink the water, then we can't even live."

"It's not just the Erie Canal that's important," he continues. "All of our connections to land, water, animals, plants and each other are important. I see how the communities that I'm part of, whether through blood or working relationships, I see how we're being removed from the worldview that our ancestors had, and that's making me sad. That Western influence on our lives is really individualized, and it's making us feel disconnected from one another and from the planet that gives us all life."

So when we talk about equality, when we talk about sustainability, when we talk about health and homelessness and hunger, we also, he says, need to talk about basic teachings, about seven generations. About the fact that we shouldn't expect to live in constant comfort — 23 degrees Celsius (73 Fahrenheit) on the thermostat, burning fossil fuels year-round to hit that sweet spot, even though exposure to cold is actually good for us — because we didn't evolve through artificially steady conditions but through harsh ones in which we worked together.

"One of the major lies that capitalists tell us is that we need an economy to survive as a species, when in fact we have survived for 99 percent of our time on this planet without economies," Joe says. "It's the *relationships* we have with one another and with the natural world that have gotten us to this point, and we've done it collectively, holding each other up and helping each other through the hard times. It's not individuals pulling themselves up by their bootstraps and making a million dollars who have pushed us forward. It's our grandmothers and grandfathers and mothers and fathers and brothers and sisters who have gotten us here, and we've forgotten that."

Joe doesn't know what the future of the Erie Canal might hold. But he thinks adhering to the American Dream should mean taking on a responsibility to know what your forebears did. And that beyond doing what he can to nurture a fuller understanding of the past, his participation is about relationship building. "If Americans want to keep the Erie Canal around, we have to find a new purpose for it. We need to help it grow in different ways. Let's make it more than what it is. Let's give it meaning.

"I don't know what this entails," he continues. "It's not *my* vision. I'm not trying to drive the car. I just want to open a door."

Brian Trzeciak wants to hold that door open, stressing that the Buffalo Maritime Center is not re-creating but instead revisiting the journey of the *Seneca Chief*. By linking the city to its maritime past in an open-minded way, the center hopes to play a broader, progressive role in the regional cultural fabric.

"We're not applauding the Erie Canal. We want to talk about its origins and impacts, good and bad. Two hundred years later, we have a chance to do something right. We always apologize for what happened in the past: 'It was a different time, they didn't know any better.' I don't want those excuses anymore. We're changing the narrative. The wedding of the waters is going to be the wedding of the cultures. We're aware of what was lost and of the responsibility to incorporate different perspectives, to go forward in a different way."

CHAPTER 25

"However tightly we pack our waste, wherever we ship it, however we divvy the blame, there's no distancing ourselves from the fact that the earth is in pain. By turn, so are we. Or, as the cyberneticist Gregory Bateson says, 'You decide that you want to get rid of the by-products of human life and that Lake Erie will be a good place to put them. You forget that the eco-mental system called Lake Erie is part of your wider eco-mental system — and that if Lake Erie is driven insane, its insanity is incorporated in the larger system of your thought and experience.'"

— Chris Dombrowski, The River You Touch

SPEAKING OF GOING FORWARD IN A DIFFERENT WAY, LET'S GET BACK TO paddleboarding because there's something else I want to tell you about Brian Trzeciak. In his spare time, he builds beautiful custom SUPs. Brian's involvement with the Buffalo Maritime Center began, he divulges, when he went looking for a place to work on a board.

More than a cool surprise, this is also a significant discovery. During my approach to Buffalo, paddling the westernmost section of the Erie Canal, almost everybody I chatted with inquired about my route back into Canada. And almost everybody cautioned me about the Niagara River, whose notoriously fast northward currents — as well as that little waterfall you may have heard of — are apparently rather dangerous. (The river basically pours Lake Erie into Lake

Ontario, a tiny constriction for so much flow.) Citing a pair of fairly recent fatal accidents, boater after boater urged me to bypass the rapids beneath the Peace Bridge and use the Black Rock Lock, on the American side of the river, to make my way north.

Amid that salvo of warnings, I kept digging for a detailed scouting report. Did I really need to use the lock if the current would be propelling me — at about five miles an hour — in the right direction? An experienced whitewater paddler, I wasn't worried about rapids or waves. But I didn't want to drown. So I solicited information from a Canadian kayaker who had posted trip reports online and thought my plan sounded doable; from Gary and Tom in Gasport, who were touchingly concerned about my safety; from the lock tender in Lockport, who lives on the Niagara River and didn't see any cause for concern; from Bud-swilling Fred at that marina on Tonawanda Creek, who said he might just fire up the fuckin' boat right then and give me a lift, goddammit; from a guy at the kayak rental kiosk just down the boardwalk from the Longshed and that guy's kayak guide friend, whom he phoned on my behalf. She looked up my proposed route on a paddling app. It didn't indicate any glaring risks. Still, I wanted to be sure, so when Brian tells me about his SUP-making side gig, I barrage him with questions. He also kayaks, I learn, and is the only person I talked to who had actually paddled under the Peace Bridge. And he tells me that I'll be fine.

At dawn the next morning, I pack up my dry bags in my hotel room across the street from the Longshed, pile them onto a luggage cart, lug them from the lobby to the start-slash-end of the Erie Canal, pump up my board and push off from shore.

Despite Brian's reassurance, I'm apprehensive about the fast and choppy flow ahead, about breaching an international border on a stretch of water that so many others told me to avoid. I don't want to become the first paddleboarder ever to boof over the lip of Niagara Falls. I don't want my mother to know where I am.

With a mild east wind at my back, I cross the neck of Lake Erie back into Canada for the first time in six weeks. Then the current takes hold of my board, pulling me beneath the Peace Bridge as I paddle vigorously not for speed but to keep the SUP's nose pointed north. The rapids are a fairly tame romp. All that fretting over a few minutes of fun? I shoot out from beneath the bridge and pull into an eddy to rest. "You went under there on *that*?" fishing guide Denis Kreze says from his boat, pointing at the bridge. "Right on."

The rest of the run is smooth and fast, 20 miles in just over four hours. When the river curves left around the tip of Navy Island, I hear a low roar and see plumes of spray rising above Niagara Falls less than two miles away. The current, which had waxed and waned with the depth and width of the channel, intensifies. My sympathetic nervous system kicks into gear. I can feel my heart pumping inside my chest and the muscles in my neck and shoulders tensing. But I'm tight to the Canadian shore — another piece of advice from everyone I had consulted, one that I heeded — and slip under a pedestrian bridge into the fast-flowing Welland River, beyond which it is illegal (and Darwin Award worthy) for watercraft to continue.

A couple minutes later, I tie my board to a public dock and phone the Canada Border Services Agency for permission to reenter the country that I have already reentered. Even though boaters are allowed to self-report upon arrival, the agent who takes my call seems confused, initially by my location — "Internet?" I suggest when she asks how to confirm my coordinates — and then by my mode of travel. (I also note that I'm adjacent to a Tim Hortons, which is a pretty useless landmark in Canada.) She puts me on hold repeatedly and asks a string of questions about my SUP: size, color, brand. It feels like I'm helping her choose which model to buy, so I enthusiastically recommend Badfish. And then, after nearly half an hour, she asks for my name and passport number, which I had assumed would have been the first two questions. Finally, I'm cleared, a process more challenging than the paddle. Why didn't anybody warn me about border bureaucracy?

It behooves me here to broach one of the fundamental character traits distinguishing Americans from Canadians. Two nautical border crossings comprise an admittedly small sample size, but there's a telling gulf between my experience in Rouses Point, New York — which can be boiled down to "Get over here! Where are you going? You're good to go!" — and the byzantine procedure at a porous border I could have casually crossed. Americans can be effusively open with random passersby; in five minutes, they'll tell you their life story and demand to know yours (especially if they're border guards). Even though we're by the book, the intimate corners of a Canadian psyche are often a closed book. And while we tend to regard our restrained manners as an admirable quality, in a world where people shy away from direct contact with strangers, I've found the in-your-face candor of our neighbors refreshing.

It's a sunny Saturday afternoon and a dozen or so people are milling about this parkette beside the Welland River, but nobody says a peep to me as I pack my gear and deflate my board. Then a small hatchback pulls up and a shaggy haired man steps out. He looks like he's been sleeping in the car. "I am Federico!" he declares immediately, reaching for my hand. "I live in Rome! I am driving across Canada and sleeping in car! Your name, what is it? Where are you going?"

Federico hung out at this spot yesterday, he tells me, collecting all the litte and trimming the weeds with a pair of scissors. Now he's dismayed that there's already more garbage on the ground. "In Italy, this place would be a gem!"

My friends Shauna and Jon Eben live in St. Catharines, not far from Niagara Falls, and they are gems, picking me up mid-heart-to-heart with Federico, pampering me at their house and, early the following morning, dropping me off at a beach on Lake Ontario.

On a map, the two-day paddle around the western tip of the lake from St. Catharines to Toronto looks relatively idiotproof. A 30-mile shot northwest along the southern shore to Burlington, at the end of the lake, and then another 30-plus miles northeast to Toronto. I've been covering these distances regularly throughout my trip, and there are no open crossings. A friend in Burlington is ready to host me for the night, and one of my brothers and his wife will be waiting for me in Toronto. The wind forecast is favorable: moderate but building from the east on the first day, and then steady but not too strong from the southwest on day two, which will push me (in theory, at least) more or less the way I want to go.

Considering the ease of my jaunt down the Niagara River, what can go wrong?

A lot, it turns out. Starting with hubris, because nothing falsely predicts the present quite like a comfortable past — a miscalculation many of us make daily.

Leaving St. Catharines, I can see the blurry Toronto skyline across the lake. As the crow flies, it's not much farther than Burlington. For a minute, paddling away from the beach with a gentle breeze at my back, I consider altering course and crossing the exposed open waters of Lake Ontario to the city where I was born — a dumb and potentially deadly idea, unless you wait for the right weather window or have boat support. Still, it's tempting. A feeling that vanishes within a couple hours as the wind picks up and shifts to my right side. The waves, which have nearly all of the lake's 200-mile fetch to develop, grow to three and then four and then five feet. Like the apocryphal frog that gets boiled alive, I don't notice the gradual increases and am now ensnared in a tempestuous cauldron.

Staying far enough from shore to avoid getting slammed into the rocks by breaking waves, yet close enough to remind myself that I'm not in the middle of an ocean, I paddle hard on my left side. For the first time since leaving home, I drop to my knees frequently for extra stability. And then, also for the first time since leaving home, even with my center of gravity low, a sneaky steep wave pitches me sideways off the SUP.

I hoist myself back onto the board, relieved that I kept my head above the surface and my sunglasses are still atop my hat; relieved that it's early August when Lake Ontario's often-frigid water temperature climbs above 70 degrees Fahrenheit (21 Celsius); and relieved that there's nobody nearby to witness my chagrin.

Then another wave sends me tumbling right back into the drink. Only this time, the paddleboard flips upside down too. A possibility, with all the weight on its deck, I had not once considered.

Bobbing beside my overturned SUP amid the swells, I take stock of the situation. I'm leashed to the board and wearing my PFD and was mindful enough before setting out to clip my dry bags to the elastic tie-down straps with carabiners, so there's no risk of anything getting lost, present company included. Worst-case scenario, I wash up on shore somewhere, maybe with a few bumps and bruises.

I swim to the SUP, put my hands beneath the near side and push skyward — a maneuver I have only attempted on an unburdened surfboard, but one that proves mercifully easy. The board is right side up, and it's a snap to shove my bags back into place.

Had it been more challenging to reconstitute my kit, I would probably have turned toward land and called it a day. The likelihood of capsizing again is high. But I don't think there's any real danger — yet — and am determined to keep going.

Back up on my feet, I have to focus on each wave as it crests, digging in with my paddle and keeping my core coiled low to remain upright and keep the SUP's nose pointed in the right direction. I don't know whether my legs are shaking because I'm frazzled or because I'm pooped or because I'm scared. These are the roughest waters I've ever paddled, the redline of my abilities, and I don't know what might happen next.

It's too undulant to eat or drink while paddling, my usual procedure on a long day. But luckily, earlier, I had spied two places for pit stops on the mostly rocky, privately owned shoreline: a picnic area in a protected inlet and a yacht club behind a breakwater. By late afternoon, after nearly eight hours of left-side paddling, and another three or four accidental plunges, I've made nearly 25 miles and am alongside Hamilton Beach, a sprawling park on the sandbar that spans the western end of Lake Ontario. A short canal halfway up the sandbar leads to my goal: the sheltered water of Burlington Bay and the marina a few minutes from my friend Alan's house.

Deciding to rest and refuel one last time and give my faltering nerves a break, I turn left and aim for Hamilton Beach. It's a holiday weekend, and though overcast and very windy, the sand is packed with families admiring the crashing waves. Shuffling toward the front of the SUP, I catch a swell as it peaks and rocket down the face, enjoying the ride ... and then wiping out near the shore as the board flips over. Once unclipped, I drag my dry bags from the surf so they don't get washed away. I look out at the waves pounding the beach (rather than at all of the people looking at me) and see a police boat hovering just offshore.

Realizing that I can't get back onto the lake — it'd be impossible to reload my board in the shallows, let alone get past the breakers — I begin to shuttle my gear away from the water. When I finally muster everything beside a bench, I'm trembling with exhaustion and adrenaline and a small, nascent taste of trauma.

That's when the police officer approaches.

"Do you know that boat is out there because of you?" he asks.

"I was kinda assuming that."

"People called about you. They saw you fall in a couple times."

I explain that falling in wasn't a big deal but concede that conditions are indeed dodgy.

"Should you be out there today?" he asks.

"I'm not sure."

"What's the plan now?"

"Call a friend."

"Good idea."

My decision to head into Hamilton Beach nags at me for the rest of the evening. I could have continued onward to the channel. I could have reached the bay behind the sandbar. Yet it had been the toughest paddle of my life, more difficult than any session on the Pacific or Atlantic; my body and brain needed a break. If I hadn't stopped, something bad could have happened. Granted, I wasn't in a remote wilderness. The people who had phoned the police were likely among the hundreds I saw barbecuing and lounging outside gorgeous lakefront homes. There were eyes on me all day; the rescue boat could have saved me. Still, was I putting them at risk needlessly? Should I have been out there?

My wise friend Alan suggests, after he and his wife, Suzanna, feed me dinner, that it was a good thing I had been pummeled. Yet another reminder that we're not really in control. Which is one of the reasons paddlers and other outdoorsy types do all sorts of dangerous things for no apparent reason. We want to be humbled and awed and remember that the universe doesn't care about what we want.

My journey into the densely populated heart of a continent isn't particularly dicey. But it scratches that itch for adventure. And it shows me that the water, amid all of the danger and destruction that it can unleash, is also still a place where people watch out for one another. Even for hapless knuckleheads like me.

There's a residual swell from the east when Alan delivers me to a small beach beside the pier in downtown Burlington. Waves still rising three or four feet. But the wind has dulled and blows from the southwest, so the rolling ridges of water are softer, gentler.

I'm laser-focused, right back on this horse, and make good time along the "west coast" of Lake Ontario. This entire stretch of shoreline is urban, development spurred by the opening in 1939 of the parallel Queen Elizabeth Way (QEW), North America's first controlled-access highway. "Throughout the 1950s, as car ownership became universal and suburbs took over the farmland, the perils of sprawl and congestion loomed ominously in the future," Ron Brown writes in a book about Lake Ontario's shoreline. "Today, with no open space left... and with the QEW almost constantly gridlocked, the future has arrived."

I follow a kayaker under an oil pipeline and into an Oakville marina, talking to Butch as I sit on the dock and snack, feet bucking up and down on my board. He's a kayak guide and was out on the lake yesterday. Butch saw a stream of boats motor past the breakwater and instantly retreat while he surfed wave after wave.

"Should I have been out there?" I ask.

"Sounds like you did fine and had some fun," he replies.

The swells diminish and so does the wind. I make 21 miles in six hours. Ten more miles to go.

Headway is slow, but soon I start to distinguish features, to recognize the city where I grew up. The CN Tower, apartment buildings and tony lakefront properties. It's a holiday Monday, and there are a lot of people on paths and in parks. Finally, I round the last promontory before the spot where my brother and his wife will retrieve me.

A surge of emotion hits. This isn't the end, but it's an end. The circle a little less broken. I tear up. But my sentimentality doesn't last. The waves from yesterday's swell and today's wind are bouncing off the breakwater that protects Sunnyside Beach. The lake is confused, snotty. My knees are like shock absorbers as the SUP bucks up and down. A mogul run to the finish line.

Laura and Ed are there. Hugs, shower, food, family. But it's a little hard to relate. Two days later, I'm still swaying.

PART IV

TORONTO TO OTTAWA

"I closed my eyes and listened. While I'm stimulated to no apparent end by the sight of rivers, it is their audible reverberations that strike the deepest chords. This must be what a monk feels when he hears the temple bell ring . . . this is the note the earth is ever sounding, calling me back to my wildest name."

— Chris Dombrowski, The River You Touch

"If we fail this test, there will be another one, and another after that, but each time the stakes will be higher and the price of failure steeper. . . . That there will be life at the end of the Petrocene Age is a certainty, but whose, and how much, and where is less clear."

—John Vaillant, Fire Weather

CHAPTER 26

"It's really interesting to sit at either Copacabana or Ipanema Beach in Rio, as kind of an anthropological study, and just watch how life goes by. You'll see all layers of society, shoulder to shoulder, enjoying the same space. Rarely are there any fights or disagreements. The poor and the rich are both happy just being in that environment. Last time I was home in Brazil, I went to the same beach every day to do a workout and meditate. I saw these two foreigners and I could tell they were European — they were pretty white. They brought a soccer ball. The first day I came, they were kicking it back and forth to one another. The second day, they picked up the local game and were trying to keep the ball in the air with their feet, chests and knees, like everybody around them was doing. The third day, they were playing with two kids from the slums."

— Antonio Lennert, founder of Surf the Greats

A THREE-MINUTE WALK EAST FROM THE HOUSE WHERE I GREW UP IN THE middle of Toronto there is a gap between a pair of properties where a mountain ash and copse of cedars shroud the entrance to a small hollow. Today, a paved path descends into this recess, but when I was a kid, it was a secret passage one could follow into a fully canopied ravine, a natural playground hidden from the eyes of adults. At the bottom of this saddle, channeled by culverts and wire cages containing coarse chunks of gray rock, there was water. I spent hours jumping over and splashing in these pools and riffles with friends, assembling dams and floating sticks down the current when the flow was fast in spring or after rain.

My childhood was innocent if not idyllic. Mind you, immigrant academic parents meant no organized hockey with my buddies and no TV in the house until I was a teenager. But my two brothers and I were given the freedom to explore, and though Mom and Dad might not be thrilled that "itinerant paddleboarder" is their middle son's career du jour, their love and support have never waned.

The old neighborhood, however, has changed. My parents' bungalow is one of few remaining originals in a sea of posh. Metastasizing square footage and double-wide driveways have diminished tree cover and the ground's ability to absorb rainfall. "For every percentage point increase in roads, parking lots and other impervious surfaces that prevent water from flowing into the ground," hydrology and geophysics researchers from Johns Hopkins University caution in a 2020 paper, "annual floods increase on average by 3.3%."

When capacious new homes were starting to colonize his community, my father spent several years fighting to ensure that zoning rules were enforced, a thorn in the side of bigger-is-better developers and buyers. Ma, a geophysicist, used to ask where the water would go. "What would these people do," I recall her saying one afternoon as drivers jockeyed aggressively for parking spaces outside the local Starbucks, "if they had to deal with any real problems?"

Although many of Toronto's ravines have been paved over, they still cover 17 percent of the city, the largest urban ravine network in the world. A "connected sanctuary," according to the official revitalization strategy for this system, that's "essential for . . . health and well-being." Toronto's ravines are akin to the canals of Venice and hills of San Francisco, Robert Fulford writes in *Accidental City*: "the heart of the city's emotional geography." Yet Torontonians "look at [their environment] in pieces and fail, through inattention, to see it whole."

Around the corner from my childhood bedroom, Burke Brook still flows into the Don River. If you cross a couple of major streets and cut through a condo complex, you can remain beside or within sight of the creek and reach a string of parks cradled between sloped woodlands of maple and cottonwood, sumac and walnut. This three-mile-long artery offers a sanctum from cars and other conveniences of the city. It also filters and transports stormwater, tamps down the area's temperature and gives biodiversity a little boost.

The Don watershed, 140 square miles and home to 1.4 million people, is among the most developed in the country. Like much of the planet, it contains multitudes of anthropogenic accelerant. But inhale the cool, earthy dampness down here in the dale. Close your eyes and listen to the chatter of robins and sparrows and the scampering of squirrels in the underbrush. You can forget topside long enough to recalibrate.

The wetlands at the mouth of the Don were fertile fishing grounds for the Wendat, an Iroquoian-language-speaking Nation who around eight centuries ago established villages on the north shore of Lake Ontario, the site of human activity for 15,000 years. Anishinaabe and Haudenosaunee Peoples also fished and hunted in what is now Toronto, and by the 1700s the Mississaugas of the Credit, a subgroup of the Anishinaabe Nation, settled around the western end of the lake.

Between 1781 and 1820, the Mississaugas of the Credit entered into eight treaties with the British, including the Toronto Purchase of 1805, expecting to share the land with settlers. But farms and communities curtailed their seasonal movement, diseases decimated their population, fish and game were depleted and their territory evaporated from 4,000,000 acres to 200.

Toronto's predecessor, the town of York, was established in 1793, which is right around when pollution began to poison the Don. Dozens of mills were constructed on the river, plus brickworks, tanneries, pork processors and eventually oil refineries. Chemical effluent, sewage and landfill seepage fermented into a brew that caught fire a couple times. In 1969, a fledgling environmental group held a mock funeral for the

Don, complete with a casket. Reported the *Toronto Telegraph*, "Judging from the smell of the 'deceased,' it was long overdue."

But like the Hudson in miniature, Canada's "most messed-with river," described thusly by historian Jennifer Bonnell, is being nursed back to health. Although the Don Valley is bifurcated by a freeway and squeezed betwixt developments, stronger environmental regulations and practices, including tree planting and habitat restoration, have induced salmon to return, so, too, scores of human visitors. The lower Don is being re-naturalized as part of a billion-dollar project that involves new flood management infrastructure, a reengineered delta that frees the waterway from the concrete corridor it had been funneled into since the 1880s, and the creation of green space where people can gather in the formerly industrial port lands. (A subsidiary of Google's parent company was granted approval to build a "smart neighborhood" in the midst of this waterfront redo but ultimately pulled the plug. The company blamed economic uncertainty; concerns about data privacy were also a factor. The latter never seems to deter my mother.)

In concert with its Great Lakes siblings, Lake Ontario's ecological trajectory mirrors that of the Don. A century ago, commercial, urban and agricultural runoff fed massive algal blooms and rendered the water increasingly unsafe for drinking and swimming. In the Southwestern Ontario town of Walkerton, seven people died from drinking tap water tainted with animal waste in 2000. That *E. coli* outbreak spurred environmental lawyer Mark Mattson to cofound Lake Ontario Waterkeeper and adopt Robert F. Kennedy Jr.'s tactics: investigate and drag offenders to court. Now called Swim Drink Fish, the group has continued to advocate for environmental protection and equitable access to blue space, in particular during the COVID-19 pandemic, along Toronto's nearly 30 miles of lakefront. The law is a tool for cleaning up polluted waters, Mark said to me during a lockdown phone interview, but encouraging personal relationships with nature is the key to lasting change.

The city is taking many progressive steps to get people to the shore, but there have been stumbles, such as the provincial government's controversial move, in 2023, to privatize a popular parcel of waterfront parkland. Ontario Place, where a glitzy new spa is being built, was one of the few childhood connections I had to the lake. (Swamp Thing mad!) I went there on countless school field trips and, as a teenager, for free outdoor concerts. I remember looking across the blue-green vastness of Lake Ontario at smudges of land on the far shore. St. Catharines, probably. Watering a seed, perhaps.

It's only in recent years, whenever I'm back home to see family, that I've started to venture down the Don to the lake. Depending on where I'm staying and how much time I have, I will walk, run or SUP along some of these waterfronts. A needle in an ancient groove. A dose of revirescence, making me feel fresh and young again.

Although I'm from Toronto, the first time I ever paddled in the city was only a few years ago, when I mapped out a route with intel from Antonio Lennert, who has eased thousands of people back to Lake Ontario. A surfer from Brazil, Antonio was surprised how few folks he saw in the water after moving here in 2008. The elevated highway running across downtown was a physical separation. "Toronto had turned its back on the lake," he says, "and forgot what it had."

People told Antonio to go "up north" to cottage country if he wanted to swim. But immigrants like him rarely have access to a cottage. "I've been to, like, five cottages in 15 years," he says.

Despite the Great Lakes tradition of dumping what you don't need down the communal drain, newcomers congregated on the lakeshore to picnic, play soccer and splash around. Swim Drink Fish confirmed that the water quality was decent, so Antonio dove in.

After discovering that one can surf on any of the Great Lakes, Antonio opened a surf and SUP store in Toronto in 2016 with a culture radically different than the scene he had experienced in Brazil. Rife with localism, territoriality and occasional outbreaks of violence, surfing wasn't kind to a young man who knew he was gay by age 14. Since its inception, the vibe at Surf the Greats has been pure inclusivity, a queer-friendly, anti-macho space that hosts events such as beach cleanups and screenings of surf films directed by women, in addition to selling gear and teaching people about water safety.

The physical shop closed its doors in spring 2024. Consumer habits had changed, Antonio had earned an MBA and wanted to coach other entrepreneurs, and his partner in life and business had passed away. He was ready to move on. Nonetheless, he showed that it's possible to nudge a heel-dragging ethos in a new direction. "It was very important to create a community where I could belong," he says, "one that reflected the rainbow of people who want to be on the water."

After paddling into Toronto via Buffalo and St. Catharines in August 2023, I biked back and forth along Lake Ontario to a series of meetings. One afternoon, after leaving Surf the Greats, I saw a woman renting SUPs and kayaks out of a shipping container on a west end beach and stopped to ask some questions. Jenifer Rudski is running a business, but the big-wave surfer is mostly on a mission to connect people to water.

Jenifer was raised in Scarborough in Toronto's east end. Her family lived in Indigenous social housing; her mother is from the Tetlit Gwich'in Nation in the Northwest Territories. Jenifer's parents were always taking their five children outdoors, in part because it was free. They hiked and biked near the lake but never swam. That was the norm in 1980s Toronto. People seldom thought it was safe to go in the water. The Great Lakes Water Quality Agreement, signed by Canada and the U.S. in 1972 to jumpstart the restoration of a basin that contains about one-fifth of the world's fresh water, was just starting to have an impact.

When Jenifer was 20, she tried surfing for the first time while on the West Coast and fell in love with the mix of adrenaline and meditation. "It's just you and the ocean," she says, squinting in the sun at Toronto's Budapest Beach on an August afternoon, long brown hair swirling in the breeze. "You have to be super present, super aware." After trips to California, Peru and Ecuador, she realized that one can not only surf but also SUP on Lake Ontario. The arc of her life changed. "Paddleboarding teaches you to stand strong on two feet but stay fluid. It has opened so many doors for me."

Jenifer left her job at an Indigenous wellness agency, took a six-month college entrepreneurship course and, with two of her sisters, opened Oceah Oceah in 2012. "We grew up with teachings about women having a responsibility as water carriers and life givers," she says. "It's part of who we are as Indigenous people. It was woven into every part of me."

Starting with three paddleboards and a custom-made trailer rack for her bike, the company has expanded to a pair of seasonal locations and a much larger fleet of rental boards and kayaks, as well as paddling tours and SUP yoga sessions. The second spot, a bus Jenifer parks beneath the white sand and clay cliffs at Bluffer's Park Beach in Scarborough, has been subject to "harassment" from bylaw officers over permitting. But it's important for her to keep it open, so she can entice locals down to the water. "And why shouldn't I be able to build socioeconomic equity?" she asks.

As much as Jenifer needs an income, she's conscious of the implications of commodifying water and is focused on cultivating community alongside the business. She teaches empowerment classes for girls and hosts paddling outings with Indigenous groups, trying to get people to pay attention to the big lake in their backyard and, hopefully, help create a ripple effect of broader stewardship.

"The world is literally on fire and flooding at the same time," she says. "I have nieces and nephews, and when we talk about how fucked the planet is, that creates an atmosphere in which kids can easily feel hopeless. I'm not sticking my head in the sand, but I think we need to start focusing on what we can do."

CHAPTER 27

~~~~~~~

"Paddleboarding opened up the whole lake to me. It made me think about how disconnected from the water we were. SUP created a relationship that I didn't think was possible."

—Jenifer Rudski, owner of Oceah Oceah

SEPTEMBER 2023. I'M BACK IN TORONTO, AND MY BROTHER ED IS DRIVING me across town to Bluffer's Park. Technically, I should have picked up my paddle where I left off, near his house in the west end, but I've crisscrossed enough of the city on a SUP to feel no shame over this shortcut.

It's been a month since I wobbled into Toronto on my paddleboard, a holding pattern during which I was never entirely present on dry land. Adrift at social gatherings, thousand-yard stares while stuck in traffic. Blue space is slowly showing me how to embrace uncertainty, but the limbo of an extended pause has left me floundering. More confused than calm, I'm ripe for another round of aquapuncture. Yet I'm not exactly rested and ready for this final leg.

A few days ago, I drove back to Ontario from Nova Scotia, where I had dropped off my daughter Daisy at university and helped her move into her first apartment. The friction between filling an overflowing shopping cart at Walmart and assembling Ikea furniture until my fingers bled versus early morning SUP surf sessions was jarring. Squeezed into a whirlwind schedule, dawn patrol on the Atlantic helped me handle the emotional weight of watching my kid grow up and frenzied box-store shopping. Now I'm hoping that getting back on the water will dampen the remaining butterflies.

Ed drops me off at Bluffer's Park, the shore cliff of Lake Iroquois, a prehistoric, proglacial forerunner of today's Lake Ontario. At daybreak on a weekday the parking lot is empty, but by the 1870s, Torontonians were already retreating to this part of the lakefront from heatwaves and "unbridled industry," Jane Fairburn reports in *Along the Shore*, arriving aboard trains or steamboats that departed at regular intervals from the busy downtown harbor. With broad sandy beaches backing onto a 300-foot-tall bluff, Scarborough's Victoria Park was a popular summer resort, according to an 1885 history of the city, and a refuge for "large numbers of pleasure seekers and wearied citizens in search of a brief respite from the toil and worry of urban life."

I pump up my board and paddle away from the boat launch above a deltaic shelf that caused dozens of shipwrecks in the 19th and early 20th centuries. Sailors staggered ashore after storms grounded their sailboats and paddle wheelers, returning once the waters had settled to salvage cargo. Sometimes pilferers arrived first, and locals would be well supplied with sugar and canned tomatoes for several seasons.

There is no such peril for me as the sun slips above the line of trees to the east and the halo of clouds on the horizon turns pink. The mercury climbs to a pleasant 20 degrees Celsius (68 Fahrenheit), the distinctive, dazzling turquoise waters of this strip of Lake Ontario are cool and refreshing, and I'm abetted by a soft but steady tailwind.

Swans and geese bob on a resplendent, ruffled blanket; hawks glide by gracefully and gulls squawk. A few sailboats drift past — not much boat traffic now that it's nearly autumn. Six million people live in the Greater Toronto Area, but the blue fringe is mostly beaches, trails and parks. Including Whitby's Intrepid Park, which I paddle past after lunch — it was the site of a top-secret Second World War spy training school called Camp X where Allied agents learned how to sabotage the enemy and where a young British naval intelligence officer named Ian Fleming may have conceived of James Bond. I like that a green space adjacent to a liquor warehouse, auto body shop and flooring retailer carries the name Intrepid, galvanizing my own covert operation.

The shoreline east of Toronto is also spiked with bits of industry: a cement plant here, a nuclear power plant there. I skirt the immense domed reactors of the Pickering Nuclear Generating Station and, after nine hours and 28 miles, stop short of the Darlington Nuclear Generating Station, having booked a campsite at the adjacent provincial park. After setting up my tent on a rise overlooking the beach, I rehydrate a bag of Cuban coconut black beans and rice (which could have been a nuclear combination inside my digestive tract had there been more than seven beans amid the rice) and sit on a driftwood log with my supper. It's soothing to be alone, at least for one night, bare toes tickling the sand, awestruck beneath an apricot sky, land-based anxieties ebbing.

Later, as I slide into a fitful sleep, the waves crashing into shore almost drown out the droning of trucks on Highway 401.

Six o'clock in the morning hits different in mid-September. It's need-headlamp dark and wear-everything nippy when I get up, but that spurs me to start paddling. Within an hour, I'm shedding layers clandestinely close to the Darlington nuclear facility, which seems secure behind a fortified fence and array of cameras. Setting aside debates about the merits of nuclear power, I'm reminded of the perspectives one can absorb in places where we're not expected to linger.

A dozen years ago, I spent a day crisscrossing Harlem on foot with a man named Matt Green, tagging along in the midst of his multiyear project to methodically walk every block of every street in New York City and submit to a "uncurated flow of stimulation and information that overwhelms our innate tendency to try to fit everything into a neat and tidy set of preconceptions." Matt and I had climbed to the rooftop of a parking garage at a chain-store retail complex and were looking down at the green waters of the East River. He hadn't planned to ascend to this perch but spotted a concrete staircase and wanted to see where it led. A police boat roared up the river, piercing the white noise from six lanes of cars and trucks on FDR Drive. We weren't enraptured by the natural world, Matt remarked, but our vantage wasn't a disheartening manifestation of humanity either. "People in Manhattan complain about stores like Costco coming in, but this is here. They should come and check it out."

Onward eastbound, looking for the bright side of exurban development, might as well check it out.

To my left, set back from the shoreline, the rampart-like edge of a subdivision-in-progress, fronted by a dramatic cliff-top trail. An anti-eco panorama of sprawl to some, but at least there's a view of the lake. Next, the Wilmot Creek retirement village, a low-slung band of homes on a bluff where seniors on front porches and golf carts wave and pickleball players interrupt their game to shout greetings. Is this the kind of active lifestyle community where I might end up? Or will erosion undercut this enclave before I reach my golden years? And will the eroding global economy undercut my meager retirement savings?

Wilmot Creek's sprightly residents are the only people I see for hours. Train tracks and the busiest highway on the continent are barely beyond sight to the north, but it's practically primordial on the waterfront. Turkey vultures soar high above and clusters of bright orange monarch butterflies muster ahead of their epic migration to Mexico. The weather is idyllic again — bright sun, light tailwind, mild temperature — but fatigue sets in by early afternoon. I'm out of SUP sync, and without the camaraderie of strangers, my crutch on the Erie Canal, it's just my sagging energy and the interminable miles ahead.

I distract myself by scouting potential rough camping sites on the mostly undeveloped rocky shoreline. The farmers up top wouldn't even know I'm here. But disembarking is formidable, waves bouncing off rocks, so I can't take many off-board breaks. Finally, on the 30th of today's miles: the concrete abutment at the entrance to Port Hope Harbour, atop which a handful of people are fishing. Curling around the end of the wall and turning up the Ganaraska River, I see at least a hundred fishers lining both banks and, farther upstream, dozens of people wading in the shallows with rods.

A fishing derby? At 5 p.m. on a Thursday?

A boil of thrashing and splashing erupts to my left. Ahead, long blue-green bodies wriggle onto rocky ledges. I look down. Hundreds of salmon are swimming upriver to spawn. The weather has started to get colder, which tells the fish (and, apparently, fishers near and far) that it's time.

The prevalence of flying fishhooks and my SUP fin scraping along the riverbed tell me it's time, so I haul myself up to a park and indulge in a rite as elemental as the annual salmon run: sponging off old friends.

I haven't seen Dianne and Michal in nearly 20 years, but when I was planning the last leg of my circuit and saw on social media that they had moved to Port Hope, I took that as a sign. So I emailed my long-ago journalism school classmates and said that I'd be passing through.

Armed with electrolyte drinks, energy bars and a roof rack for my board, Dianne and Michal scoop me up and stop at a brewpub on the drive back to their house, then stuff me with burgers, potatoes, pie and butter tarts. A sports nutritionist might not endorse this diet, but my friends are triathletes, runners and paddlers, and Michal holds the world record for the fastest marathon while juggling, so I am in good hands. Swamp Thing happy.

In the morning, after making me a pair of eyeball-rattling double espressos and cramming my dry bag with leftovers, Dianne and Michal hop onto their SUPs for a send-off. We depart from a pocket beach beside the outflow of the Ganaraska. Lisa and I came to this spot frequently with our daughters when they were young, a swim and picnic stop on the drive between Toronto and Ottawa. One Sunday, there was a tent. A middle-aged man in a suit with a British accent walked over and told us that he was driving across the country and had decided this was a fine place to camp. A young police officer had pulled up as he was erecting the tent and informed him that this was not legal, and our well-dressed white raconteur replied that he intended to sleep, have breakfast at the café next door, go to the church up the hill, then be on his way. The officer let him stay.

I chuckle about that exchange every time I drive past Port Hope. A riparian heritage minute: the laid-back arm of Canadian law. Yet it's also a troubling reminder that with a growing number of encampments in communities throughout the continent, all travelers are not treated the same.

Michal accompanies me to the next town, keeping pace on a much shorter board and demonstrating that juggling translates into paddling fitness decidedly more than the other way around. He turns back at Cobourg, a community marketed to American ferry-borne vacationers in the 1870s as a "forested fresh air retreat." Now I'm alone atop bedazzled crystalline waters, transfixed by parallel lines of sandy ridges on the lakebed, a topography punctuated by large flat planes of limestone splayed with cracks and crevices.

I look up long enough to see a beat-up, graffiti-covered yellow school bus jettisoned on a beach, its raised rear end buried in dense foliage, its nose ripped off and front wide open near the edge of the lake. There are no roads nearby and the internet can't tell me how it got here (and the outernet signals in the hinterlands of Canada seem to be a lot weaker). While I might be able to find out by making a few phone calls, the bus's *Into the Wild* aura keeps my sleuthing in check. We'll never really know why Chris McCandless, the subject of Jon Krakauer's best-selling book, holed up and ultimately died in an abandoned bus in the Alaskan wilderness. But McCandless seems to have reached at least one conclusion. Found among his belongings was a note he had scribbled: "happiness only real when shared."

McCandless was a smart, troubled young man who seems to have turned his back on modern society in a search for some sort of enlightenment. A wilderness chronicle that has a lot in common with the outdoor adventure canon. We go into the unknown, accept reasonable risks and rely on DIY skills to foster resilience and personal growth by navigating tough times. That's how British psychologists Paula Reid and Hanna Kampman distill the expedition mindset in a 2020 paper. Most of us go into the wild (or, in my case, into the mild) for some variation of these reasons, and we emerge with some variation of these outcomes. What doesn't kill us, we hope, will make us stronger. What matters is how we respond to setbacks. And, as McCandless realized, alone and emaciated, none of it matters without others, however wobbly and off-key our communities may be.

About an hour past the bus, I paddle beneath a conveyor belt that's used to load limestone onto ships. A quarry that's operated, a local newspaper quips, by "one of those rare companies where the deeper it digs itself into a hole, the more successful it becomes."

Twenty-four miles into another wearying day, I dig deep for an open-water crossing. A six-mile east-south-east line will take me straight to my campsite at Presqu'ile Provincial Park, midway down a long peninsula that unfurls into the lake. Paddling along the shore would add another three or four miles. The only problem is the south-southwest crosswind. And the après-butter-tart sugar crash.

Twenty-four hundred left-side paddle strokes and two unexpectedly pleasurable hours later, I reach the limestone shoals that protect the peninsula and make landfall at golden hour.

The next day: a tale of two crossings.

First, a zippy 10-mile downwinder southeast from Presqu'ile to Pikes Point, skimming over cerulean wavelets. To my left: a phalanx of sand. Right: the great blue beyond and, eventually, Rochester, New York. At Pikes Point, where a smooth limestone shelf adorned with a forlorn chrome barbecue sticks out into the lake, I make a left into an east-southeast bearing, aiming for Outlet Beach at Sandbanks Provincial Park, where, conveniently, Lisa and some friends are camping for the weekend. But the wind has shifted and is now blowing fiercely from the southwest. Here at the eastern end of the lake, that gives waves plenty of fetch to amass upon.

I try to maintain my line to the bay where my wife, conviviality and coolers full of food await, but the crosswind and mounting swells push me northeast toward a dune. It's the world's largest freshwater baymouth barrier dune, in fact, but of more immediate consequence, it's a Sahara-esque span of sand without road access. Paddling three miles takes approximately an hour; walking three miles along a beach dragging all my crap would take approximately forever. I've SUPed here before in similar conditions, but those were short outings on a much more maneuverable hard-shell racing board unencumbered by dry bags. With all the weight on my SUP, it's impossible to pivot my nose to the correct orientation. I had hoped to ride the waves into the campground to a hero's welcome. That's impossible, but I don't have any bandwidth for brooding, expending all of my energy to make it as close as possible to a parking lot and avoid an embarrassing "Can you retrieve me in a dune buggy?" call to the park's emergency line.

Four hours, a dozen grueling left-side-paddling miles and God-knows-how-many strokes after departing Pikes Point, I surf-crash into crowded Lakeshore Beach. Rescuing my SUP and bags from the pounding waves triggers flashbacks to my inglorious landing in Hamilton last month. I wait until the heaving in my chest subsides and call for a pickup. It doesn't matter that I failed to glide up onto the correct beach. My dear friends Andy and Jan are on their way. Happiness is best when shared.

A cold-water Caribbean in the middle of Canada, Sandbanks Provincial Park is the jewel of Ontario's Prince Edward County, a 400-square-mile tilted limestone plain that juts out into the lake, rising from sea level in the west to lofty cliffs in the east. Lisa and I camp here regularly and love biking around the pastoral backroads, stopping at some of the breweries, wineries and distilleries that have turned this once-quiet agricultural region into a boozy tourist mecca.

With a mild climate and long growing season, this headland had a booming barley business in the 19th century, supplying American breweries a short sail to the south. It was also a hideout for rum-runners during Prohibition. Men would load their boats with whiskey and beer and, under the cover of night, slip across the marine border just 10 miles distant. Evading U.S. coast guard cutters, they'd transfer their cargo to fishing vessels, and it'd be on its way to New York City or Erie Canal groggeries.

Prince Edward County's wild, rock-strewn southern coastline was conducive to smuggling, but it's an obstacle to me. Paddling around its bulk would take all day — if I'm lucky. The wind forecast is calling for 15 knots from the north, which could send me back to New York. So I decide to sleep in and get a lift to a put-in that's close to my next port.

Jan delivers me to a cheese shop on the Black River. There's a kayak rental service across the road, but the owner asks for $10 to launch from his dock. "I'm running a business," he says with a shrug, although so were all the Americans who let me camp on their properties without charging. On principle, I walk back across the street and settle for a marshy slope and wedge of smoked gouda. An hour later, I'm tying up my SUP in a vacant slip at the Waupoos Marina, where I've booked an Airbnb. The second *B* stands for *boat*.

When I climb onto my sailboat, the man in the neighboring fishing boat — leather ballcap and a biker vest with his name, Derek, spelled out in block letters — glances up from his tinkering. "Looks like you're on an adventure."

I summarize my voyage, and we start trading the-sea-was-angry stories. A retired marine mechanic and licensed commercial pilot, Derek handily has me beat. This marina, where he worked for 20 years, is on a long isthmus separated from the mainland by Adolphus Reach. To cruise into Picton, the biggest town in the county, one must navigate the gap between the finger of land we're on and Amherst Island to the east and then U-turn so you're heading southwest. When the wind is coming from the southwest, the prevailing direction, a significant percentage of Lake Ontario is forced through this narrow, shallow opening. Derek and his wife were motoring through the gap in a yacht one day, made the turn and were slammed by a train of waves that reached their bridge, 20 feet above the water. "This lake can be more nasty than the ocean," he says. "Be careful and try to get going early before the winds build."

I thank Derek for his advice.

"No, you've got to pay for advice. I just gave you my opinion, and that's free."

Before heading home, without me mooching, Derek hands over a can of beer. Also free.

CHAPTER 28

~~~~~~

"Proponents of a movement called Deep Adaptation argue that climate chaos, followed by societal breakdown, is imminent. They are sounding the alarm not to incite panic, but to inspire a conversation about what comes next. It's an opportunity to rethink everything, to prepare for radical change in ways that reduce conflict and trauma. One facet of such radical acceptance is to admit that water always wins. That admission is not weakness. Instead, it's the foundation for strength because it opens us up to innovative solutions. The way we are relating to water and the natural world is not innate. We create our narrative, and we can change it."

— Erica Gies, Water Always Wins

MY ALARM RINGS AT 5 A.M., AND I'M ON THE WATER BEFORE 6 WITH AN ambitious 35-mile day ahead. It's still dark, but when the sun rises an hour later, the clouds turn rosy. Red sky at morning, sailors . . . something something?

It's dead calm, however, and I shoot past ominous gray cliffs and through the treacherous gap Derek had warned me about. Now I'm paddling alongside boulder beaches, farm fields and wind turbines on the northern shore of Amherst Island — a low-lying limestone extension of Prince Edward County's eastern tip — on yet another postcard-perfect day. My body and brain are back in the SUP zone, and I've had sufficient human contact to stave off loneliness.

A dozen miles long, Amherst Island had nearly 1,300 residents in the 1860s. It was an early exemplar of vertical integration with three shipbuilders, a pair of taverns and an economy built around exporting barley to the U.S. When that trade began to decline around the turn of the century, the population started its slow decline to less than 500. Amherst is now mostly a sedate agricultural and cottage community, and my only excitement comes when I pass the ferry terminal a little too close to an incoming vessel. The glare I receive from the captain is not the kind of human contact I'm seeking. A north wind slows my crossing to the mainland, but I take a break in the lee of the Brother Islands and reach the city of Kingston's suburbs by late afternoon.

A horizon of expensive homes and expansive lawns doesn't feel like much of a payoff after 10 hours of paddling. For a few minutes, I'm jealous of the locals arriving home from the office, hungering for their hot meals and soft couches. But continuing eastward, the urban texture modulates and draws me in. I pass the gunmetal walls of a circa 1833 former penitentiary now open for tours and funky modernist buildings that contain a theater, gallery and café. I pass the university residence where my mother lived for a summer in the late 1960s ("I thought you were writing a book about water," she says when I ask her to reminisce) and stop at Gord Edgar Downie Pier, a concrete pad with pool ladders, linked to a park by a wooden footbridge. A man wearing surgical scrubs pulls up on a bicycle, strips into a bathing suit and leaps in.

"How's the water?" I ask — an inquiry to which in Canada the customary response is "It's warm once you get in." Which is, most of the time, considering our oft frigid lakes, a brazen attempt to trick friends into joining you. "It's warm once you get *out*" would be a more accurate response.

"It's getting colder but not that bad yet," the swimmer, Chris, replies. "How come I'm the only one in here?"

Treading water, Chris tells me that he works at the nearby hospital. Since this fenced-off brownfield was converted into the country's first deep-water urban swimming pier in 2018 — a project championed by Swim Drink Fish and named in honor of local rock band the Tragically Hip's late beloved frontman — he has made a habit of taking a dip on his ride home. This spot has transformed the city, Chris says, adding that on hot days it's packed with students from Queen's University, located directly across the street. He recently saw a group of young men roll their buddy into the lake in a shopping cart and worries about accidents. "We pay a price for our freedoms."

The sky has been darkening and thunder is now rumbling this way from the west, so I bolt toward the downtown harbor on a gusty tailwind. Offshore from a yacht club, I see a pair of neoprene-hooded heads bobbing in the water and apply the brakes.

Val Hamilton and Mary Ann Higgs, both in their 70s, are testing their wetsuits, purchased recently so they can extend the swimming season.

"We're not just old ladies — we're serious old ladies!" Mary Ann says.

Twenty years ago, to get a break from her busy job and crowded household, Val tells me that she spent a month swimming across more than 20 different lakes in the area. "They all smelled different! Some were more compost-y."

I take their photo and get a phone number, and when we talk several months later, Val divulges that she was in the midst of radiation therapy for breast cancer when I happened upon them. Radiation creates a lot of heat in the body, she explains. Your lymph nodes can swell, reducing mobility. To keep her arms limber, she swam in Lake Ontario every day during her four weeks of treatment. "I told every doctor, and they all said, 'Good idea.'"

Sometimes the gray-haired long-time friends have to change into their bathing suits or wetsuits in parking lots, and they don't care who sees them. "That might encourage the young people, to see us grandmas going in," says Val. "Once we make a date, we keep it, even if it's cold. It's good to have a companion."

"And you can bring anything you want in a thermos, I'm just saying," adds Mary Ann.

During her treatment, awash in lacustrine churn, Val saw treading water as a metaphor for life. "You'd think by our 70s it'd be all peace and harmony," she says. "But it's not. It's still hard."

The rain starts while I'm hovering beside the pair, but it's not hard to paddle around the corner to Kingston's Confederation Basin Marina, where I commandeer a wagon and wheel my bags to the hotel next door. Standing in the check-in line in the shiny lobby, dripping rain and sweat amid women in heels and men in suits, I smell a tad . . . compost-y.

Kingston, population 132,000, is an old city. In the 17th century, when Europeans started settling in this traditional homeland of Anishinaabe, Haudenosaunee and Huron-Wendat Peoples, they quickly cottoned on to its desirable location, where Lake Ontario tapers into the St. Lawrence River and where the Cataraqui River drains down through the Canadian Shield from the north. By the early 1800s, Kingston was a busy British port for exporting raw material and importing colonial migrants. With the American border nearby, it also had a significant military presence. In 1841, it became the first capital of a new province called Canada. Two years later, the queen of England moved the seat of government downriver to Montreal because Kingston was deemed vulnerable to attack by water.

That short-lived status not only left a legacy of grand limestone buildings and naval fortifications, it also dictated the city's early attitudes toward water. When Kingston was in line to be named capital, it was ravaged by cholera, typhoid and fires. One in 16 people died in an 1830 cholera outbreak; 40 buildings were destroyed and 45 people left homeless in an 1840 inferno. The solution, to mollify the political kingmakers, was pumped water. Yet another example of how people in decades past, when confronted by monumental undertakings, rolled up their sleeves and got busy.

The city's first waterworks opened in 1849, too late for its long-term leadership aspirations but good for residents who previously had to dig wells, collect lake water themselves or buy it from commercial carriers. One of the soon-to-be country's first water utilities, initially privately owned, helped curtail waterborne diseases and deadly blazes. Kingston's original waterworks, a handsome red-brick building a couple blocks from my hotel, is now the PumpHouse Museum. The old water intake pipes are still in the lake, and there are grooves in the floor where firemen would drag in coal to fire the engines. "We're telling the whole water story," curator Miranda Riley tells me, "in the place where it actually happened."

I popped into the museum on my walk down the shore to Richardson Beach, where the recent restoration of a historic bathhouse and swimming spot adds a new page to this story. Like Toronto, Buffalo and just about every community I visited on my paddle, there's a growing recognition that access to local waters will play a vital role in so many facets of Kingston's future.

Until the 1970s, the city had a hopping beach scene: lifeguard towers, hot dog stands, show up before noon or you won't find a parking spot. Then Lake Ontario's water quality deteriorated and people retreated home to backyard pools and television sets. Completed in 2023, the Richardson Beach reno has rejuvenated a place where people had been hanging out for centuries. The bathhouse, circa 1919, is a squat stone building with sleek changerooms and a light-filled foyer. Stairs lead down to a cobble beach that gives way to smooth flat bedrock. There are tiers of curved wooden benches beside the stairs — "gathering and lounging amenities," in the parlance of Neal Unsworth, Kingston's manager of parks and shoreline, who is sitting beside me on one of the benches, pointing out various rock and concrete features that protect the physical integrity of the waterline.

"Storms seem to be getting worse and lasting longer, and water levels are getting a little higher some years," says Neal, a tall man with a trim beard. "The lake acts like a bathtub, and at this end the water can sloosh up when the wind blows from the southwest, which is frequent. The mass of water comes and you get wave action and erosion occurring."

Richardson Beach is a flagship among nearly 140 projects outlined in the city's 30-year, $64-million waterfront master plan, an effort to enhance pockets of blue space along 174 miles of shoreline within the municipal boundary — an assortment of lakefront, riverbanks, bays and marshes — of which less than one-quarter is public. The

Gord Downie pier, a polluted former coal dock where people would go to swim anyway, including perhaps a teenaged Gord Downie, was an early win. The next high-profile job will be the construction of a path atop the long L-shaped breakwater that protects the marina where my SUP is parked. "Unless you have access to a boat, it's kind of a rare thing to look back at your city from the water," says Neal. "We've found that the majority of waterfront users don't actually go in the water. They just want to be as close as they can get, whether they're walking, jogging, sitting or just looking out over the lake. Access and egress to and from the water is also important, but how good the public space is at the shore, that can add a ton of joy to the whole experience."

Beyond these signature developments, Neal emphasizes the value of "teeny-weeny" blue and green acupunctures, such as parkettes where streets dead-end at Lake Ontario. These are quicker, cheaper and provide more widespread entry. And either large or small, all of these projects generally include an element of shoreline protection, for which there is a spectrum of approaches from gray (concrete and steel) to green (plantings). "We don't just dump rocks," says Neal. "Every single section of the shore is different: different surfaces, different wave frequency and intensity. In some places we use a hybrid design, integrating ballast like rocks into soils covered with vegetation to build shorelines that can withstand whatever Mother Nature throws at them. It's green and provides habitat, but it's got some heavy armor built into it."

These interventions embody the tactics that Erica Gies documents in *Water Always Wins*. Rather than lean on engineering, "nature can be our buffer," she argues, citing a report from the Global Commission on Adaptation. Headquartered in Rotterdam on the largest floating office in the world, the commission avows that the natural environment is our best defense "against floods, droughts, hurricanes, heat waves and other mounting impacts of climate change."

Giving space near homes and businesses back to water "creates more pliant boundaries to absorb floods and to keep local water supply robust," writes Gies. "Water fluctuations are just part of natural cycles, not disasters, if human activities aren't devastated." What's more, organic systems such as wetlands and ravines are more complex than single-purpose installations, like dams, and provide a range of concurrent benefits: mitigating floods and droughts, filtering water, holding soil in place, sequestering carbon dioxide, providing habitat for plants and animals, relieving human stress. And because healthy natural ecosystems can maintain themselves, "if we give them space to do their thing," they are often cheaper to preserve than concrete, which can't always handle today's weather extremes.

Gies envisions a tapestry of small projects across the waterscape, not centralized infrastructure. Her mantra: "More is more."

Five years ago, design and health researcher Jenny Roe helped conduct an experiment in West Palm Beach, Florida. A section of the downtown waterfront was modified with a few low-cost additions: tables and chairs, plants that provided shade and buffered traffic sound, and wooden "fascination frames" that encouraged people to stop and gaze out at the harbor. Study participants walked through the pop-up and also walked along part of the waterfront that had not been improved. Using a mood scale to capture subjective well-being plus smartwatches to track heart rate variability, the research team found that stress reduction was markedly higher in the enhanced space.

It was a small study, Jenny cautioned me when we spoke not long after the project, but it showed that a simple change can have a discernible positive impact. And it gives urban planners and public health advocates a window into how they "can take full advantage of underused, underperforming, or otherwise neglected water spaces in a city."

Jenny, you might remember, is the University of Virginia environmental psychologist who told me how blue space triggers our parasympathetic nervous system, sparking a sense of boundless possibilities coupled with contentment and harmony. She has conducted experiments involving subjects looking at images of blue, green and gray urban spaces while wearing headsets that capture cortical brain activity, signals that can be translated into alpha waves (which indicate relaxation) and beta waves (higher cognitive attention demands). And she has layered all these insights into *Restorative Cities*, which should be required reading at every city hall.

Coauthored with psychiatrist and public health researcher Layla McCay, the book reminds readers that the critical importance of urban outdoor spaces and the vast spectrum of needs within any sizable community were both laid bare during the COVID-19 pandemic. The pandemic also showed us how cities and towns can be flexible with their infrastructure — say, wrestling real estate away from cars — and reap the benefits. In a chapter devoted to "the blue city," Roe and McCay note that access to water may be particularly good for the emotional wellness of children and seniors. That improving access for all will likely generate social connections and cohesion. And that greener, "soft-engineered" water infrastructure can bolster our health and, at the same time, municipal budgets.

Neal Unsworth is proud of the work Kingston is doing on its waterfront. He has watched families at Richardson Beach, curious how they use the space. Grandparents and parents sit on the comfortable benches; kids climb on the rocks and splash in the water. "Some people stay there far longer than they probably planned to," he says. (Probably, Roe and McCay would suggest, because of the "unique magic and wonder" of water.)

As a municipal manager, Neal believes that while public space is a planning priority today, this wave of interest could crest and be pushed aside by other needs, such as housing. "That's the nature of society. People may not be committed to what they were talking about five years ago. And a city government is just like any other branch of society: we just respond to what the public wants. If they have enough of this, they may want something else."

Neal has to run to a meeting, so I change into my bathing suit and wade out on the bedrock shelf, then sprawl forward and submerge my torso and head beneath the waves. The sky is cloudy and the wind brisk, but the water is warm once you get in.

~

While I was at the PumpHouse Museum and Richardson Beach, Queen's University global development researcher David McDonald was touring Kingston's current wastewater treatment plant with a group of students. The field trip was part of a new course he created, Living Lake Ontario, an attempt to get young people to think about historical and contemporary issues related to the lake, from access to clean water and urban planning to climate change.

"We had a conversation about who gets diarrhea from contaminated drinking water and who doesn't and where and why," David tells me at a pub that evening, wearing a long-sleeved T-shirt and, with tussled short gray hair, looking very much like a prof who's as comfortable atop a windsurfing board as in a classroom. "It's such a simple thing to treat water, yet we still don't do it for everybody. I want students to focus on water as a physical entity — what happens when they flush the toilet — but also to think about the beauty of water and all of its many biological, economic and spiritual faces."

David's research focuses on who owns water and electrical utilities and who delivers services such as health care in various countries around the world, and how governments assess whether a public or private model will be more effective. Just like in Kingston, most early waterworks in North America and Europe were private until, around the 1860s, municipal leaders began to realize this was dodgy. In London, England, he says, there were nine competing water services at one point; firefighters would only be able to get water from certain hydrants. Buildings burned, people died. Kingston's waterworks were purchased by the city in 1887, part of an international groundswell of municipalizations that continued until a surge of privatization in the neoliberal 1980s and 1990s. Now David is seeing "remunicipalizations," especially in the United Sates, often at the behest of conservative politicians who conclude that it's cheaper than backstopping the profit motives of corporations. "These pragmatic bureaucrats are looking at the numbers and saying, 'Let's bring it back in house; our job is to save money.' It's not ideological opposition to privatization. It's hard-nosed accounting."

When he's not working or windsurfing, David runs Kingston's Water Access Group, a community organization that promotes public blue space. He credits the group's activism — a series of mass swims, water-themed art shows, dinners at local restaurants featuring fish from Lake Ontario — with convincing the city that a comprehensive waterfront plan was needed. "It was like pushing against a wall at first. I think they finally realized it makes sense. Or maybe they were seeing the dollar signs from tourism."

But while David loves Kingston's master plan, he feels its timeline is far too long and its funding way too low, especially considering that the city recently spent more than the blueprint's total budget to widen a two-mile length of road. "My job is to make sure water never cycles out of favor," he says. "There's never a lack of interest, only a lack of political commitment."

There was another mass swim at the Richardson Beach grand reopening in June 2023. The mayor and federal and provincial elected representatives were there, and when David took the podium, he looked at the politicians and said it was ridiculous how slowly the plan was rolling out. "People cheered. We have to keep the heat on." There's nothing in the plan, he says, about improving public transit to help low-income families get to the lake. "This isn't the end of the story. How are we going to make this space truly accessible and more broadly used? That's the next challenge for Kingston."

Responding to the assertion that today's interest in public spaces could soon ebb, David acknowledges that things come and go. But he also suggests that thinking "nothing is special" is indicative of an engineering mindset, adding, "There's something magic about water."

Once a stretch of shoreline is developed for residential or commercial use, he says, it will likely never be public again. That heightens the need to remain vigilant, to preserve and enhance the blue spaces that exist. Swimming or sitting in the shade at Richardson Beach is no panacea. But a network of places like this — more is more — could help push the pendulum, in tandem with hard-nosed accounting.

Fighting climate change requires public education, good legislation and collective action, says David, which goes against the tides of our individualized, market-oriented world. "It's beyond the municipality's pay grade," he says, "to really think about these things." But to him, highlighting the importance of water — say, to university students who hop into shopping carts at Gord Downie pier — is a back door to getting them to think about environmental justice. "Because water impacts so many aspects of our lives, it's a good segue into conversations about industry, health, food, recreation, about things that underlie so many central aspects of our lives. Water is kind of a canary."

I bounce my Big Idea off David: that water slows us down and provides an opportunity for connection, which could help lead toward collective action.

"There's a contradiction, an unpleasant dialectic associated with water," he replies. "It's both a unifying force and a lens into shocking inequality. Not only who doesn't have access to clean water, but also who has time to paddleboard. Nothing personal: I'm a privileged white male too. Water is both a primordial bond for humanity and a revealing indicator of injustice. Maybe that's the heart of the tension I have. Sometimes I feel very bougie talking about water and why it's great, so maybe I overcompensate by talking about the injustices associated with it."

CHAPTER 29

"First, there were the exploring parties through the dark, swampy, and entangled forest, overgrown with underwood, through which it was necessary at one moment to cut a way, and the next to wade in deep water, the only direction being the compass; then, in the winter, surveying on the ice the lakes and streams through which the canal was to pass, hardly able to move the screws of the instruments for cold, impeded with the snow and heavy clothing . . . in spring, the passing of rapids in canoes, and sometimes upset in them; carrying them round others when it was impossible 'to shoot,' scorched with the sun, bitten with insects, drinking poisonous creek-water, agues wasting the frame — but worse than all, the officers on the line of the canal lived at intervals of 10 miles so that they had no companion but their stove-pipe. . . . Think of that, my friends, who complain of dull stations — think of the wilderness of the Rideau!"

— Sir James Alexander, Transatlantic Sketches

I HAVE DRIVEN THROUGH KINGSTON ON HIGHWAY 401 AT LEAST 100 TIMES. The car descends into a broad valley with marshy shoulders and, on a six-lane bridge, races over the Cataraqui River at 75 miles per hour. But I have never set foot in this valley, and I suppose I still haven't, paddling between a pair of concrete piers under the 401 with a red navigation buoy to my right and a green one to my left. The start-slash-end of the Rideau Canal. A UNESCO World Heritage Site and a national historic site. My local.

Built between 1827 and 1832, just a few years after the Champlain and Erie Canals, the Rideau has a different birth story than its American cousins. With the War of 1812 not far in the rearview, the British were concerned about the looming Yankee presence on the south side of the St. Lawrence River, a vital shipping route from the Atlantic Ocean to the Great Lakes. Lieutenant Colonel John By was tasked with constructing a 125-mile water link from Kingston to Ottawa (which, until 1855, was named Bytown, after the selfsame royal engineer). The canal — a medley of rivers, lakes and 16 miles of man-made channels — would allow the Brits to move troops and supplies between Lake Ontario and Montreal with less vulnerability to American attacks.

Explorer Sir John Franklin laid the canal's ceremonial first stone in one of the Ottawa locks, having just arrived by canoe down the Kichi Sipi from the Arctic. Fortuitously passing through town, Sir John applied the final knock to a one-and-three-quarter-ton block in front of "as large and respectable a gathering of spectators as had ever been witnessed at this place," a proto photo op before there were any cameras in this part of the country. But there were lots of picks, shovels, chisels, sledgehammers, wheelbarrows and dynamite. Some 4,000 sappers, miners, masons, stonecutters and general laborers quarried, dug and blasted after the dignitaries dispersed. They built dams to raise water levels and locks to allow boats to travel up and down, and six construction seasons later, the job was done.

Largely Irish immigrants and French Canadian, up to 5,000 people worked on the canal every year. They had to contend with swampy terrain — malaria killed 500 of the estimated 1,000 who died during construction — and penny-pinching funders in the British Ordnance Department. The final bill for the project was £822,000, well above optimistic initial estimates and the most expensive military-financed undertaking in any British colony. Summoned to a parliamentary inquiry in London, By was cleared of all charges of financial impropriety, but the Rideau remains a presaging early example of cost overruns on infrastructure projects in Canada's national capital region.

By the time this bypass was completed, tensions had eased between the Brits and Americans and the frontier was fairly peaceful. Its original purpose moot, which seems to happen whenever anybody digs a canal, the Rideau soon became a busy commercial conduit for steamboats, often towing barges loaded with timber or coal. With 47 locks and 24 dams, the waterway overcame a 272-foot rise from the Ottawa River to its summit at Upper Rideau Lake and a 160-foot drop to Kingston. And much like the Erie, it opened a wide swath of lands to colonial settlement.

There were people along this route already: Algonquin in the northern section and Algonquin, Iroquois, Mississauga and Mohawk in the Cataraqui watershed. Human presence in the region dates back about 10,000 years, shortly after the glaciers retreated. Archaic projectile points found on the shore of Little Rideau Lake, near the middle of the waterway, have been radiocarbon dated to 6000 BCE. Indigenous Peoples hunted and fished up and down the Rideau corridor, traveling from camp to camp via the bountiful small lakes and rivers. But in the 1830s, while protesting the steady influx of newcomers, the Grand Chief of the Algonquins "was forced to relinquish control over his people's vast traditional hunting ground, including the entire Rideau River drainage basin," writes Randy Boswell, an Ottawa-based history journalist.

All of this territory is within the 14,000 square-mile land claim the Algonquins of Ontario are currently negotiating with the federal and provincial governments. They are seeking control over large tracts of crown land, millions of dollars in compensation and defined rights to harvest natural resources — a thorny legal and political process that could ultimately lead to the "re-Indigenization" of a big chunk of Ontario. No private property will be taken from anybody when this claim is settled, the feds say, and navigable waterways will be maintained — a long-standing law in Canada. Though it's the result of a 19th-century parliamentary fight for the right to float timber down an Ontario stream, it's a law that our forebears got right.

~

Heading up the rock- and tree-lined channel north of Highway 401, the Rideau Canal is downright cozy this morning compared to Lake Ontario, with no big wind or waves to toss me around. The din of traffic fades, replaced by twittering from the green crowns of oak and maple under a radiant, bluebird sky.

It's a paddler's nirvana, and I've spent the past two nights in a plush hotel bed, so why am I feeling bleary?

The brilliant sun that's been blessing me since Toronto is part of the problem. Regular applications of sunscreen have safeguarded my skin, but I forgot my SPF lip balm. This might not strike you as a crucial piece of survival equipment, but remember the lion with the thorn in its paw? A sore has formed at the corner of my mouth, and judging by an escalating headache, it might be getting infected. My lip, an Achilles' heel.

At Kingston Mills, where a flight of four locks raises boats 45 feet up a narrow granite gorge, I'm faced with one of the main differences between the Rideau and New York's canals, as pertaining to paddleboarders. Policy on both sides of the border has yet to declare SUPs lock-worthy vessels. But while generously supportive of my trip, Parks Canada, the Rideau system's manager since 1972, isn't willing to bend the rules like my New York State Canal Corp. friends. (One of whom, in our first of several calls, may have said that my trip sounded "fucking awesome!") The upshot of this Canuck officiousness is that I have no choice but to portage.

At least there's a low dock, making it easy for paddlers to get onto and off the water. Chalk one up for Canada. And because almost all of the locks on the Rideau are still manually operated, with staff cranking open the heavy gates by hand, it's usually faster to walk anyway. It takes me 20 minutes to carry two loads up a steep path to the top. Locking through would have taken an hour.

Upstream, I set out across Colonel By Lake and a section of the canal called River Styx, a pair of meres formed by flooding above the dam at Kingston Mills, the largest expanse of drowned land on the Rideau. The littoral zone is flecked with lily pads. Trees on the shoreline are just starting to show their warm autumn colors, ablaze in the midday sun. A lone grey heron and bevy of honking milky-white swans take flight. But even though it's heavenly, and today's leg a scant 15 miles, I'm running on fumes. And I'm not the only traveler who has struggled here. In his *Observations on the Rideau Canal*, published in 1834, Dr. Edward John Barker complained about this desolate part of the route, where "the total absence of human life inspires anything but pleasure. . . . all is solitude, save the scream of water fowl or the snorting of the fiery steam-boat as she wends her way among the trees in these dreary waters."

Maybe I don't have it so bad.

At Lower Brewers lock, without me asking, a young lock tender named Elijah prophetically shares the door code to the "oTENTik" glamping unit that Parks Canada has reserved for me at Upper Brewers, less than two miles ahead. When I arrive, I find the brown canvas A-frame tent-cabin hybrid on a gorgeous rocky point between the lock channel and river. Inside on the raised floor are a blond wooden table and chairs and, on an array of bunks, six soft-but-not-too-soft mattresses. Also, once I open the windows, a pine-scented breeze, the indoor plumbing version of forest bathing.

There's a houseboat tied to the wall beside the upstream gates of the lock and two older couples are playing cards at a picnic table, but I don't hear anybody as I reboot with a swim, don long underwear and boil water for a bag of broccoli cheddar rice. A woman walks by with her dog; a teenaged boy casts a line, then wanders away. The air is cool and the canal is a burnished mirror, a fusion of trees, water and sky, slanting rays alighting on a golden pocket of birch on the far shore. My hotel and the restaurant meals I had in Kingston were exquisite, but I can't think of any place more perfect than this patch of quiescence.

The distance on tap the next day is barely a dozen miles, the shortest daily output of my entire journey, a walk in the park, a paddle in the pool, for all intents a morning or evening session portioned out over a blank slate. With no haste to depart, I cocoon inside my sleeping bag, then dawdle over breakfast, sitting in an Adirondack chair and watching the sun burn mist off the glazed water.

"Too often boaters, including paddlers, get into a Point A to Point B mentality — rushing between locks," Ken Watson writes in his guide to the canal. "That's not the way to do the Rideau. You may discover things of interest that delay you."

Languorous reflection, on this trip and in general, is rare for me. Making miles or checking things off a to-do list provides purpose. Now in the final stretch back to Ottawa, with no interviews booked nor any particularly long days on the agenda, a discordant duality settles in: we all want time to do nothing, yet we also want to bask in the afterglow of productivity. Satisfying these contradictory instincts feels out of reach right now. Maybe balance is elusive because I'm almost home and am uneasy about the inevitable return to reality. Maybe it's that I'm on familiar terrain, having crisscrossed the Rideau by car on weekend outings for 15 years, stopping in parks and tiny towns, swimming at lock stations and skipping stones over slack-water channels. Is there anything fresh ahead?

I paddle lazily away from the campsite around midmorning. The weather is flawless again — barely any breeze, puffy cartoon clouds, endless blue — but this does not perk me up. Like a 45 rpm record spinning at 33, the globe seems off-kilter. I trundle past trippy, postimpressionistic Group of Seven rocky islets topped with spindly pines. Shoreline trees shimmer, as if changing color before my eyes. A couple of cottagers wave, a kayaker raises her blade as she glides past in the opposite direction: no chitchat, ghostly apparitions.

You'd think I could take a break, sit on my SUP, dangle my feet in the water, chew on a blade of grass, soak up this scene and then leisurely make my way north into the wondrous autumn. But my sluggishness starts to feel more like wooziness, and not discounting the anvil of ennui, I blame my now-throbbing lip for this malaise.

North of the Brass Point swing bridge, I detour east to the village of Seeley's Bay, tie up in the harbor and lurch along sunbaked empty streets toward a drugstore in a strip mall beside the highway. A dog curled up on the sidewalk raises its head as I pass, yawns, then goes right back to sleep.

The apothecarist — a gray-haired woman who may have been dispensing ointments and tinctures here when steamboats and stagecoaches brought people to the village — leans in real close after I explain my infirmity. Her nose is practically touching my lip. A little too intimate, perhaps, for the post-COVID world, but an old-fashioned attention to detail that I appreciate.

"How long has it been like that?" she asks.

"Dunno. Two or three days."

She tilts closer, eyelashes fluttering against my cheek.

"Saltwater rinse. Warm compress. Vaseline and Tylenol. I don't recommend medication that people don't need."

Still feeling like crap but no longer fearing collapse, I pop some pills and backtrack up Seeley's Bay, a toe poking east at the bottom of Whitefish Lake. Unlike the Erie and Champlain Canals, the Rideau still follows its original two-century-old path. Thousands upon thousands of boats of all shapes and sizes have plied the four-mile stretch between my pharmacological port of call and the base of Jones Falls. Plodding the length of the lake, I could be the slowest.

The crooked rocky rapids of Jones Falls were a head-scratcher for canal engineers. After drafting several iterations, they designed a 350-foot-long, 60-foot-high arched dam made of neatly cut sandstone blocks — the tallest dam of its kind in North America at the time — and a set of four locks. Jones Falls was "the scene of the greatest of all the achievements of Colonel By," writes historian Robert Legget, "a piece of construction which today still evokes the admiration of all who know even the rudiments of the practice of civil engineering."

Not in the mood for engineering, I'm instead admiring the long low dock, across a slender bay from the bottom lock, where overnight guests have been stepping ashore for nearly 150 years. And where a pair of newly minted blue space stewards have jumped in with both feet.

Hotel Kenney, a yellow wood-framed inn flanking a handful of cottages and wood-paneled motel rooms, opened as a fishing lodge in 1877. Four generations of Kenneys ran the resort, sporadically expanding and upgrading, and hosting countless "brothers of the rod," as well as a British princess and a former U.S. president, among other nautical tourists. It was a classic Canadian summer hotel; a 1914 pamphlet advertised rates of $2 to $3 per day for "cool piazzas, excellent cuisine, modern sanitary arrangements . . . and live bait always on hand." But it was already fraying when the Kenney family sold it to one of their regular customers, a clothing store owner from Martha's Vineyard, at auction in 2008. Then the global economy tanked, hitting Eastern Ontario tourism hard. Ten years later, it went out of business.

Jeff Day had his eye on the vacant property for a while. He grew up in the area, worked in hospitality management in Toronto for two decades, ran a nearby inn for a few years and, with his partner, chef Core Lee, closed the deal on Hotel Kenney in 2022.

It needed a bit of work.

"Last year was the year of the roof. Every building had to get a new roof," Jeff says to me beneath a mounted ram's head in the cozy lounge after I've showered, napped and taken more Tylenol. "It was literally raining in one cabin after we bought it, the first time we walked in."

Jeff is chatty and warm, despite being run ragged trying to fix up the hotel. Tomorrow, he and Core will be serving lunch in their sprawling dining room to 120 people on a bus tour. The couple need large groups to bankroll the reno, but they also want locals to feel comfortable sitting down to dinner on the glassed-in veranda, a hangout that, alongside the handful of jobs they've created, can contribute to the community's social evolution. "We're working owners," says Jeff. "Core is in the kitchen, and I'm at the front desk. We saw the potential of this neglected place and this forgotten part of the province."

After I wolf down a bowl of delicious-but-not-great-for-an-infected-lip chicken curry, Core pops over to my table. He grew up in Toronto, working in large restaurants run by his Guyanese-Chinese family, so the forthcoming luncheon crowd isn't daunting. Nor is being a fish out of the water in predominantly white and outwardly hetero rural Ontario. "Having a hotel and a restaurant to play with, this is the most fun you can have in a job," he says, beaming. "Until you need to write the checks."

Like pirate impresario Thomas "Tomtuga" Bruggman on the Erie, Core is a canal dreamer. He wants to orchestrate a progressive multistage wedding aboard a pontoon boat descending the Jones Falls locks; to plate a formal dinner on the 200-foot-long timber pedestrian bridge below the falls; to set up a stage on the front lawn and throw silent dance parties under the starshine. Live music! Comedy shows! Razzmatazz!

"It's a little too sleepy around here," Core says with a faraway smile. "Life has to be fun. Otherwise it's depressing."

Energized by the bacon and eggs with avocado-feta toast that Core rustles up at a respectable 9 a.m., I climb the steep slope beside the locks and ease into a sun-splashed pool above Jones Falls. Schools of tiny fish dart about in the lucent greenish water, spellbinding in their glasshouse aquarium. I cross a small lake and curl through a narrow tree-lined passage to another set of locks. Tied to the wall is a boat with a SUP bungeed to its side. A couple reading books sit on lawn chairs under an umbrella on the shore. They look up and nod as I slip past.

A second lake brings me to Chaffey's Lock, a quintessential oasis, Legget writes, for "a silent swim in the cool of the headpond on a broiling day . . . or a lazy half-hour on the high bank [that] will drive time out of mind in real enjoyment." I eat lunch in the shade on the high bank and stroll next door to an old-school ice cream parlor — lime-green walls, upholstered chrome stools, marbled Formica — that was the centerpiece of another resort resurrection.

Built as a private residence in the late 1800s, the Opinicon became a fishing club and, in 1920, a lodge. A scattering of rustic cabins around a clapboard green-and-tan mansion, the hotel was the grande dame of the Rideau, with a classy dining room overlooking a lake, where local young women served prime rib and fried perch and were courted by tourists. Picture *Dirty Dancing*, only with no dancing. The place remained pretty much the same for decades: it had a dinner bell, no TVs, a legendary team of fishing guides and the iconic ice cream counter. Eventually, aging facilities and a slumping economy dragged down the bottom line. In 2012, after the death of the matriarch of the family that had always owned the lodge, its doors were closed and her daughters decided to sell.

Fiona McKeen's arrival in 2015 felt providential. A public servant from Ottawa on maternity leave, she had grown up cottaging in the area and saw the spur-of-the-moment purchase of a dilapidated resort as a way to preserve the carefree summers of her childhood for her own kids. With deep pockets, Fiona and her husband, Tobi Lütke, the founder and CEO of e-commerce megacorp Shopify, were able to backstop a sizable chunk of the local economy (contractors galore, dozens of jobs for front-of-house and maintenance staff, local suppliers for the kitchen) without the need for profit. "I just want to pick up this place, dust it off and help it get back on its feet," Fiona told me a decade ago when I wrote about the Opinicon's rebirth.

Her optimism was contagious; the buzzy makeover was stylish. People flocked to the resort — diners, overnight guests, boaters, wedding parties — until COVID-19 threw a wrench into this trajectory. Accommodation is no longer available; it's just a restaurant and pub, with an ice cream parlor and concerts on the front porch, and a fence now cordons off much of the property. A transformation story, it seems, that's still unfolding. As Tobi said to me years ago at the fresh-from-the-ashes Opinicon, with the understated precision of a German software engineer turned tech billionaire, "New ventures always end up being much more of a puzzle than you expected."

No room at this inn, I push onward across lakes, around locks and through slender serpentine channels, unsure where I'll sleep. By early evening, I'm on Big Rideau Lake, the largest on the canal. The air is still, so I head into the middle of a yawning bay toward Colonel By Island, where paddlers are permitted to camp. There's nobody else on the water, and I'm expecting solitude: a naked swim, a quiet dinner, a slug of bourbon. But it's a Friday night and the dock, jammed with houseboats and cabin cruisers, beats with predinner bustle.

"Please don't tell me where you came from on *that* thing," says a guy grilling steaks on his aft deck.

He's being comical, but that's a new one, even for a fellow Canadian: somebody explicitly asking me *not* to share my story. Were he American, I might be regaling new friends over rib eye this evening. Motioning uphill with his barbecue tongs, he indicates where I might find some flat ground to camp.

There's a boarded-up house on the island — a mid-1900s getaway for a New York City taxi tycoon and his celebrity pals — and I settle under a towering elm on its rambling lawn. At 10 p.m., all of the boaters turn off their music and lights and the silver moon, a few days shy of full, spotlights my tent in silence.

CHAPTER 30

"I moved back to Canada and went out that fall on Big Rideau Lake. It felt almost like returning home. I had missed the seasons so much; I had missed the colors. It felt like everything in life had led me to come back to this place. There's a German word, waldeinsamkeit, that has no analog in the English language — it means being alone in the forest and having a total sense of peace and contentment. That's how I felt being back on an Ontario lake, and now my job was to focus on how to protect these waters after they had done so much for me."

— Jordanna Bergman, aquatic conservation scientist

A FEW YEARS AGO, I SPENT A DAY IN AN ALUMINUM SKIFF ON BIG RIDEAU Lake with a group of biology professors and students from Carleton University. They were catching and tagging fish to better understand the movement of several species on the Rideau system, part of a much larger research collaboration aimed at determining the impacts of human activities on the health of the waterway. Ultimately, their goal was to help Parks Canada come up with effective management policies for everything from wildlife conservation to flooding. I was on the boat to ask questions and take pictures for an article, an escape from the office into the summer sunshine.

I watched PhD student Jordanna Bergman catch a northern pike and, after another student immobilized the fish by cradling it with a pair of low-voltage electric gloves, make an incision. Jordanna implanted a cylindrical two-centimeter-long acoustic transmitter into its belly, sutured the slit and gently lowered the pike over the side of the boat, where it swam out of sight.

A string of submerged telemetry receivers set up along a 40-mile stretch of the Rideau tracked the fish's travels over the next few months. Because of all the locks and dams on the canal, researchers have myriad questions about the movement of game fish such as the northern pike and invasive species like the round goby. They also want to assess the pressures that other fauna and flora face from cottages, shoreline communities and fishers, and to share recommendations with officials who make decisions about the waterway.

"It takes a lot of time, but this is what you need to do to start to change things," Jordanna said to me on the boat. "That one fish you tag could help thousands of other fish. I love doing science for the sake of science, but I also want to leave the world a little bit better after my short time here."

"I think fishing and science are very similar," chimed in one of her supervisors, Steven Cooke, a principal investigator on the overarching Rideau project, who was captaining the boat. "Fishing is about the unknown. You don't know what you're going to get on the end of your line. Science is also about mystery and uncertainty.

"This canal both fragments and connects," he added. "It fragments bodies of water that should be linked and connects others that shouldn't. That makes it very interesting to study."

There are a lot of competing priorities for Parks Canada to juggle on the Rideau: supporting biodiversity and habitat restoration, slowing the spread of invasive species, preserving historical features and encouraging recreational use that surrounding communities rely on, including an angling industry that generates about $2.2 billion in Ontario every year. Administering a 19th-century canal in the 21st century isn't easy. The agency's most recent management plan, from 2022, calls for the development of sustainable, low-impact recreational activities and for the conservation of the Rideau's cultural heritage, among other objectives. It also stresses the need for integrated decision-making about water — levels and flow, shoreline development, climate change mitigation — based on systematic data collection.

Five years after I met her, Jordanna is driving across Nebraska with a PhD on her CV and a postdoc awaiting on the West Coast. She grew up in Ontario and Florida, fell in love with lakes and then the ocean, became a divemaster and marine biologist, and came back to Canada for grad school. "I literally knew nothing about the Rideau," she says to me during her cross-continent move. "When Steve interviewed me over the phone, I didn't even know what word he was saying. I was trying to Google 'r-e-e-d-o-o.' But the more I learned about our project leading to direct conservation outcomes, the more I wanted to dive in."

Turns out Jordanna spent a fair bit of time diving into the Rideau in her scuba gear and wetsuit, deploying telemetry receivers at the bottom of rivers and lakes. Acoustically tagged fish emit a ping every 20 or so seconds. If they pass close enough to a receiver, their location is logged. In clear lakes, Jordanna saw perch and pike, bluegills and bass. The urban lock stations harbored lawn chairs, bikes, shopping carts and, for her, a bout with pink eye. The lock research revealed that while gated chambers and water-control dams limit fish connectivity, especially multi-lock flights or those with larger vertical rises, they do not restrict it altogether.

The results of this study are difficult to summarize, but Jordanna takes a shot. More fish swam downstream through locks than upstream; some species rarely attempted to pass through these barriers; and one teeny, tiny round goby made a break for it uphill — perhaps because the gates are manually operated, she speculates, so lock masters keep them open when they can to avoid additional toil when a boat approaches. In many instances, she says, distilling disparate data into suggestions for Parks Canada will involve listening to a cross section of stakeholders about the changes they're seeing — local knowledge that academics and governments have become much more open to — and devising evidence-based, geographically specific strategies.

Take, for example, the invasive common carp. The species, which has the potential to decimate the spawning grounds of other fish, appears to be drawn away from locks by the high-flow oxygenated waters below dams. They're ostariophysans, a family with well-developed hearing, Jordanna says, and may also be deterred by the noise of lock stations. The common carp is already prevalent through Ontario, but its even more destructive relative, the Asian carp, is knocking at the door of the Great Lakes system via the Chicago River. If it gets in, some of these insights could help guide deterrence measures on the Rideau without shutting the door to navigation.

"Hopefully this research will show us some small key things we can do to keep fish populations healthy," says Jordanna, echoing both Simon Bell's acupunctural vision and the more-is-more ethos of Erica Gies. Plus, with hundreds of millions of dollars of infrastructure work scheduled on the canal over the next few years, there's an opportunity to stitch what Steven Cooke calls "conservation gains" into bricks-and-mortar maintenance.

The paper that emerged from Jordanna's PhD research notes that we're in the midst of the world's sixth mass extinction and that "biodiversity losses are most extreme in freshwater ecosystems, with freshwater fish experiencing some of the greatest losses." Invasive species and barriers to connectivity are two of the biggest threats. They often act synergistically and can be exacerbated by climate change, so understanding the entire system is the key to an effective response. "The Rideau is small, but there are about 37,000 miles of historic canals and 370,000 miles of navigable rivers worldwide," Jordanna says, "and they face similar problems: habitat degradation, pollution, biodiversity decline, climate change. Any finding we reach, we hope it's useful for others who are striving to strike a balance between conservation and human needs."

No dice with the weather gods when I awake on Colonel By Island. My lucky streak, 10 consecutive days of favorable conditions, has screeched to a halt. The wind is whooshing hard from the northeast, my direction of travel most of the way to Ottawa.

I'm on the board early, scooting back and forth between parallel shorelines on the constricted northern section of Big Rideau Lake, seeking cover behind paltry promontories, my first protracted grind since leaving Toronto. This blowback was overdue, I tell myself, mining energy from my limited muscular reserves. It's a four-hour, 10-mile slog to the hamlet of Rideau Ferry. "Wasn't so bad," I conclude myopically upon arrival.

A concrete highway bridge has long since replaced the ferry that used to ply the narrow neck between Big Rideau and Lower Rideau Lakes (wagons paid 15 pence, foot passengers three apiece), but a cluster of public docks and adjacent shops make this an enduring port of call. The boat I paddled past yesterday with a SUP lashed to its hip is at the dock.

Anne and Kevin see me land and walk over, curious about my journey, and vice versa. The semiretired couple are languidly returning to a marina south of Ottawa, averaging more or less the same daily mileage as I do. Along the way, Anne is stopping to paddle. Last year, she SUPed from Kingston to Ottawa over 10 days, sleeping and waiting out storms on the boat.

"I puttered along as her support crew," says Kevin.

"That's the way to do it," Anne says.

I think they're onto something.

Kevin and Anne motor off as I tuck into a sandwich from the general store, then plunge back into an escalating headwind. Four days out of Kingston, the Precambrian rock has morphed into flatter, less dramatic fens and farms — a landscape that reminds me of home, just an hour's drive away. But in paddling distance, Lower Rideau Lake is nowhere near home, and it's a shallow, wavy, swearing-out-loud-to-myself struggle to traverse. (Motherfu— . . . sorry, Mom.) Two bemused, camouflage-clad duck hunters anchored in the reeds chortle as they watch me flail by.

The tendril flowing out of the northeastern tip of the lake — the start of the Rideau River proper, which drains into the Ottawa — offers a touch of shelter but not much of a break, bearing pretty much straight into the wind. Even the slender man-made channel to the Poonamalie lock demands head-down paddling to make progress. Anne and Kevin are sitting beside their moored boat, reading under their umbrella. I'm envious, but three miles farther, I'm in Smiths Falls, aboard my own bateau pour la nuit.

The handle "Smiths Falls" is a red herring. The town was founded in the late 1700s by Lieutenant Thomas Smyth, a United Empire Loyalist who sided with the Brits in the American Revolution and was granted land north of the border when booted out of the U.S. Then Lieutenant Colonel By came through and the once-magnificent falls were diverted into a series of locks. Somewhere along the line, Smyth became Smith and the apostrophe vanished.

Things have been coming and going in Smiths Falls ever since then. The Rideau Canal powered mills and led to markets. This attracted people, factories and trains. In 1885, a main line on the Canadian Pacific railroad linked the burgeoning working-class town to Toronto and Montreal. Coca-Cola made soda pop, RCA Victor pressed records and a gargantuan Hershey's factory put it on the map. Families from across Canada, mine included, stopped for tours and bags full of broken chocolate bars during summertime road trips.

But as in so many communities in this part of the world, traditional industries began migrating overseas in the 1960s. Even the Hershey's plant shut down in 2007, eliminating hundreds of jobs in the name of "global supply chain transformation" just half a year after the company had announced record profits. (Smiths Falls, population 9,000, lost roughly 1,700 jobs during this long decline, nearly 40 percent of its active labor force.) Ten years after the country's largest chocolate factory closed, Canopy Growth converted the 700,000-square-foot facility into Canada's largest indoor cannabis grow op. The jobs, spin-off spending and affordable housing attracted new residents, an economic glimmer. And though Canopy has already gone bust in the legal weed gold rush, selling the factory back to Hershey's in 2023, the pandemic spotlit the possibilities of remote work, and the trains that arrived on the heels of the canal remain conducive to occasional commuting.

In an article published in a journal called *Just Labour*, Arif E. Jinha suggests that the canal can serve "as a powerful symbol for the need to work innovatively around the less tangible obstacles globalization presents to small towns across North America. Navigation is all about knowing the environment and looking ahead. . . . The challenge of re-establishing a sustainable economy in Smiths Falls and the surrounding region will likely not be met by ignoring its unique local geography and history."

Ringed by public space where both locals and tourists congregate, the canal remains the heart of Smiths Falls. Lock master Sebastien helps me portage across a busy road, carrying a couple bags and lowering the checkered barriers that stop traffic. Now I'm paddling into the downtown boat basin, dotted by islands and pedestrian bridges at the foot of an attractive wide sloping main street. Parks Canada's canal HQ and visitor center are here, and in 2017, European houseboat company Le Boat set up its first North American base on a purpose-built set of docks on the other side of the water.

Unlike the local cannabis sector, the houseboat business is thriving. I've seen Le Boat's sleek white vessels every day since leaving Kingston, and the company has agreed to let me sleep on one tonight. I tie up beside a Horizon 2 cruiser and step into the cabin through a sliding screen door on the rear deck. It's just as sleek and white in the salon and bedrooms; Swamp Thing feels like fish not in water. I squeeze into a tiny shower and emerge in time to greet Lisa and our daughter Maggie, who have driven down from Ottawa for the night.

Sunset is stunning from the boat's rooftop deck, salmon-pink striations across a bruised-purple sky. But I'm beat and still somewhat feverish; Lisa slipped on the stairs at home, rushing to leave with too much on the go, and is nursing a deep bloody gash on her shin; and Maggie, who just had four wisdom teeth removed, is doped up on painkillers and subsisting on mush. I had hoped this brief reunion would propel me into the last three days of paddling. Instead, we're the walking wounded, limping along our own paths.

Which for me, in the morning, is directly back into the teeth of a northeaster.

The six miles from Smiths Falls to the Kilmarnock lock and swing bridge are some of the hardest paddling I've ever done. Especially the wide lake-like stretch near the end, where there is no eluding the relentless wind. Those waves at the eastern end of Lake Ontario were fearsome; this is backbreaking. A test. Purgatory. So close to the finish of a long journey on a typically tranquil section of the Rideau River, I dig and dig.

"Just keep paddling," my friend Karl Kruger had sagely said to me before embarking on another leg of his SUP expedition through the Northwest Passage. "Put the blade in, pull on it, then do it again and again and again."

This keeps things simple. Not pleasurable, but it quashes spiraling dread. Eventually, mercifully, here's Kilmarnock. And hello, tied to the wall, umbrella and books unfurled, here's Anne and Kevin, having leapfrogged past me when I got bogged down taking an inside line through some weeds on a wide corner. Their smiles spur me onward. Until wind gusts bring me to a stop, then push me rearward.

Fed up, pissed off, pleading, I talk back.

"C'mon!"

"Really?"

"You gotta be fucking kidding me."

Sorry again, Mom.

A punishing three-hour battle brings me to the village of Merrickville, where a crowd befitting a sunny Sunday afternoon is spilled onto the parks and sidewalks that flank the canal. I stagger ashore to portage, then Swamp Thing through the aisles of a supermarket, chug two bottles of Gatorade, eat seven mini cinnamon buns and lay down in the shade before beginning the final few miles to another oTENTik. On the board, I think about distance and time and gravity and energy and paddle strokes and angles and physics and hydration and calories and my fingers and hands and feet and then it all kind of blurs together and I'm not thinking at all.

At one final portage, my ninth lock of the day, haggard but happy, I sit on the edge of the dock before hefting my SUP out of the water. On the stone-block point where the river splits, flowing left to the lock and right over a dam, there's a woman with three young kids. She's setting up fishing rods for the kids, leaning over them one by one until they're ready to cast and then moving onto the next. Teaching three children to fish must be tricky, so many small hands grasping for your attention. From afar, she seems tender and serene, the kids so full of wonder.

CHAPTER 31

"Fishing makes us less the hostages to the horrors of making a living. In some Jungian sense it returns us to the aesthetics of the ancient art of gathering and hunting for food. It is a time warp we may step into for a little peace."

— Jim Harrison, poet and novelist

MY FATHER LEARNED HOW TO FISH FROM HIS FATHER. HE WAS BORN AND raised in a large city in South America — Dad doesn't want me to name the country, in case the government decides to shake down expats for back taxes — and would join his father on Sunday morning trips to the lake.

"I wasn't much help in the boat," Julio said at the dining room table in the house where I grew up during a recent visit. "I always managed to throw my line on top of somebody else's and make a big mess, and my father would very patiently untangle it."

"What's the appeal of fishing?" I ask.

"I tried it a few times after I came to Canada. Eh, I could take it or leave it."

My father's parents left Poland before the Second World War, settling, like many Jews, in . . . South America. He's even more circumspect about his childhood than my mother. But I've got him cornered at the table under the pretext of talking about fishing and am trying to segue into other subjects. Like his path to Toronto.

In the early 1960s, the political future was "shaky" in "South America," so Dad joined two friends working toward their PhDs in theoretical physics in New York City. He's got no problem telling me about quantum mechanics and meeting researchers in Oppenheimer's circle, but when I ask about the physics student he was set up with on a blind date at the Schillers' house in Hoboken, the details are skimpy. "It was a dinner party, there were other people . . . Ask your mother. You should rely on her for 90 percent of my memories."

The U.S. was embroiled in the Vietnam War by then and my father could have been conscripted if his student visa expired. Despite the frigid January weather, a short postdoc in Saskatchewan sold my freshly married parents on Canada. Dad landed a university position in Toronto, then began teaching high school and, with my mom, gave my brothers and me a loving upbringing in this house around the corner from Burke Brook.

Now both in their 80s and long retired, my parents' happy place is a cabin on a lake northeast of the city. It's a shanty with no electricity, dodgy cell service and a woodstove on a small bay with barely any trace of the neighbors amid the forested shorelines. I could probably identify the lake by its loamy smell.

My mom reads and cooks, gardens and watches the hummingbirds. Dad tinkers all day, fixing pumps, digging holes, cutting trees, and then holds court during long family dinners, diagramming and explaining the intricacies of his latest jerry-rigged invention, cannibalizing parts from one machine to create something ingenious. He is currently working on a flush toilet for the outhouse, with materials salvaged from the dump.

This bare-bones shtetl simplicity is mostly Dad's doing, and although infuriating at times, my paddling journey has given me new appreciation for minimalist comforts. For his perennial pedagogical lo-fi demonstration of how to hunker down together and keep our footprints as light as possible.

When I'm at the cottage, I'm usually the first one awake and immediately head down to the lake for a swim. Then I watch Dad wheel a small solar panel into position on the deck to juice up an old car battery that's used to run a few electric lights and recharge phones. He made a sign on a piece of graph paper and taped it to the burlap wall beside the power bar: "20th century feeding trough for 21st century devices."

Late afternoons, we gather on the dock with snacks and drinks — rather, on the *docks*, a precarious series of wooden decks, bridges and rafts that my dad has built and refined for three decades — and look out over the water.

"Why do you love the cottage so much?"

"Ask your mother."

Heads cocked, white blazes on red-brown faces, the horses stare at me like I'm loopy, a trio of chestnuts peering over the fence at the water's edge as I snail past. Monday morning, downstream from the Upper Nicholsons lock station, where I slept in an oTENTik. The wind has amped up even more, and I'm the only fool on the river, sticking tight to shore, a futile attempt to dodge the SUP-stalling blasts. I consider wading through the shallows and towing my board by its leash, but most of the riverside properties don't seem welcoming. "No trespassing. Violators will be shot," one sign cautions. "Survivors will be shot again."

Other signs are more hospitable but equally blunt: "Welcome to our porch. No peeing off porch."

It takes me nearly six hours to cover 11 miles. This is where the whole body-acting-like-a-sail part of paddleboarding really sucks. Crawling would be quicker.

At Becketts Landing, I nose under a bridge and come to a dead stop in the wind. Retreating behind a concrete abutment, I sit on my board, feet anchored in the rocks, downcast, defeated. Anne and Kevin motor down the middle of the Rideau and appear to be assessing my status. I'm tempted to flag them down, to climb into their boat, to commute my commute, but instead I flash a feeble thumbs-up. They wave sympathetically and cruise beneath the bridge.

After resting and refueling, I launch back into the fray, grinding downstream foot by foot. Shoreline trees sway, marsh grasses whistle and cresting waves streak across the frothy surface, thwacking into my SUP. The wind today tops 20 knots, funneling down the valley and buffeting my body. But even in this mess, tucked into a small cove, there's a man in a kayak, casting a line.

I see anglers *everywhere* on my SUP journey. Usually, albeit not in this gale, I stop and say hello. I've had sublime experiences the few times I fished on magazine assignments: casting for char at midnight in Nunavut, landing a 30-pound salmon off the coast of Haida Gwaii. But there are many things about fishing that I don't understand. For instance, how hunting animals for sport is actually good for the planet. Lisa Goodier, a professional guide who works the Rideau and Ottawa Rivers, has agreed to fill in some of the blanks.

A year after I started paddleboarding toward Montreal, I'm in Lisa's boat, trying to catch whatever is biting on a warm, blustery late-spring afternoon. Bouncing away from a public boat launch, wearing a black ballcap and blue hoodie, Lisa tells me that she fell in love with fishing a dozen years ago, when her girlfriend bought her a session with veteran muskellunge guide John Anderson as a birthday present.

The biggest member of the pike family, torpedo-shaped musky can grow to 50-plus inches and more than 60 pounds. Their large mouths are filled with sharp teeth. Called "the fish of ten thousand casts," they're cunning and hard to catch, ambush predators at the top of the region's freshwater food chain.

It was November the first time Lisa fished for musky. Cold and getting dark after a luckless day on the water, she was ready to go home. "Don't give up hope," Anderson counseled. She cast and saw a flash of fish.

Lisa cranked on the rod, but her scarf got tangled in the reel. It broke, the braided line went slack, and she thought her shot at a giant fish was gone. Pulling in the loose line, she realized the fish was still hooked. Anderson grabbed a net and scooped up a 47-inch musky. "I've never experienced an adrenaline rush like that," Lisa says. "I was buzzing for hours and hours. That moment changed my life."

She bought a boat, then a bigger one, thrilled by the chase and entranced by long days on the river. Soon, she was working for Anderson's Ottawa River Musky Factory (tagline: "We produce big fish") and volunteering for a charity, Blue Fish Canada, that protects water and wild fish stocks through education and outreach. Staffing booths at boat shows, Lisa taught people how to catch and release properly, how to selectively harvest and about issues impacting water quality and connectivity. We rarely eat musky; they're boney and, as an apex species, contain a fair share of mercury. But if pursued responsibly, especially in the Ottawa River watershed, where there's a self-sustaining population, the sport doesn't degrade the ecosystem. And whether we fish for pleasure or for food, it opens a doorway into blue space.

On the Rideau or Hudson or any river, lake or ocean, fishers generally want to protect their waterways. They report oddities to local watchdog organizations and serve as eyes, ears and hands for scientists. Because the Rideau is much cleaner than it used to be, there are more people on the water these days. Sometimes, competing uses create conflict, including squabbles between anglers and cottagers. But when clashing groups sit down together — for instance, at workshops where waterfront property owners and bass tournament organizers air their beefs — a mutual love can help spawn consensus.

"It's a matter of respect for one another, for fish and for the water," says Lisa. "That's easier said than done. But the health of these rivers shows that even when things go wrong, we can make them right."

Lisa pilots her boat into a sheltered cove, spears a worm on a hook and passes me a rod. It's not musky season yet, so we're using smaller tackle, hoping for bass, pike or walleye. She clicks on the auto deploy trolling motor, which will keep us in place, and looks at a live sonar image of what's happening beneath and around the hull. Not much, it turns out.

"Sorry, I tend to bring bad luck." I shrug.

"Oh, you're one of *those* guys."

Lisa became a guide to share her passion. Sometimes, grown men celebrate with childlike joy when they finally catch a musky, and she's always eager to take kids onto the water. It gets them outside, away from screens, a gateway to a non-virtual aquatic world. And overturning my assumption, being a woman in a traditionally masculine field has probably helped, she says, with people in the industry reaching out to support her. Another barrier eroded in blue space.

We leave the cove I have jinxed and try trolling in a couple different spots, "bottom bouncing" my lure on the riverbed, then circle back and stop just off an island. Pitching up and down in the chop, I flip open the bail on my reel and let the weighted hook on my pickerel rig drop shot 22 feet. Within a minute, there's a bite. Lisa coaches me on technique, and riding a surge of adrenaline, I pull up a foot-long catfish. Its white underbelly is soft, its fins sharp, and with a flick of its tail, it swims away after I lower it back into the water. Next drop, another catfish on my hook. This time, Lisa busts out a short ruler that's inadequate for musky — "First time I've used it," she says with a laugh — and measures a whiskered 17-inch whopper.

"We just got your first catfish *and* your personal best," she says. "The good news is that it won't be hard to beat your personal best."

CHAPTER 32

~~~~

"For all the hours I've spent on moving water, a thimbleful: that's all I've managed to ascertain. My failure to glean more, my stone-headedness, does not deter me, though, and I keep planting myself bankside or on the currents to listen."

— Chris Dombrowski, The River You Touch

NOT FAR BEYOND BECKETTS LANDING, I'M MIRED IN A MAT OF VEGETATION river right, peeling bundles of weeds off my fin while getting blasted by the wind. A police boat going the other direction zips past — gunning, perhaps, for the guy fishing from his kayak. No rescue pending for me, I paddle full bore for two hours, covering less than two miles toward the Pirate Cove Marina. I feel like one of those meme-mocked cyclists who celebrates a racing victory prematurely, turning to taunt his rivals and then wiping out before crossing the wire. After nearly 10 weeks of paddling, will I stall before getting to the checkered flag?

Anne and Kevin watch me limp into their home port's sheltered harbor. Their boat is docked and the jeep's half packed. I breathe out deeply and pulse my splayed fingers, cramped into claws.

"Need anything?" Anne asks from shore. "A ride?"

"We live a few minutes from the Long Island locks," Kevin says. "It'd be easy to take you there."

I consult my map and phone, entering time, distance and wind data into the frazzled calculator in my brain, and meekly accept their offer.

There's no space in the vehicle for my gear, so Kevin drives to their house to unload while I deflate and roll up my SUP. Anne and I continue the sporadic conversation we've been having about paddle-boarding over the past four days. Whatever the vessel, she and her husband treasure slow trips up and down the Rideau. They're both divers and ex-military, and they have traveled the world, Anne says, but they never tire of the river in their backyard.

When we're driving north, I ask why they're going out of their way for a stranger who's not in any real trouble.

"It's nothing," says Kevin. "Just what anybody would do for us, I hope."

The locks where they drop me off are a frequent turnaround spot on my paddles up the Rideau from the city. A series of wooden staircases descend beside three chambers, and there's a grassy point at the bottom, away from the parking lot, that's ideal for tenting. During training runs, I gulped water and sat in the shade here regularly. Today, with the bloodred sun starting to sink toward the forested contours on the far shore, yellow leaves reflecting in the dark green water, there's a dude at a picnic table strumming his guitar, a mellow serenade as I set up camp.

Muscles sore and face windburned, I'm ready for bed before dark, upbraiding myself for cadging a ride, yet aware that had I continued paddling, I'd have been on the water for another three or four more hours. Just like in Buffalo and on Lake Champlain, where I took Ubers, or Hamilton, where I phoned a friend, these shortcuts weren't shortcomings, just the means to an end.

Last morning. Last mug of instant coffee, last bowl of instant oatmeal, last time stowing my sleeping bag and tent, last time donning sour-smelling paddling clothing, last time filling up my water bottles in a bathroom sink. I'm moving slowly, methodically, savoring the routine. Also: my fingers don't quite work right and this is the only pace I can manage.

It's 15 miles to the end of the canal, and I know every curve and bridge ahead, but there's a surreal luster to the landscape, an ethereal sheen of drooping willows painted atop the glassy Rideau. As if I've never been here before.

My first time ever paddling in Ottawa was aboard a stubby whitewater kayak I borrowed from a neighbor. It was April, and Sawmill Creek, a glorified drainage ditch near my house, was gushing with spring runoff. I drove to a big-box shopping mall, carried the kayak through an LRT station and put in on a stormwater pond. The downstream run through tangled ravines and oxbows strewn with shopping carts and tires took four hours. Muddy, soaked and shivering, I emerged from this fissure just before the creek spills into the Rideau River, beside a busy intersection that I pass through multiple times some days. Blinking, cowed by a cacophony of cars, it felt like I was entering a foreign world.

Stashing the kayak at an auto shop, I took a bus back to the mall where I had parked my van. The paddle took four hours, my drive to pick up the boat only 10 minutes.

Either from the cold or the sewage, or both, I was sick for a good while after that transit. It was probably just a bad case of the sniffles, but maybe I was exposed to something else in the water. Something that tweaked my DNA. A mutation that activated the swamp gene.

On the five-mile stretch from Long Island to the next lock at Black Rapids, I see one canoe in the water and count 10 planes in the sky. When my daughter Maggie had a weekly gymnastics class near here, I'd drop her off and sneak out for a quick paddle on warm autumn nights, my headlamp the only luminance under a black sky. Then: an ear-splitting noise and blinking lights from above. Granted, it's right beside the international airport, but paddling here always conjures Kim Stanley Robinson's speculative cli-fi novel *The Ministry for the Future*. After heat waves kill millions, an eco-terrorist group uses drone swarms to crash jets and container ships in protest of continuing carbon emissions. It's brutal, but it works, a warped version of the trolley problem: is it OK to kill one person if you save five, or 300 airline passengers to save 300 million?

Another scene from the book stands out: the opening, in near-future Uttar Pradesh, India, where people are dropping dead in the intolerable heat, and a group of locals submerge their bodies in a superheated lake in a desperate, ill-fated attempt to stay alive.

We don't need to look to fiction or the future to encounter such catastrophic devastation. My summer of SUP coincided with devastating wildfires across Canada and the prominence of John Vaillant's masterpiece *Fire Weather*, which deconstructs our collective addiction to hydrocarbons and the prospect, whether we embrace it or not, of a reckoning. "Over the past century and a half, we have recalibrated our lives, culture, and economy to the point that we now feel both dependent on and entitled to the luxury of fire in waiting," Vaillant writes. "In the developed world, it has become an unspoken expectation that one of government's jobs is to provide cheap and abundant energy, especially fossil fuels. It's hard for most people to imagine an alternative. What if I have to change my behavior? What if it's unpleasant? What if it's somehow . . . less?"

Rising seas are flooding coastlines, overflowing rivers are wreaking havoc, warming water is fueling intense hurricanes, but I'd seek refuge in blue space if the cities and forests are burning. Maybe my parents' cabin, where there's nothing wrong with less.

It's four miles from Black Rapids to the next lock at Hog's Back Falls. I'm still clocking landmarks but now, out-of-bodily hovering above my board, I'm equal parts relieved and wistful when I arrive.

A thunderous cataract in spring, Hog's Back is where the Rideau River forks with the artificial canal, charting parallel pathways to the Ottawa River, five miles distant. In 1826, it took a survey party three days to bushwhack here from the Ottawa, "meeting with various gullies, and huge swamps, to get through which . . . [we] waded, and were obliged to crawl on our hands and knees under the brushwood." A short railway, likely the first in Canada, was built to carry stone to the falls from a quarry. Building a dam that could retain water to a depth of 50 feet across a swift-flowing river was an engineering stunt that had yet to be attempted in North America. It collapsed twice during construction, the second time after By had fired the original contractor and taken over the project.

I skinny-dip one final time and portage around the falls. Onward from here I'll be in a concrete channel lined by busy multiuse paths, atop murky slack water where swimming is neither permitted nor wise. After a mile, I'm at a pair of locks adjacent to the Carleton University campus, a triangle of land cradled between the canal and Rideau River.

A few years ago, a friend of mine took her class outside to sit by a set of rapids on the Pasapkedjiwanong — Algonquin for "the water that runs between the rocks," replaced by the name Rideau in an act of colonial erasure. She asked her students to think about their relationships to the river.

Initially skeptical, one student later reflected that she "has begun to see how Indigenous values of relationality and reciprocity between human and more-than-human agents could reshape her understanding of literature," English prof Jan Schroeder wrote in the university's *Raven Magazine*. "One thing this could mean for us in English — or any program — is questioning the division between nature and culture that structures knowledge in the Western university."

The global rights-of-nature movement also questions such divisions, advocating for the recognition that ecosystems and natural communities are not ownable properties but rather entities with the right to exist and flourish. One of the movement's more tantalizing directions is the proliferation of personhood campaigns for rivers — the drive to give watercourses a set of specific protections, including the right to flow and be free from pollution.

In a TED Talk, University of Waterloo legal scholar Kelsey Leonard questions the morality of a society that grants the right to be heard in a court of law to multinationals but not nature. "If you can grant that to a corporation, why not the Great Lakes?" asks Leonard, a citizen of the Shinnecock Nation on New York's Long Island. "Why not the many waterways across our planet that we depend on to survive?"

One of her mentors, Anishinaabe Elder Josephine Mandamin, who walked around the Great Lakes to raise awareness about environmental degradation, told Leonard about a prophecy: an ounce of water will one day be worth more than an ounce of gold. When Leonard suggested that we're in the time of prophecy already, Mandamin (aka Grandmother Water Walker) replied, "So what are you going to do about it?"

Leonard believes recognizing water as a living relation and granting it personhood will help address some of the injustices we see in the world today, including racial and class inequality, to say nothing of the impacts of climate change. A change in legal status, she argues, can support the development of holistic water quality standards and begin to dismantle the harms of exclusive ownership. Most of all, it will protect water from us, "from human beings that would do it harm," and begin to reverse the "accepted hierarchy" of our dominance over nature.

This transformation demands that we amend the ways in which we connect to water, says Leonard. "It's the first medicine that each of us as human beings are exposed to. We are all born with a natal connection to water, but somewhere along the way we lost that connection, and we have to work to restore it."

She imagines a world where we go to the blue space closest to our homes and ask, "What have I done for the water today?"

Leaving the Carleton campus behind, shorelines aflame with crimson and orange leaves, I skim the side of Dows Lake. Now a sparkling pond on the edge of a prosperous neighborhood, this used to be Dows Great Swamp — a dismal wilderness where a bushwhacking group of surveyors spent Christmas in 1826. "There, on the bushy hemlock would we lie down . . . [and] some would fall asleep, others to sleep and snore; and after having lain an hour or so on one side, some one would cry *Spoon!* — the order to turn to the other — which was often an agreeable order, if a spike of tree-root or such substance stuck up between the ribs."

I tamp down a swampy urge to bivouac — alone — for an extra night at Dows Lake and prolong my trip. Paddling under an arterial road, I enter a pinch point 80 feet across — the "Notch of the Mountain" to canal engineers, a depression in a ridge that was a convenient location for a deep cut. I've walked, biked, run, paddled and skated the final few miles of the Rideau Canal hundreds of times, hemmed in by ornamental lampposts topped with large globes. This cleft, where Lisa picks rosehips in the fall, and where I surf the ricocheting wakes of tour boats, is half an hour by foot from my house. Suddenly, it feels like I'm simply out on a short sojourn. I close my eyes. When I open them, will the whole trip be just a dream?

"Holy crap!" a passing canoeist startles me. "I've seen people paddle the Yukon River with way less gear."

He asks where I'm going.

"The Ottawa River."

"Where did you start?"

"The Ottawa River."

"Huh?"

"Beautiful day," I reply, then move on.

It could be the surge of endorphins, or the lingering effects of my lip infection, or wind-induced Stockholm syndrome, or that I'm *home* after so many weeks on so many different waterways, but a giddy sensation cascades through my body, from the top of my sweaty head to the wrinkled base of my feet; a harmonious thrum, a web of incandescent filaments between me and all those ducks and geese and gulls and herons, the mosquitoes and snakes and spiders and damselflies, the marinas and parks and museums and locks and islands and harbors and cities and towns; between me and Chris Aubichon, biking beyond the arbitrary limits of potential and the horror stories we're fed about the world; between me and Maris Jacobs, soaring alongside her ancestors in a kayak like a knife through soft butter; between me and Cole Delisle, coaxing his animal and plant relations back to Tekakwitha Island; me and Art Cohn on Lake Champlain, yearning for the simple connections between human beings and our history and the things we've done right and done wrong; me and Kate Morse in Schuylerville, fixing some of the problems in her part of the world; me and the crew of the *Edna A*, wielding wrenches and navigating through the waves and cycles of time and space; me and Lisa Cline at the Hudson River Maritime Museum, trying to get people to slow down and pay attention and open a hatch into their brains; me and Patricia Finnerty and the spirit of Pete Seeger, giving people a home in every port; me and Duane Martinez in the resurgent wilds of Quassaick Creek and Chev Dixon on the reclaimed waters of the Hudson River and Oscar Hernandez standing his ground on the shores of Hoboken; me and Len Tantillo, fighting to bring back a splash of old Albany; me and Joe on his chair in St. Johnsville and Rob sharing his Mountain Dew at lock E22 and Matt Donahue embracing me on his boat in Weedsport and the Walkers enveloping me with love in their farmhouse and Sue and Doug keeping an eye on me in Albion; me and Brian Trzeciak in Buffalo trying to shake loose from the old excuses and Joe Stahlman remembering all the grandmothers and grandfathers and mothers and fathers and brothers and sisters who have gotten us here; me and my grandparents and parents and siblings and children and cousins near and far, removed and yet not really removed, all of us flowing astride an enduring force like no other.

So much of the modern world pulls our attention somewhere else, and that somewhere else is often unsettling. Our nervous systems travel through time and space and can't process what they encounter. A visit to blue space can be an escape, but it's also a lodestone, pulling us back to the present. To presence. Look to the horizon and breathe in the boundless possibility, but also savor the sense that, at least for a short spell, home is *here*.

Did I emerge from my trip more resilient? Am I better equipped to manage the uncertainties of a fractured, warming world? To keep my head above the current after pushing off from shore?

Personal growth usually accrues after the fact, rarely in the moment. But whenever I faced a rough patch on the water or a setback on land, the need to focus on the impasse at hand was a visceral reminder of the virtues of staying grounded. Drilled into me repeatedly, that lesson took. I've also got some newly whetted tools for holding off angst — humility, determination, gratitude — and new techniques to try. I can pick up garbage, volunteer for a nonprofit, use social media to commune without falling into the rabbit hole. And while my body allows, I can always go for a paddle.

Blue acupuncture is not one-size-fits-all, but it can improve our health and the health of our communities. What works in Kahnawake may not fly in Newburgh or Manhattan or Albion or Smiths Falls, but in bang-for-our-bucks accounting, well-executed aquatic interventions are hard to beat. Established projects like Hudson Crossing Park are flourishing; fledgling efforts like the Quassaick Creek trail are still taking root; rewatering downtown Albany remains a dream. But they're all knit from the same connective thread, a lifeblood lapping around our feet.

In my book about walking, I tried to distill everything I had learned and settled on three words: walk more, anywhere. The essence of blue space? Just two words, in Latin: solvitur aqua. It is solved by water.

After all, we're one rambling, short-sighted, dysfunctional human family, but each of us is about 60 percent water.

Beer is about 90 percent water, and though there are fewer groggeries in Ottawa than on the Erie Canal in days of yore, I stop for a pint to forestall a premature finale.

At 5 p.m., Lisa and some friends will be waiting for me at mile zero, the top of a flight of eight locks that drop to the Ottawa River, and I can't arrive at the finish line until then.

Hidden behind a stone archway near downtown, there's a small inlet with a creek-side bistro. I sit on the patio and contemplate the currents and tides that came before and swirl ahead.

Back on the canal, I turn a corner and the wind is pushing me. Figures. A boost when I'm trying to go slow.

I pause, holding onto an iron fence, then paddle beneath a trio of bridges. Lisa and a small clutch of pals are standing on a dock. There's a sign with my name on it, a bottle of champagne. Kisses, hugs, a toast. I step away from the group and stand atop the gate of the uppermost lock, where the water begins its staircase down to the Ottawa and then the St. Lawrence and eventually the Atlantic. The end of the canal. Or the beginning. Or just another waypoint on an infinite circle.

ACKNOWLEDGMENTS

NO PADDLEBOARDER IS AN ISLAND. THE VOYAGE AT THE HEART OF THIS book and the distillation of everything that I experienced would not have been possible without the boundless goodwill of countless individuals. Many of these inspiring people appear in the preceding pages. Thanking them all here would necessitate a whole other book. But some people supported me from behind the scenes, while others were particularly vital.

I bounced this project off three watermen before diving into the planning. Canoe guru Max Finkelstein deemed my route feasible during a January paddle amid the ice pans on the Ottawa River; I was wearing a drysuit aboard my SUP while Max stood in his canoe wearing cross-country ski attire, yet I still consider him a voice of reason. Sailor, doctor and writer Kevin Patterson affirmed that the narrative could hold water, and I am grateful for his ongoing mentorship from afar. Writer and paddleboarder Bruce Kirkby got into the granular details with me over the phone, recommending specific gear and providing a big-hearted adventurer's perspective.

Bruce's main paddleboarding partner, Norm Hann, is the first SUP instructor I learned from. Thank you, Norm, for not only teaching me proper technique (which I'm still working on), but also for instilling a respect for this sport and all the places it can take us. (Small world: Norm is friends with SUP coach and recreation therapist Alex Chandler, who helped me understand connections between paddling and mental health.)

A long list of people and tourism agencies generously provided accommodations during my trip: Emili Bellefleur at Tourism Montreal, Frédéric Pichette at Tourisme Montérégie, Michelle Kearns at Visit Buffalo Niagara, Laywah Ang at the Ontario Tourism Marketing Partnership and Steve Weir at the province's RTO9 regional tourism organization, Lauren Riddell at tartanbond on behalf of Tourism Kingston, Karen Feeley and Guy Thériault at Parks Canada. Thanks as well to Bill Sweitzer at the New York State Canal Corporation and Shane Mahar at the New York Power Authority — you guys rock!

To everybody who welcomed me into Kahnawake, niá:wen for showing me your community and sharing your stories. I can't wait to paddle over for another visit.

Mona Caron from the Erie Canalway National Heritage Corridor provided indispensable logistical advice and introduced me to several key contacts, among them canal stewards Beth, Sara and Rick Walker, who felt like family the moment I met them.

My actual American family also became unwitting accomplices. Laura and Janet Schiller, their respective husbands, David and Lee, and their brother Kenneth welcomed me into their homes and lives. Join us up here in Canada anytime!

Patricia Finnerty in Newburgh, New York, offered her spare room to a stranger — an act of kindness magnified by the fact that I arrived during an unprecedent rainstorm in the lower Hudson Valley.

While in the home stretch of the writing process — an ordeal that made the paddling seem like a walk in the park — I bunked for a week at the Gibraltar Point Centre for the Arts on Toronto Island. Thank you, ArtHubs, for keeping spaces like this alive.

Writer, editor and mentor Rick Boychuk read this book in chunks as it was coming together. His sage advice kept me on track. Jesus, bravo: I thought Rick was an amazing editor when I started working with him two decades ago, and he keeps getting better.

My masterful agent, Martha Webb at CookeMcDermid, talked through this idea with me at various points over the past five years and believed in it from the start. She helped channel my excitement, found a home for the book I wanted to write and coaxed me down from the ledge (as did Andrée Germain!).

My calm-amid-the-storm editor, Jen Knoch at ECW Press, was also willing to listen to my thoughts about blue space over the years as *Water Borne* took shape. A keen-eyed wordsmith, deep thinker, community activist, amateur psychologist and more, Jen was a perfect partner for this journey, as she was with *Born to Walk* in 2015. See you in 10 years for the next one, Jen?

ECW's digital and art director Jess Albert, sales and rights director Emily Ferko and the rest of the crew made sure my words could find an audience. Thanks as well to co-publishers Jack David and David Caron for having me back. And to the Ontario Arts Council for chipping in!

A few magazines published my stories in the lead-up to this book being born. Thank you Kristin Schnelten at *Mountain Life*, Kaydi Pyette at *Paddling Magazine*, Kellie Davenport at *re:porter* and Sarah Brown at *Canadian Geographic*.

Several gear companies made the trip as smooth as possible. Thanks to Mike Harvey, one of the owners of Badfish SUP, who didn't hesitate to give me the ideal board; Peter Allen of Blackfish Paddles, who put a pair of sweet paddles into the mail right away; Jo Salamon at Mountain Equipment Company for the recommendations and kid-in-a-candy-store shopping spree; Darren Thompson at Hammer Nutrition Canada for the care package; Laura Fergusson at Mustang Survival for the world's best dry bag; and to Vaikobi Ocean Performance co-founder Adrienne Langley and Trailhead Paddle Shack co-owner Jason Yarrington for the generous deals.

Nobody has been more generous to me throughout this project than my family. I hope you get a feel for my parents from reading this book; they're unique and brilliant and I love them oh so dearly, even if neither will get on a paddleboard. My brothers, sisters-in-law, niece and nephews — your homes and hugs are always safe harbor. My daughters, Maggie and Daisy, dealt with my absence for a few months with aplomb (though they took a while to notice I was gone). Maybe they'll join me on the next long paddle?

To my wife, Lisa, who knew how encompassing this project would be but gave me an enthusiastic green light anyway: you were with me from the start and stuck around, in good times and bad. A writer, editor and my go-to first reader, your beautiful voice rings through this book and me. I love you, Lisa, to the end of the river and back.

And thank you to all the citizens of blue space, including anybody I've neglected to mention here. I'll see you down at the shore.

WORKS CITED

Albany Riverfront Collaborative. "Albany Reimagined." albanyriverfrontcollaborative.com.

American Battlefield Trust. "Valcour Island." battlefields.org/learn/revolutionary-war/battles/valcour-island.

Barker, Edward John. *Observations on the Rideau Canal.* Office of the British Whig, 1834.

Beach, Allan Penfield. *Lake Champlain as Centuries Pass.* Lake Champlain Maritime Museum, 1994.

Behringer, Wolfgang. *Tambora and the Year without a Summer: How a Volcano Plunged the World into Crisis.* Polity Press, 2019.

Bell, Simon, et al. "Urban Blue Acupuncture: A Protocol for Evaluating a Complex Landscape Design Intervention to Improve Health and Wellbeing in a Coastal Community." *Sustainability,* May 2020.

Bell, Simon, et al., eds. *Urban Blue Spaces: Planning and Design for Water, Health and Well-Being.* Routledge, 2021.

Berge, Chloe. "This Canadian River Is Now Legally a Person. It's Not the Only One." *National Geographic,* April 15, 2022.

Bergman, Jordanna, et al. "Ecological Connectivity of Invasive and Native Fishes in a Historic Navigation Waterway." Canadian Journal of Fisheries and Aquatic Sciences, February 2024.

BlueHealth. "Urban Regeneration: Teats Hill." bluehealth2020.eu/projects/urban-beach-regeneration.

Blum, Annalise, et al. "Causal Effect of Impervious Cover on Annual Flood Magnitude for the United States." *Geophysical Research Letters,* February 2020.

Bonnell, Jennifer. *Reclaiming the Don: An Environmental History of Toronto's Don River Valley*. University of Toronto Press, 2014.

Boswell, Randy. "Reimagining the Rideau — A River's Resurgent Indigenous Identity." *Ottawa Citizen*, August 9, 2021.

Boyle, Robert. *The Hudson River: A Natural and Unnatural History*. W. W. Norton & Co., 1979.

Brazil, Rachel. "The Weirdness of Water." *Chemistry World*, April 2020.

Brown, Ron. *From Queenston to Kingston: The Hidden Heritage of Lake Ontario's Shoreline*. Dundurn, 2010.

Calarco, Tom. *The Search for the Underground Railroad in Upstate New York*. History Press, 2014.

Coss, Richard, and Craig Keller. "Transient Decreases in Blood Pressure and Heart Rate with Increased Subjective Level of Relaxation While Viewing Water Compared with Adjacent Ground." *Journal of Environmental Psychology*, June 2022.

Childers, Jodi. "How Pete Seeger Turned Green." *Jacobin*, May 2023.

City of Kingston. "Kingston's Waterfront Master Plan." April 2016.

City of Little Falls. "Born of Water." thisislittlefalls.com/history.

Cronin, John, and Robert F. Kennedy Jr. *The Riverkeepers: Two Activists Fight to Reclaim Our Environment as a Basic Human Right*. Scribner, 1997.

Crow, Scott, ed. *Setting Sights: Histories and Reflections on Community Armed Self-Defence*. PM Press, 2018.

Davison, Sophie, Mathew White et al. "Concern About the Human Health Implications of Marine Biodiversity Loss Is Higher Among Less Educated and Poorer Citizens: Results from a 14-Country Study in Europe." *Frontiers in Marine Science*, April 2023.

Deer, Ka'nhehsí:io. "By the Rapids: Restoring Kahnawake's Bay and Life on the Water." CBC News, October 2020.

Desfor, Gene, and Jennefer Laidley, eds. *Reshaping Toronto's Waterfront*. University of Toronto Press, 2011.

Dombrowski, Chris. *The River You Touch: Making a Life on Moving Water*. Milkweed Editions, 2023.

Downey, Allan. "How Mohawk Ironworkers from Kahnawake Helped Build New York's Skyline." *CBC Ideas*, September 2022.

DuLong, Jessica. *My River Chronicles: Rediscovering America on the Hudson*. Free Press, 2009.

Dunwell, Frances. *The Hudson: America's River*. Columbia University Press, 2008.

Egan, Dan. *The Death and Life of the Great Lakes*. W. W. Norton, 2018.

Erie Canal Museum. "Exploring Abolition along the Empire State Trail." February 2023. eriecanalmuseum.org/exploring-abolition-along-the-empire-state-trail.

Erie Canalway National Heritage Corridor. "A National Treasure." eriecanalway.org/learn/history-culture.

Fairburn, Jane. *Along the Shore: Rediscovering Toronto's Waterfront Heritage*. ECW Press, 2013.

Fian, Leonie, Mathew White et al. "Nature Visits, but Not Residential Greenness, Are Associated with Reduced Income-Related Inequalities in Subjective Well-Being." *Heath & Place*, January 2024.

Finnerty, Ryan. "Remembering the Secret History of the Underground Railroad in the North Country." North Country Public Radio, February 2022.

Fleming, L. E., P. J. Landrigan et al. "How Can a Healthy Ocean Improve Human Health and Enhance Wellbeing on a Rapidly Changing Planet?" World Resources Institute. 2024.

Foley, Denis, and Andrew Wolfe. "Raiders of the Lost Lock: Researchers in New York Unearth Part of the Old Erie Canal." *Offshore*, February 2003.

Foner, Eric. *Gateway to Freedom: The Hidden History of the Underground Railroad*. W. W. Norton, 1996.

Fox, Liam. "The Economic Roller-Coaster of a Small Ontario Town Fuelled by Chocolate and Cannabis." Canadian Press, September 18, 2023.

Friends of Albany History. "Albany's D&H Building and How It Grew." June 2019.

Fulford, Robert. *Accidental City: The Transformation of Toronto*. Macfarlane Walter & Ross, 1995.

Georgiou, Michail, et al. "Mechanisms of Impact of Blue Spaces on Human Health: A Systematic Literature Review and Meta-Analysis." *International Journal of Environmental Research and Public Health*, March 2021.

Gies, Erica. *Water Always Wins: Thriving in an Age of Drought and Deluge.* University of Chicago Press, 2022.

Goldenberg, Suzanne. "Pete Seeger's Greatest Legacy? Saving New York's Hudson River." *The Guardian*, January 29, 2014.

Hauptman, Laurence M. *Conspiracy of Interests: Iroquois Dispossession and the Rise of New York State.* Syracuse University Press, 2001.

Heat-Moon, William Least. *River-Horse: A Voyage Across America.* Houghton Mifflin, 1999.

Hogan, Holly. *Message in a Bottle: Ocean Dispatches from a Seabird Biologist.* Knopf Canada, 2023.

Hudson River Maritime Museum. "History of the Sloop Clearwater." *History Blog*, May 14, 2020. hrmm.org/history-blog/history-of-the-sloop-clearwater.

Hudson River Maritime Museum. "The Hudson River Sloop." *History Blog*, November 2016. hrmm.org/history-blog/the-hudson-river-sloop.

Humphreys, Barbara, and Fiona Spalding-Smith. *Legacy in Stone: The Rideau Corridor.* Boston Mills Press, 1999.

Hunt, Elle. "Blue Spaces: Why Time Spent Near Water Is the Secret of Happiness." *Guardian*, November 3, 2019.

Jardim, Clara. "Interview with Yuval Harari, the Author of *Sapiens, Homo Deus, 21 Lessons for the 21st Century* and the New *Sapiens: A Graphic History*." *Uma Revista*, 2021.

Jenish, D'Arcy. "Inland Superhighway." *Canadian Geographic*, July/August 2009.

Jinha, Arif. "Smiths Falls in the World: A Study of Globalization in a Rural Canadian Town." *Just Labour*, October 2009.

Kahnawà:ke Environment Protection Office. "Tekakwitha Island and Bay Restoration." June 2023. kahnawakeenvironment.com/project/tekakwithabayandislandrestoration.

Kaplan, Rachel, and Stephen Kaplan. *The Experience of Nature: A Psychological Perspective.* Cambridge University Press, 1989.

Kelly, Jack. *Valcour: The 1776 Campaign That Saved the Cause of Liberty.* St. Martin's Press, 2021.

Klein, Seth. *A Good War: Mobilizing Canada for the Climate Emergency.* ECW Press, 2020.

Koeppel, Gerard. *Bond of Union: Building the Erie Canal and the American Empire.* Da Capo Press, 2009.

Kolbert, Elizabeth. "Sleeping with the Enemy." *The New Yorker,* August 2011.

Krakauer, Jon. *Into the Wild.* Anchor, 1997.

Kunstler, James Howard. "Schuylerville Stands Still." *The New York Times,* March 25, 1990.

Lake Champlain Maritime Museum. "Commercial Era (1823–1945)." lcmm.org/explore/lake-champlain-history/commercial-era-1823-1945.

Larkin, Daniel. "The Railroads and New York's Canals." Consider the Source New York: Teaching with Historical Records.

Legget, Robert. *Rideau Waterway.* University of Toronto Press, 2001.

Leonard, Kelsey. "Why Lakes and Rivers Should Have the Same Rights as Humans." TED, December 2019.

LeWine, Howard. "Understanding the Stress Response: Chronic Activation of This Survival Mechanism Impairs Health." Harvard Health Publishing, April 2024.

MacGregor, Roy. "Bringing Toronto's Don River Back from the Dead." *The Globe and Mail,* August 12, 2016.

Maclear, Kyo. "Singing in December." CBC Books/Governor General's Literary Awards, February 2024.

Marcus, Ben. *The Art of Stand Up Paddling: A Complete Guide to SUP on Lakes, Rivers, and Oceans.* Falcon Guides, 2012.

Marsh, James H., and Nathan Baker. "Ottawa River." *The Canadian Encyclopedia,* December 2006.

McGrath, Ben. *Riverman: An American Odyssey.* Knopf, 2022.

Medina, John. *Brain Rules: 12 Principles for Surviving and Thriving at Work, Home, and School*. Pear Press, 2014.

Mitchell, Rich. "What Is Equigenesis and How Might It Help Narrow Health Inequalities?" The Centre for Research on Environment Society and Health, November 2013.

Mock, Jillian. "Why Doctors Are Prescribing Nature Walks." *Time*, April 2022.

Neuzil, Mark, and Norman Sims. *Canoes: A Natural History in North America*. University of Minnesota Press, 2016.

Nichols, Wallace J. *Blue Mind: The Surprising Science That Shows How Being Near, In, On, or Under Water Can Make You Happier, Healthier, More Connected, and Better at What You Do*. Little, Brown, 2014.

Nutsford, Daniel, et al. "Residential Exposure to Visible Blue Space (but Not Green Space) Associated with Lower Psychological Distress in a Capital City." *Health & Place*, May 2016.

NYS Canal Corporation. *Reimagine the Canals Task Force Report*. January 2020.

NYS Department of Environmental Conservation. "The Hudson Estuary: A River That Flows Two Ways." dec.ny.gov/nature/waterbodies/oceans-estuaries/hudson-estuary.

Office of the Director of National Intelligence. "Benedict Arnold: A Name Synonymous with Treason." intel.gov/evolution-of-espionage/revolutionary-war/british-espionage/benedict-arnold.

Oneida Lake Association. "About Oneida Lake." oneidalakeassociation.org/About%20Oneida%20Lake.html.

Oosterom, Nelle. "Rideau Canal: A Post-War of 1812 Waterway Built at a Huge Human Cost." *Canada's History*, January 2011.

Parks Canada. "Rideau Canal Draft Management Plan." February 2022.

Pasanena, Tytti, Mathew White et al. "Neighbourhood Blue Space, Health and Wellbeing: The Mediating Role of Different Types of Physical Activity." *Environment International*, October 2019.

Pearson, Amber, et al. "Effects of Freshwater Blue Spaces May Be Beneficial for Mental Health: A First, Ecological Study in the North American Great Lakes Region." *PLOS ONE*, August 2019.

Peck, Mary. *From War to Winterlude, 150 Years on the Rideau Canal.* Public Archives Canada, 1982.

Railway Museum of Eastern Ontario. "Smiths Falls Railway History." rmeo.org/smith-falls-railway-history/.

Ray, Sarah Jaquette. "Climate Anxiety Is an Overwhelmingly White Phenomenon." *Scientific American*, March 2021.

Reid, Paula, and Hanna Kampman. "Exploring the Psychology of Extended-Period Expeditionary Adventurers: Going Knowingly into the Unknown." *Psychology of Sport and Exercise*, January 2020.

Riverkeeper. "Hudson River PCBs." riverkeeper.org/campaigns/stop-polluters/pcbs.

Roe, Jenny, and Layla McCay. *Restorative Cities: Urban Design for Mental Health and Wellbeing.* Bloomsbury, 2021.

Roe, Jenny, et al. "The Restorative Health Benefits of a Tactical Urban Intervention: An Urban Waterfront Study." *Frontiers in Built Environment*, June 2019.

Rogers, Kara. "Biophilia Hypothesis." *Britannica*, October 2010.

Roos, Dave. "How the Erie Canal Was Built with Raw Labor and Amateur Engineering." History, April 2021.

Rubinstein, Dan. "Blue Space Is the New Green Space." *The Walrus*, June 2021.

Rubinstein, Dan. *Born to Walk: The Transformative Power of a Pedestrian Act.* ECW Press, 2015.

Rubinstein, Dan. "Peak Paddling in the B.C. Rainforest." *enRoute*, June 2019.

Rubinstein, Dan. "Shopify Owners Revive the Iconic Opinicon Resort." *Cottage Life*, August 2020.

Rubinstein, Dan. "What It's Like to Paddleboard from Washington to Tofino." *Western Living*, September 2019.

Rubinstein, Dan. "Where the Wild Fish Go." Carleton Newsroom, July 2019.

Rush, Elizabeth. *Rising: Dispatches from the New American Shore.* Milkweed Editions, 2018.

Salles, Joaquim. "Flood. Retreat. Repeat." *Grist*, September 2022.

Schroeder, Janice. "Take Me to the River: What My Students Learned from Pasapkedjiwanong." *Raven Magazine*, Winter 2020.

Sheriff, Carol. *The Artificial River: The Erie Canal and the Paradox of Progress, 1817–1862*. Hill and Wang, 1996.

Smith, Laurence C. *Rivers of Power: How a Natural Force Raised Kingdoms, Destroyed Civilizations, and Shapes Our World*. Little, Brown, 2020.

Solnit, Rebecca. "Why Climate Despair Is a Luxury." *The New Statesman*, July 2023.

Stehl, Patricia, Mathew White et al. "From Childhood Blue Space Exposure to Adult Environmentalism: The Role of Nature Connectedness and Nature Contact." *Journal of Environmental Psychology*, February 2024.

Steuteville, Robert. "Bold Campaign for Highway Removal." *Public Square: A CNU Journal*, March 2022.

Steuteville, Robert. "Freeway Ramp Becomes Park, Connecting City to Its River." *Public Square: A CNU Journal*, May 2023.

Sweeney, Peter. *The Sweeney Diary: The 1839 to 1850 Journal of Rideau Lockmaster Peter Sweeney*. Friends of the Rideau, 2008.

Taylor, Eric B. *Rivers Run Through Us: A Natural and Human History of Great Rivers of North America*. Rocky Mountain Books, 2021.

Teron, Lemir, and Renée Barry. "Visualising Heritage: A Critical Discourse Analysis of Place, Race, and Nationhood along the Erie Canal." *Local Environment: The International Journal of Justice and Sustainability*, February 2023.

Toronto and Region Conservation Authority. "Don River Watershed." trca.ca/conservation/watershed-management/don-river.

Ulrich, R.S. "View Through a Window May Influence Recovery from Surgery." *Science*, April 1984.

U.S. Fish & Wildlife Service. "Bald Eagle." fws.gov/sites/default/files/documents/bald-eagle-fact-sheet.pdf, February 2021.

U.S. Fish and Wildlife Service. "Montezuma National Wildlife Refuge." fws.gov/refuge/montezuma/about-us.

Vaillant, John. *Fire Weather: The Making of a Beast*. Knopf Canada, 2023.

Vaucher, Jean. "History of Ships: Prehistoric Craft." www.iro.umontreal.ca/~vaucher/History/Ships/Prehistoric_Craft.

Watson, Gordon. "Palaeo-Indian and Archaic Occupations of the Rideau Lakes." *Ontario Archaeology*, 1990.

Watson, Ken. "Death: A Rideau Mythconception." *Rideau Reflections*, Winter/Spring 2010.

Watson, Ken. *Engineered Landscapes: The Rideau Canal's Transformation of a Wilderness Waterway*. 2006.

Watson, Ken. *Watson's Paddling Guide to the Rideau Canal*. 2012.

Wheeler, Benedict, Mathew White et al. "Does Living by the Coast Improve Health and Wellbeing?" *Health & Place*, September 2012.

White, Mathew, et al. "The 'Blue Gym': What Can Blue Space Do for You and What Can You Do for Blue Space?" *Journal of the Marine Biological Association of the United Kingdom*, January 2016.

White, Mathew, et al. "Blue Space, Health and Well-being: A Narrative Overview and Synthesis of Potential Benefits." *Environmental Research*, December 2020.

White, Mathew, et al. "Coastal Proximity, Health and Well-being: Results from a Longitudinal Panel Survey." *Health & Place*, June 2013.

Wybenga, Darin. "Mississaugas of the Credit First Nation." *The Canadian Encyclopedia*, September 2022.

Yetto, Nick. "A Brief History of the Erie Canal." *Smithsonian Magazine*, March 2023.

York, Geoffrey, and Laureen Pindera. *People of the Pines: The Warriors and the Legacy of Oka*. Little, Brown, 1992.

LISA GREGOIRE

Dan Rubinstein is an Ottawa-based writer, editor and stand-up paddleboarder. His first book, *Born to Walk*, was a finalist for the Ottawa Book Awards and Kobo Emerging Writer Prize. He's also a National Magazine Award–winning journalist who contributes to publications such as *The Walrus*, *The Globe and Mail* and *enRoute*, and he's a former editor at *Canadian Geographic* magazine.

Entertainment. Writing. Culture. ────────────

ECW is a proudly independent, Canadian-owned book publisher. We know great writing can improve people's lives, and we're passionate about sharing original, exciting, and insightful writing across genres.

──────────────────── **Thanks for reading along!**

We want our books not just to sustain our imaginations, but to help construct a healthier, more just world, and so we've become a certified B Corporation, meaning we meet a high standard of social and environmental responsibility — and we're going to keep aiming higher. We believe books can drive change, but the way we make them can too.

Being a B Corp means that the act of publishing this book should be a force for good — for the planet, for our communities, and for the people that worked to make this book. For example, everyone who worked on this book was paid at least a living wage. You can learn more at the Ontario Living Wage Network.

This book is also available as a Global Certified Accessible™ (GCA) ebook. ECW Press's ebooks are screen reader friendly and are built to meet the needs of those who are unable to read standard print due to blindness, low vision, dyslexia, or a physical disability.

This book is printed on FSC®-certified paper. It contains recycled materials, and other controlled sources, is processed chlorine free, and is manufactured using biogas energy.

For every copy of this book sold, 1% of the cover price will be donated to Kateri Food Basket, a non-profit that supports community food security in Kahnawake, QC.

ECW's office is situated on land that was the traditional territory of many nations, including the Wendat, the Anishinaabeg, Haudenosaunee, Chippewa, Métis, and current treaty holders the Mississaugas of the Credit. In the 1880s, the land was developed as part of a growing community around St. Matthew's Anglican and other churches. Starting in the 1950s, our neighbourhood was transformed by immigrants fleeing the Vietnam War and Chinese Canadians dispossessed by the building of Nathan Phillips Square and the subsequent rise in real estate value in other Chinatowns. We are grateful to those who cared for the land before us and are proud to be working amidst this mix of cultures.

ecwpress.com